Report
to UNESCO
of the
International
Commission
on Education
for the
Twenty-first
Century

LEARNING: THE TREASURE WITHIN

LEARNING: THE

TREASURE WITHIN

Report to UNESCO of
the International Commission
on Education for
the Twenty-first Century

UNESCO PUBLISHING

The members of the Commission are responsible
for the choice and the presentation of the facts contained
in this book and for the opinions expressed therein,
which are not necessarily those of UNESCO and do not
commit the Organization.

Published in 1996 by the United Nations Educational,
Scientific and Cultural Organization
7, place de Fontenoy, 75352 Paris 07 SP, France

Graphic design by Jean-Francis Chériez
Composition and page make-up by Susanne Almeida-Klein
Printed by Presses Universitaires de France, Vendôme

ISBN 92-3-103274-7 (UNESCO)
ISBN 0-11-984387-0 (HMSO)

On completing this report, we wish to express our profound gratitude to Federico Mayor, Director-General of UNESCO. We admire his convictions and we share his goal of rekindling the ardour that lay behind the founding of the Organization, in order to serve peace and international understanding by means of the preservation and expansion of education, science and culture for all of humanity.

This report was his idea, and in conferring its preparation on us, he placed our task in the overall framework of his action as head of UNESCO.

He enabled us to conduct our inquiry in complete independence, while ensuring we had the support necessary for our work. We hope that the result is faithful to the inspiration that was behind it. If this report contributes to invigorating a debate that is indispensable, nationally and internationally, on the future of education, we will have at least partially fulfilled the confidence placed in us by the Director-General of UNESCO.

The Members of the Commission

Conter

Education:
the necessary Utopia   Jacques Delors   13

PART ONE: OUTLOOKS

1. From the local community to a world society   39

2. From social cohesion to democratic participation   53

8. Choices for education: the political factor

9. International co-operation: educating the global village

EPILOGUE

APPENDICES

13

acques Delors

Education: the necessary Utopia

In confronting the many challenges that the future holds in store, humankind sees in education an indispensable asset in its attempt to attain the ideals of peace, freedom and social justice. As it concludes its work, the Commission affirms its belief that education has a fundamental role to play in personal and social development. The Commission does not see education as a miracle cure or a magic formula opening the door to a world in which all ideals will be attained, but as one of the principal means available to foster a deeper and more harmonious form of human development and thereby to reduce poverty, exclusion, ignorance, oppression and war.

At a time when educational policies are being sharply criticized or pushed – for economic and financial reasons – down to the bottom of the agenda, the Commission wishes to share this conviction with the widest possible audience, through its analyses, discussions and recommendations.

Does the point need to be emphasized? The Commission was thinking principally about the children and young people who will take over from today's generation of adults, the latter being all too inclined to concentrate on their own problems. Education is also an expression of affection for children and young people, whom we need to welcome into society, unreservedly offering them the place that is theirs by right therein – a place in the education system, to be sure, but also in the family, the local community and the nation. This elementary duty needs to be constantly brought to mind, so that greater attention is paid to it, even when choosing between political, economic and financial options. In the words of a poet: 'The Child is father of the Man'.

Our century has been as much one of sound and fury as of economic and social progress – progress that in any case has not been equally shared. At the dawn of a new century the prospect of which evokes both anguish and hope, it is essential that all people with a sense of responsibility turn their attention to both the aims and the means of education. It is the view of the Commission that, while education is an ongoing process of improving knowledge and skills, it is also – perhaps primarily – an exceptional means of bringing about personal development and building relationships among individuals, groups and nations.

This view was explicitly adopted by the members of the Commission when they accepted their mandate. They wished moreover, by the arguments they adduced, to stress the pivotal role of UNESCO, a role that stems directly from the ideas on which UNESCO was founded, based upon the hope for a world that is a better place to live in, where people will have learned to respect the rights of women and men, to show mutual understanding, and to use advances in knowledge to foster human development rather than to create further distinctions between people.

Our Commission had the perhaps impossible task of overcoming the obstacles presented by the extraordinary diversity of situations in the world and trying to arrive at analyses that are universally valid and conclusions acceptable to everyone.

Nevertheless, the Commission did its best to project its thinking on to a future dominated by globalization, to choose those questions that everyone is asking and to lay down some guidelines that can be applied both within national contexts and on a worldwide scale.

Looking ahead

Some remarkable scientific discoveries and breakthroughs have been made during the last twenty-five years. Many countries have emerged from underdevelopment, and standards of living have continued to rise, albeit at rates differing considerably from country to country. Despite this, the prevailing mood of disenchantment forms a sharp contrast with the hopes born in the years just after the Second World War.

It may therefore be said that, in economic and social terms, progress has brought with it disillusionment. This is evident in rising unemployment and in the exclusion of growing numbers of people in the rich countries. It is underscored by the continuing inequalities in development throughout the world.[1] While humankind is increasingly aware of the threats facing its natural environment, the resources needed to put matters right have not yet been allocated, despite a series of international meetings, such as the United Nations Conference on Environment and Development (UNCED), held in Rio de Janeiro in 1992, and despite the serious warnings of natural disasters or major industrial accidents. The truth is that all-out economic growth can no longer be viewed as the ideal way of reconciling material progress with equity, respect for the human condition and respect for the natural assets that we have a duty to hand on in good condition to future generations.

We have by no means grasped all the implications of this as regards both the ends and means of sustainable development and new forms of international co-operation. This issue will constitute one of the major intellectual and political challenges of the next century.

That should not, however, cause the developing countries to disregard the classic forces driving growth, in particular as regards their need to enter the world of science and technology, with all this implies in terms of cultural adaptation and the modernization of mentalities.

Those who believed that the end of the Cold War held out the

1. According to UNCTAD studies, average income in the least-developed countries (560 million inhabitants) is falling. The estimated figure is $300 a year per inhabitant as against $906 for developing countries and $21,598 for the industrialized countries.

prospect of a better and more peaceful world have another reason for disenchantment and disillusionment. It is simply not an adequate consolation or excuse to repeat that history is tragic; that is something everyone knows or should know. Although the death toll in the last world war was 50 million, we must also remember that since 1945 some 20 million people have died in around 150 wars, both before and after the fall of the Berlin Wall. It hardly matters whether these are new risks or old risks. Tensions smoulder and then flare up between nations and ethnic groups, or as a result of a build-up of social and economic injustices. Against a background of growing interdependence among peoples and the globalization of problems, decision-makers have a duty to assess these risks and take action to ward them off.

But how can we learn to live together in the 'global village' if we cannot manage to live together in the communities to which we naturally belong – the nation, the region, the city, the village, the neighbourhood? Do we want to make a contribution to public life and can we do so? That question is central to democracy. The will to participate, it should be remembered, must come from each person's sense of responsibility; but whereas democracy has conquered new territory in lands formerly in the grip of totalitarianism and despotic rule, it is showing signs of languishing in countries which have had democratic institutions for many decades, as if there were a constant need for new beginnings and as if everything has to be renewed or reinvented.

How could these great challenges not be a cause for concern in educational policy-making? How could the Commission fail to highlight the ways in which educational policies can help to create a better world, by contributing to sustainable human development, mutual understanding among peoples and a renewal of practical democracy?

Tensions to be overcome

To this end, we have to confront, the better to overcome them, the main tensions that, although they are not new, will be central to the problems of the twenty-first century, namely:

• The tension between the global and the local: people need gradually to become world citizens without losing their roots and while continuing to play an active part in the life of their nation and their local community.

• The tension between the universal and the individual: culture is steadily being globalized, but as yet only partially. We cannot ignore the promises of globalization nor its risks, not the least of which is the risk of forgetting the unique character of individual human beings; it is for them to choose their own future and achieve their full potential within the carefully tended wealth of their traditions and their own cultures which, unless we are careful, can be endangered by contemporary developments.

• The tension between tradition and modernity, which is part of the same problem: how is it possible to adapt to change without turning one's back on the past, how can autonomy be acquired in complementarity with the free development of others and how can scientific progress be assimilated? This is the spirit in which the challenges of the new information technologies must be met.

• The tension between long-term and short-term considerations: this has always existed but today it is sustained by the predominance of the ephemeral and the instantaneous, in a world where an over-abundance of transient information and emotions continually keeps the spotlight on immediate problems. Public opinion cries out for quick answers and ready solutions, whereas many problems call for a patient, concerted, negotiated strategy of reform. This is precisely the case where education policies are concerned.

• The tension between, on the one hand, the need for competition, and on the other, the concern for equality of opportunity: this is a classic issue, which has been facing both economic and social policy-makers and educational policy-makers since the beginning of the century. Solutions have sometimes been proposed but they have never stood the test of time. Today, the Commission ventures to claim that the pressures of competition have caused many of those in positions of authority to lose sight of their mission, which is to give each human being the means to take full advantage of every opportunity. This has led us, within the terms of reference of the report, to rethink and update the concept of lifelong education so as to reconcile three forces: competition, which provides incentives; co-operation, which gives strength; and solidarity, which unites.

• The tension between the extraordinary expansion of knowledge and human beings' capacity to assimilate it: the Commission was unable to resist the temptation to add some new subjects for study, such as self-knowledge, ways to ensure physical and psychological well-being or ways to an improved understanding of the natural environment and to preserving it better. Since there is already increasing pressure on curricula, any clear-sighted reform strategy must involve making choices, providing always that the essential features of a basic education that teaches pupils how to improve their lives through knowledge, through experiment and through the development of their own personal cultures are preserved.

• Lastly – another perennial factor – the tension between the spiritual and the material: often without realizing it, the world has a longing, often unexpressed, for an ideal and for values that we shall term 'moral'. It is thus education's noble task to encourage each and every one, acting in accordance with their traditions and convictions and paying full respect to pluralism, to lift their minds and spirits to the plane of the universal and, in some measure, to transcend themselves. It is no exaggeration on the Commission's part to say that the survival of humanity depends thereon.

Designing and building our common future

People today have a dizzying feeling of being torn between a globalization whose manifestations they can see and sometimes have to endure, and their search for roots, reference points and a sense of belonging.

Education has to face up to this problem now more than ever as a world society struggles painfully to be born: education is at the heart of both personal and community development; its mission is to enable each of us, without exception, to develop all our talents to the full and to realize our creative potential, including responsibility for our own lives and achievement of our personal aims.

This aim transcends all others. Its achievement, though long and difficult, will be an essential contribution to the search for a more just world, a better world to live in. The Commission wishes to stress this point strongly, at a time when some are being assailed by serious doubts as to the opportunities opened up by education.

It is true that many other problems have to be solved, and we shall come back to them, but this report has been prepared at a time when, faced with so many misfortunes caused by war, crime and under-development, humankind is apparently hesitating between continuing headlong along the same path and resignation. Let us offer people another way.

There is, therefore, every reason to place renewed emphasis on the moral and cultural dimensions of education, enabling each person to grasp the individuality of other people and to understand the world's erratic progression towards a certain unity; but this process must begin with self-understanding through an inner voyage whose milestones are knowledge, meditation and the practice of self-criticism.

This message should guide educational thinking, in conjunction with the establishment of wider and more far-reaching forms of international co-operation which will be discussed below.

Seen in this context, everything falls into place, whether it be the requirements of science and technology, knowledge of self and of the environment, or the development of skills enabling each person to function effectively in a family, as a citizen or as a productive member of society.

This all goes to show that the Commission in no way undervalues the central role of brainpower and innovation, the transition to a knowledge-driven society, the endogenous processes that make it possible to accumulate knowledge, to incorporate new discoveries and to apply them in different areas of human activity, from those related to health and the environment to the production of goods and services. It is also aware of the limits, and even the failures, of attempts to transfer technologies to the most impoverished countries, precisely because of the endogenous nature of methods for the accumulation and application of knowledge. This is why it is necessary, among other things, to become familiar at an early age with science and the uses of science, and with the difficult task of assimilating progress in such a way that human identity and integrity are fully respected. Here, too, the ethical issues must not be overlooked.

It also shows that the Commission is aware of the contribution that education must make to economic and social development. The education system is all too often blamed for unemployment. This observation is only partly true; above all it should not obscure the other political, economic and social prerequisites for achieving full employment or enabling the economies of underdeveloped countries to take off. As for education, the Commission believes that valid responses to the problems of mismatch between supply and demand on the labour market can come from a more flexible system that allows greater curricular diversity and builds bridges between different types of education, or between working life and further training. Such flexibility would also help to reduce school failure and the tremendous wastage of human potential resulting from it.

Such improvements, desirable and feasible as they are, do not, however, obviate the need for intellectual innovation and the implementation of a model of sustainable development based on the specific characteristics of each country. Given the present and foreseeable advances in science and technology, and the growing importance of knowledge and other intangibles in the production of goods and services, we need to rethink the place of work and its changing status in tomorrow's society. To create tomorrow's society, imagination will have to keep ahead of technological progress in order to avoid further increases in unemployment and social exclusion or inequalities in development.

For all these reasons, it seems to us that the concept of an education pursued throughout life, with all its advantages in terms of flexibility, diversity and availability at different times and in different places, should command wide support. There is a need to rethink and broaden the notion of lifelong education. Not only must it adapt to changes in the nature of work, but it must also constitute a continuous process of forming whole human beings – their knowledge and aptitudes, as well as the critical faculty and the ability to act. It should enable people to develop awareness of themselves and their environment and encourage them to play their social role at work and in the community.

In this context, the Commission discussed the need to advance towards a 'learning society'. The truth is that every aspect of life, at both the individual and the social level, offers opportunities for both learning and doing. It is thus very tempting to focus too much on this side of the question, stressing the educational potential of the modern media, the world of work or cultural and leisure pursuits, even to the extent of overlooking a number of fundamental truths: although people need to take every opportunity for learning and self-improvement, they will not be able to make good use of all these potential resources unless they have received a sound basic education. Better still, school should impart both the desire for, and pleasure in, learning, the ability to learn how to learn, and intellectual curiosity. One might even imagine a society in which each individual would be in turn both teacher and learner.

For this to come about, nothing can replace the formal education system, where each individual is introduced to the many forms of knowledge. There is no substitute for the teacher–pupil relationship, which is underpinned by authority and developed through dialogue. This has been argued time and time again by the great classical thinkers who have studied the question of education. It is the responsibility of the teacher to impart to the pupil the knowledge that humankind has acquired about itself and about nature and everything of importance that it has created and invented.

Learning throughout life: the heartbeat of society

The concept of learning throughout life thus emerges as one of the keys to the twenty-first century. It goes beyond the traditional distinction between initial and continuing education. It meets the challenges posed by a rapidly changing world. This is not a new insight, since previous reports on education have emphasized the need for people to return to education in order to deal with new situations arising in their personal and working lives. That need is still felt and is even becoming stronger. The only way of satisfying it is for each individual to learn how to learn.

But there is a further requirement: the far-reaching changes in the traditional patterns of life require of us a better understanding of other people and the world at large; they demand mutual understanding, peaceful interchange and, indeed, harmony – the very things that are most lacking in our world today.

Having adopted this position, the Commission has put greater emphasis on one of the four pillars that it proposes and describes as the foundations of education: *learning to live together*, by developing an understanding of others and their history, traditions and spiritual values and, on this basis, creating a new spirit which, guided by recognition of our growing interdependence and a common analysis of the risks and challenges of the future, would induce people to implement common projects or to manage the inevitable conflicts in an intelligent and peaceful way. Utopia, some might think, but it is a necessary Utopia, indeed a vital one if we are to escape from a dangerous cycle sustained by cynicism or by resignation.

While the Commission has indeed a vision of the kind of education that would create and underlay this new spirit, it has not disregarded the other three pillars of education which provide, as it were, the bases for learning to live together.

The first of these is *learning to know*. Given the rapid changes brought about by scientific progress and the new forms of economic and social activity, the emphasis has to be on combining a sufficiently broad general education with the possibility of in-depth work on a selected number of subjects. Such a general background provides, so to speak, the passport to lifelong education, in so far as it gives people a taste – but also lays the foundations – for learning throughout life.

Learning to do is another pillar. In addition to learning to do a job of work, it should, more generally, entail the acquisition of a competence that enables people to deal with a variety of situations, often unforeseeable, and to work in teams, a feature to which educational methods do not at present pay enough attention. In many cases, such competence and skills are more readily acquired if pupils and students have the opportunity to try out and develop their abilities by becoming involved in work experience schemes or social work while they are still in education, whence the increased importance that should be attached to all methods of alternating study with work.

Last, but far from least, is the fourth pillar: *learning to be.* This was the dominant theme of the Edgar Faure report *Learning to Be: The World of Education Today and Tomorrow,* published by UNESCO in 1972. Its recommendations are still very relevant, for in the twenty-first century everyone will need to exercise greater independence and judgement combined with a stronger sense of personal responsibility for the attainment of common goals. Our report stresses a further imperative: none of the talents which are hidden like buried treasure in every person must be left untapped. These are, to name but a few: memory, reasoning power, imagination, physical ability, aesthetic sense, the aptitude to communicate with others and the natural charisma of the group leader, which again goes to prove the need for greater self-knowledge.

The Commission has alluded to another Utopian idea: a

learning society founded on the acquisition, renewal and use of knowledge. These are three aspects that ought to be emphasized in the educational process. As the development of the 'information society' is increasing the opportunities for access to data and facts, education should enable everyone to gather information and to select, arrange, manage and use it.

While education should, therefore, constantly adapt to changes in society, it must not fail to pass on the attainments, foundations and benefits of human experience.

Faced with a growing and at the same time increasingly quality-minded demand for education, how can educational policies achieve the twin aims of high educational standards and equity? These were the questions that the Commission addressed concerning courses of study, educational methods and content, and prerequisites for the effectiveness of education.

The stages and bridges of learning: a fresh approach

By focusing its recommendations on the concept of learning throughout life, the Commission did not intend to convey the idea that by such a qualitative leap one could avoid reflecting on the different levels of education. On the contrary, it has set out to reassert some of the major principles advanced by UNESCO, such as the vital need for basic education, to urge a review of the role of secondary education and to examine the issues raised by developments in higher education, particularly the phenomenon of mass higher education.

Quite simply, learning throughout life makes it possible to organize the various stages of education to provide for passage from one stage to another and to diversify the paths through the system, while enhancing the value of each. This could be a way of avoiding the invidious choice between selection by ability, which increases the number of academic failures and the risks of exclusion, and the same education for all, which can inhibit talent.

The foregoing in no way detracts from the excellent definition

of *basic learning needs* produced in 1990 at the World Conference
on Education for All (Jomtien, Thailand):

These needs comprise both essential learning tools (such as literacy, oral
expression, numeracy, and problem solving) and the basic learning content
(such as knowledge, skills, values, and attitudes) required by human beings to
be able to survive, to develop their full capacities, to live and work in dignity,
to participate fully in development, to improve the quality of their lives, to
make informed decisions, and to continue learning. (World Declaration on
Education for All, Art. 1, para. 1.)

This is certainly an impressive catalogue, but it does not necessarily
imply an overloading of curricula. The teacher–pupil relationship, the
learning available in children's local environment, and an effective use
of modern media (where they exist) can in conjunction contribute to the
personal and intellectual development of each pupil. The 'three Rs'
– reading, writing and arithmetic – are given their full due. The
combination of conventional teaching and out-of-school approaches
should enable children to experience the three dimensions of education
– the ethical and cultural, the scientific and technological, and the
economic and social.

To put it another way, education is also a social experience through
which children learn about themselves, develop interpersonal skills and
acquire basic knowledge and skills. This experience should begin in
early childhood, in different forms depending on the situation, but
always with the involvement of families and local communities.

Two observations which the Commission sees as important should
be added at this stage.

Basic education should be extended, worldwide, to the 900 million
illiterate adults, the 130 million children not enrolled in school, and
the more than 100 million children who drop out prematurely from
school. This vast undertaking is a priority for the technical assistance and partnership projects carried out as part of international
co-operation.

Basic education is of course an issue in all countries, including the industrialized ones. From this initial stage onwards, educational contents should be designed to stimulate a love of learning and knowledge and thus develop the desire and provide the opportunities for learning throughout life.

This brings us to one of the major problem areas in any reform, that of the policies to be applied to the period of adolescence and youth, between primary education and work or higher education. To coin a phrase, *secondary schools* cut rather a sorry figure in educational thinking. They are the target of considerable criticism and they provoke a considerable amount of frustration.

Among the sources of frustration are the increased and increasingly diversified requirements, leading to rapid growth in enrolments and overcrowded curricula – whence the familiar problems associated with mass education, which the less-developed countries cannot easily solve at either the financial or the organizational level. There is also the distress felt by school-leavers who face a shortage of opportunities, a distress increased by an all-or-nothing obsession with getting into higher education. Mass unemployment in many countries only adds to the malaise. The Commission stresses its alarm at a trend that is leading, in both rural and urban areas, in both developing and industrialized countries, not only to unemployment but also to the under-utilization of human resources.

The Commission is convinced that the only way out of this difficult situation is a very broad diversification of the types of study available. This reflects one of the Commission's major concerns, which is to make the most of all forms of talent so as to reduce academic failure and prevent the far-too-widespread feeling among young people that they are excluded, left with no prospects.

These various types should include both conventional education, which focuses more on abstraction and conceptualization, and approaches that alternate school with work experience in a way that brings out additional abilities and inclinations. In any event, there should be bridges between these approaches so that errors – all too frequent – in the choice of direction can be corrected.

The Commission also believes that the prospect of being able to go back to education or training would alter the general climate by assuring young people that their fate is not sealed forever between the ages of 14 and 20.

Higher education should be seen from this same angle.

A first point to remember is that, side by side with universities, there are other types of higher education institutions in many countries. Some cream off the most able students while others were set up to provide specifically targeted, high-quality vocational training, lasting between two and four years. Such diversification undeniably meets the needs of society and the economy as manifested both at the national and at the regional levels.

Increasingly stringent selection in order to ease the pressures brought about by mass higher education in the wealthiest countries is neither politically nor socially acceptable. One of the main drawbacks of such an approach is that many young people are shut out from the educational process before they have been able to obtain a recognized diploma; they are therefore in the desperate predicament of having obtained neither a formal qualification nor a training appropriate for the job market.

The evolution of enrolments therefore needs to be managed, but it can be kept within limits as a result of secondary education reform, along the broad lines proposed by the Commission.

Universities would contribute to this process by diversifying what they offer:

• as scientific establishments and centres of learning, from where students go on to theoretical or applied research or teaching;

• as establishments offering occupational qualifications, combining high-level knowledge and skills, with courses and content continually tailored to the needs of the economy;

• as some of the main meeting-places for learning throughout life, opening their doors to adults who wish either to resume their studies or to adapt and develop their knowledge or to satisfy their taste for learning in all areas of cultural life; and

- as leading partners in international co-operation, facilitating exchanges of teachers and students and ensuring that the best teaching is made widely available through international professorships.

In this way, universities would transcend what is wrongly held to be the conflict between the logic of public service and the logic of the job market. They would also reclaim their intellectual and social vocation as, in a sense, guarantors of universal values and the cultural heritage. The Commission sees these as cogent reasons for urging greater university autonomy.

Having formulated these proposals, the Commission emphasizes that these issues take on a special significance in poor countries, where universities have a decisive role to play. In developing countries, universities must learn from their own past and analyse their countries' difficulties, engaging in research aimed at finding solutions to the most acute among them. It is also incumbent on them to propose a renewed vision of development that will enable their countries to build a genuinely better future. They must provide the vocational and technological training of the future leaders and the higher- and middle-level education required if their countries are to escape from their present treadmills of poverty and underdevelopment. It is particularly necessary to devise new development models for regions such as sub-Saharan Africa, as has already been done for some Eastern Asian countries, on a case-by-case basis.

Getting the reform strategies right

While neither underestimating the need to manage short-term constraints nor disregarding the need to adapt existing systems, the Commission wishes to emphasize the necessity of a more long-term approach if the reforms required are to succeed. By the same token, it stresses the fact that too many reforms one after another can be the death of reform, since they do not allow the system the time needed either to absorb change or to get all the parties concerned involved in the process. Furthermore, past failures show that many reformers adopt an approach that is either too radical or too theoretical, ignoring what can be usefully learned from experience or rejecting past achievements. As a result, teachers, parents and pupils are disoriented and less than willing to accept and implement reform.

The main parties contributing to the success of educational reforms are, first of all, the local community, including parents, school heads and teachers; secondly, the public authorities; and thirdly, the international community. Many past failures have been due to insufficient involvement of one or more of these partners. Attempts to impose educational reforms from the top down, or from outside, have obviously failed. The countries where the process has been relatively successful are those that obtained a determined commitment from local communities, parents and teachers, backed up by continuing dialogue and various forms of outside financial, technical or professional assistance. It is obvious that the local community plays a paramount role in any successful reform strategy.

Local community participation in assessing needs by means of a dialogue with the public authorities and groups concerned in society is a first, essential stage in broadening access to education and improving its quality. Continuing the dialogue by way of the media, community discussions, parent education and on-the-job teacher training usually helps to create awareness, sharpen judgement and develop local capacities. When communities assume greater responsibility for their own development, they learn to appreciate the role of education both as a way of achieving societal objectives and as a desirable improvement of the quality of life.

In this respect, the Commission stresses the value of a cautious measure of decentralization in helping to increase educational establishments' responsibilities and their scope for innovation.

In any event, no reform can succeed without the co-operation and active participation of teachers. This is one reason why the Commission recommends that the social, cultural and material status of educators should be considered as a matter of priority.

We are asking a great deal, too much even, of teachers, when we expect them to make good the failings of other institutions which also have a responsibility for the education and training of young people. The demands made on teachers are considerable, at the very time when the outside world is increasingly encroaching upon the school, particularly through the new communication and information media. Thus, the young people with whom the teacher has to deal, though receiving less parental or religious guidance, are also better informed. Teachers have to take this new situation into account if they are to be heeded and understood by young people, give them a taste for learning, and show them that information and knowledge are two different things and that knowledge requires effort, concentration, discipline and determination.

Rightly or wrongly, teachers feel isolated, not just because teaching is an individual activity, but also because of the expectations aroused by education and the criticisms which are, often unjustly, directed at them. Above all, teachers want their dignity to be respected. Most teachers are members of unions – in some cases, powerful unions – which are, undeniably, committed to the protection of their corporate interests. Even so, there is a need for the dialogue between society and teachers, and between the public authorities and teachers' unions, to be both strengthened and seen in a new light.

Admittedly, the renewal of this kind of dialogue is no easy task, but it is one that must needs be carried out in order to put an end to the teachers' feelings of isolation and frustration, to make change acceptable and to ensure that everyone contributes to the success of the necessary reforms.

It is appropriate in this context to add some recommendations concerning the content of teacher training, access by teachers to continuing education, the improvement of the status of teachers responsible for basic education, and greater involvement of teachers in disadvantaged and marginalized groups, where they can help to improve the integration of children and adolescents in society.

This is also a plea for the education system to be provided not only with well-trained teachers but also with the wherewithal for delivering education of a high standard, including books, modern communication media, a suitable cultural and economic environment and so forth.

Conscious of the situation in schools today, the Commission lays great emphasis on the quantity and quality of traditional teaching materials such as books, and on new media such as information technologies, which should be used with discernment and with active pupil participation. For their part, teachers should work in teams, particularly in secondary schools, thereby helping to achieve the necessary flexibility in the courses of study on offer, thus obviating many failures, bringing out some of the pupils' natural talents, and providing better academic and career guidance with a view to learning continued throughout life.

The improvement of education, seen in this light, requires policy-makers to face up squarely to their responsibilities. They cannot leave it to market forces or to some kind of self-regulation to put things right when they go wrong.

It is on the strength of its belief in the importance of policy-makers that the Commission has stressed the permanence of values, the challenges of future demands, and the duties of teachers and society; they alone, taking all the factors into consideration, can generate the public-interests debates that education – since it concerns everyone, since it is our future that is at stake and since education can help to improve the lot of one and all – so badly needs.

This naturally leads us to focus on the role of the public authorities. They must propose clear options and, after broad consultation with all those involved, choose policies that, regardless of whether the education system is public, private or mixed, show the way, establish the system's foundations and its main thrusts, and regulate the system through the necessary adjustments.

Naturally, all public policy decisions have financial repercussions. The Commission does not underestimate this difficulty. Without entering into the complexities of various systems, it holds the view that education is a public good that should be available to all. Once this principle is accepted, public and private funding may be combined, according to different formulae that take into account each country's traditions, stage of development, ways of life and income distribution.

All the choices to be made should, in any event, be predicated upon the fundamental principle of equality of opportunity.

During the discussions, I made a more radical proposal. As learning throughout life gradually becomes a reality, all young persons could be allocated a study-time entitlement at the start of their education, entitling them to a certain number of years of education. Their entitlement would be credited to an account at an institution that would manage a 'capital' of time available for each individual, together with the appropriate funds. Everyone could use their capital, on the basis of their previous educational experience, as they saw fit. Some of the capital could be set aside to enable people to receive continuing education during their adult lives. Each person could increase his or her capital through deposits at the 'bank' under a kind of educational savings scheme. After thorough discussion, the Commission supported this idea, though it was aware of the potential risks, even to equality of opportunity. As things stand today, a study-time entitlement could be granted at the end of compulsory schooling, so as to enable adolescents to choose a path without signing away their future.

In general, however, if after the essential step forward taken by the Jomtien Conference on basic education one had to point to an emergency situation, it would be to secondary education that we would turn our attention, given that the fate of millions of boys and girls is decided between the time they leave primary school and the time they either start work or go on to higher education. This is where the crunch comes in our education systems, either because those systems are too élitist or because they fail to come to terms with massive enrolments because of inertia and total inability to adapt. At a time when these young people are struggling with the problems of adolescence, when they feel, in a sense, mature but are in fact still immature, when instead of being carefree they are worried about their future, the important thing is to provide them with places where they can learn and discover, to give them the wherewithal to think about their future and prepare for it, and to offer them a choice of pathways suited to their abilities. It is also important to ensure that the avenues ahead of them are not blocked and that remedial action and in-course correction of their educational careers are at all times possible.

Broadening international co-operation in the global village

The Commission noted the growing tendency, in the political and economic spheres, to resort to international action as a way of finding satisfactory solutions to problems that have a global dimension, if only because of the growing interdependence that has so often been emphasized. It also regretted the inadequacy of results and stressed the need for reform of international institutions to make their action more effective.

The same applies, *mutatis mutandis*, to the social and educational fields. Emphasis has been deliberately placed on the importance of the World Summit for Social Development, held in Copenhagen in March 1995. Education occupies a prominent place in the guidelines adopted there and this prompted the Commission to formulate, in this respect, recommendations concerning:

• a policy of strong encouragement for the education of girls and women, following directly on from the recommendations of the Fourth World Conference on Women (Beijing, September 1995);

• the allocation of a minimum percentage of development aid (a quarter of the total) to fund education: this slanting in the direction of education should also apply to international funding institutions, first and foremost the World Bank, which already plays an important role;

• the development of 'debt-for-education swaps' to offset the adverse effects of adjustment policies and policies for reducing internal and external deficits upon public spending on education;

• the widespread introduction of the new 'information society' technologies in all countries, to prevent yet another gap opening up between rich countries and poor countries; and

• tapping into the outstanding potential offered by non-governmental organizations, and hence by grass-roots initiatives, which could provide a valuable backup to international co-operation.

These few suggestions should be seen in the context of partnership rather than aid. After so many failures and so much waste, experience militates in favour of partnership, globalization makes it inescapable, and there are some encouraging examples, such as the successful co-operation and exchanges within regional groupings, the European Union being a case in point.

Another justification for partnership is that it can lead to a 'win-win situation': whilst industrialized countries can assist developing countries by the input of their successful experiences, their technologies and financial and material resources, they can learn from the developing countries ways of passing on their cultural heritage, approaches to the socialization of children and, more fundamentally, different cultures and ways of life.

The Commission expresses the hope that the Member States will give UNESCO the necessary resources to enable it to foster both the spirit of partnership and partnership in action, along the lines suggested by the Commission to the Twenty-eighth Session of the General Conference. UNESCO can do this by publicizing successful innovations and helping to establish networks on the basis of grass-roots initiatives by non-governmental organizations, whether aiming to develop education of a high standard (UNESCO professorships) or to stimulate research partnerships.

We also believe it has a central role to play in developing the new information technologies in such a way that they serve the interests of quality education.

More fundamentally, however, UNESCO will serve peace and mutual understanding by emphasizing the value of education as a manifestation of the spirit of concord, stemming from the will to live together, as active members of our global village, thinking and organizing for the good of future generations. It is in this way that UNESCO will contribute to a culture of peace.

For the title of its report, the Commission turned to one of La Fontaine's fables, *The Ploughman and his Children*:

> *Be sure (the ploughman said), not to sell the inheritance*
> *Our forebears left to us:*
> *A treasure lies concealed therein.*

Readapting slightly the words of the poet, who was lauding the virtues of hard work, and referring instead to education – that is, everything that humanity has learned about itself – we could have him say:

> *But the old man was wise*
> *To show them before he died*
> *That learning is the treasure.*

Jacques Delors
Chairman of the Commission

Outlooks

Chapter 1

From the local community to a world society

There exists today a global arena in which, whether we like it or not, the destiny of every individual is to some extent played out. World-wide economic, scientific, cultural and political interdependence – dictated by the opening up, under the pressure of free-trade theories of economic and financial frontiers, reinforced by the break-up of the Soviet bloc and finding an instrument in the new information technologies – is becoming ever more securely established. Whereas the average person is somewhat bemused by this phenomenon, it is one that leaders have to face on a daily basis. What is more, the widespread realization that international relations are now globalized is itself a dimension of the phenomenon. Despite its latent promise, the emergence of this new world, difficult to apprehend and even more difficult to predict, is creating a climate of uncertainty, not to say apprehension, which renders the search for a truly global approach to problems even more half-hearted.

An increasingly crowded planet

The State
World
ulation
)3, New
k, UNFPA,
3.

Before referring to the many forms that globalization takes in the world today, we shall take a look at some statistics[1] that show the brisk pace of world population growth, for this is in a way the backdrop against which the problems are developing. Despite a slight decline in fertility rates in the past two decades, the world's population, by virtue of its previous growth, has continued to swell. Standing at 5.57 billion in 1993, it is expected to reach 6.25 billion in the year 2000 and hit the 10 billion mark by 2050.

Within that global picture there are sharp variations between regions. The developing countries' share of population growth rose from 77 per cent in 1950 to 93 per cent in 1990, and will account for 95 per cent by the end of the century. Conversely, population growth has slowed down in the industrialized countries – and even halted in some – and their fertility rates are at or below the replacement level. The proportion of over-65s will shoot up in these low-growth countries from 12 per cent in 1990 to 16 per cent in 2010 and 19 per cent in 2025. This ageing of the population will undoubtedly have repercussions not only on lifestyles and standards of living, but also on the financing of public expenditure. The absolute number of young people under the age of 15 has grown by leaps and bounds, from 700 million in 1950 to 1.7 billion in 1990. This accounts for the unprecedented pressure on education systems and the demands on them which stretch to the limit, and sometimes outstrip, their capacity to deliver. Today more than 1 billion young people – nearly one-fifth of the population – are attending school, as against a mere 300 million in 1953.[2]

Such growth in the world's population at a point in history when technology is shrinking time and space is bringing the many activities that go on in the world into an ever closer

The evolution of the age-structure of the world's population, 1980-2010 (percentages)

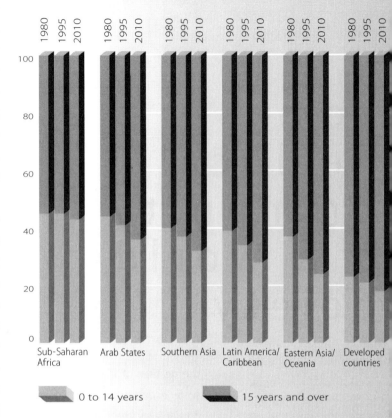

Figures compiled by UNESCO's Division of Statistics. The regions correspond to UNESCO's nomenclature. The countries of the former Soviet Union are considered as developed countries, and those that are in Asia are also included there.

2. *World Education Report 1995,* Paris, UNESCO 1995.

relationship and, without our necessarily realizing it, gives certain decisions a planetary dimension. Never before will their consequences, good or bad, have touched the lives of so many.

Towards the globalization of human activity

In the course of the past twenty-five years, the phenomenon of globalization made its appearance first of all in the economic sphere. Deregulation and the opening-out of financial markets, hastened by developments in information technology, soon gave rise to the feeling that those markets were no longer watertight compartments within one vast world capital market dominated by a handful of major financial centres. This meant that all economies were dependent on the movements of a steadily growing mass of capital, shifting from one financial centre to another at high speed, in accordance with interest-rate differentials and speculative forecasts. Subject to a logic of their own which stresses short-termism, the global financial markets no longer simply reflect the constraints of a given country's economy, but sometimes seem to dictate the terms of national economic policies.

This opening-up of frontiers has slowly but surely affected trade and industry. Foreign-exchange markets immediately pass all currency fluctuations on to the raw materials and commodity markets, and, generally speaking, economic interdependence means that the industrial crises of the most developed countries reverberate throughout the world. The large corporations have had to take those uncertainties and new types of risk into account in framing their strategies.

The resulting situation has depressed the economies of certain industrialized countries and, consequently, those of the developing countries that provide them with their raw materials. At the same time, the expansion of world trade has been beneficial to a number of countries. Growth in world exports between 1970 and 1993 was on average 1.5 percentage points higher than that of the gross domestic product (GDP), with an even greater difference in some countries, especially in the period 1980–93: almost three percentage points higher in the case of the Republic of Korea and seven points higher in the case of Thailand. World growth would thus appear to have been largely export-driven, particularly in the countries where growth has been the greatest. The share of exports of goods and services in GDP rose from 14 per cent in 1970 to 21 per cent in 1991 for all economies, and in the case of China the rise was from 3 to 24 per cent, in the case of Indonesia from 13 to 28 per cent, and in Malaysia from 42 to 80 per cent.[3] These figures clearly substantiate the notion of world interdependence.

At the same time, globalization has redrawn the world economic map. New centres of vigorous growth, based on world trade, have emerged on the Pacific rim. The North–South divide has become less clear-cut, as most observers contend that the developing countries should nowadays be classified in a series of different categories that could vary, according to whether the criterion applied is per capita GDP, the pace of development or the criteria of sustainable human development established by the United Nations Development Programme (UNDP). This means, for instance, that the question of sub-Saharan Africa's place in the global economy can no longer be discussed in the same terms as that of the Latin American countries. All in all, globalization, which dictates that every country must be able to claim some special advantages in order to participate in the development of international economic relations, makes the disparity between winners and losers in the development game even more blatant.

These disparities are tending to be exacerbated by another aspect of globalization: the establishment of science and technology networks that link up research centres to major business enterprises the world over. By and large, it is those who have a contribution to make to such networks, be it information or funding, that are able to join. Researchers or business people in the poorest countries may well find themselves excluded, with the result that the knowledge gap widens, which in turn leaves those deprived of knowledge cast adrift, far from where the action is.

Lastly, an even more acute threat is the fact that crime is also becoming globalized. The ease with which information and money now cross frontiers facilitates the illegal trade in drugs, arms, nuclear materials and even human beings, as well as the establishment of terrorist and criminal networks and the spread of money-laundering.

3. *World Development Report 1995. Workers in an Integrating World* (published for the World Bank), New York/Oxford, Oxford University Press, 1995.

Universal communication

New technologies have brought humankind into the age of universal communication: by abolishing distance, they are instrumental in shaping the societies of tomorrow which, because of those technologies, will have nothing in common with any model from the past. The most accurate, up-to-date information can be made available to anyone, anywhere in the world, often in real time, and reaches the most remote regions. Interactive media will soon make it possible not only to send and receive information, but to engage in dialogue, discussion and the transmission of information and knowledge unconstrained by distance or operating time. Let us not forget, however, that a very large underprivileged population remains excluded from these developments, in areas without electricity for instance. Let us also remember that over half of the world's population has no access to the various services available via telephone systems.

The free flow of images and words worldwide, which prefigures the world of tomorrow, its disturbing aspects included, has transformed not only international relations but people's understanding of the world. It is one of the foremost accelerators of globalization and yet it has its negative side. Information systems are still relatively costly, it is difficult for many countries to gain entry to them and control of them bestows on the great powers or the private interests that possess them real cultural or political leverage, particularly over people who have not had the benefit of the type of education that would equip them to arrange the information they receive by order of importance and to interpret or evaluate it. The fact that a handful of countries enjoy a virtual monopoly of the cultural industries and that their products are distributed throughout the world to an ever-growing audience is a powerful factor in the erosion of cultural distinctiveness. Predictable and all too often very trivial though it may be, this spurious 'world culture' nevertheless conveys implicit value systems, and may well produce a sense of dispossession and loss of identity in those exposed to it.

Education undoubtedly has an important role to play in any attempt to deal with the booming, intertwining communication networks which, by allowing the world to listen in on itself, truly make all people neighbours.

The many faces of global interdependence

Initially observed in economic and technological activity, the worldwide interweaving of decisions and actions, public and private, is slowly but surely gaining ground in other fields of human activity. Its implications for the environment extend well beyond national frontiers and it is a fact that the adverse effects of industrialization are very inequitably distributed, often affecting the least-developed countries most.

There are other manifestations of the globalization of problems which have societal repercussions that directly affect education systems. International migrations are a case in point. Reaching a long way back in history, in forms that vary widely depending on the time and the region, large-scale population movements not only continue to this day but seem likely to escalate.[4] Migratory pressures are on the increase: uneven economic growth in the world by no means eases the disparities between nations but instead exacerbates them. A great many other factors are involved here, such as the persistence of rapid population growth in a considerable part of the developing world; continuing depopulation of the countryside or the marginalization of rural areas; accelerated urbanization; the attraction of the lifestyles and sometimes the values of the more prosperous countries, as glimpsed through the media; and faster and cheaper transport. In addition to 'economic' migrants, when conflicts break out there are political refugees and asylum-seekers who, in the 1980s and 1990s, accounted for the bulk of international migrations in certain parts of the world. For example, Africa today has over 5 million refugees, most of whom are women and children.[5] A complex social process by virtue of the displacement and consequent mixing of populations, an economic process of world importance in the same way as trade in raw materials or manufactured goods and a human odyssey frequently fraught with drama for those involved, migrations have more drastic repercussions than the statistics suggest, both on the countries of origin and on the host countries, particularly, in the latter case, where education is concerned. Because migration is a daily, living metaphor of global interdependence, the welcome extended to migrants by the receiving countries and the migrants' capacity for integration into their new human environment are benchmarks against which a modern society's

4. *The State of World Population 1993*, op. cit.

5. Pan-African Conference on the Education of Girls, Ouagadougou, Burkina Faso, 28 March to 1 April 1993, *Educating Girls and Women in Africa*, Paris, UNICEF/UNESCO, 1995. (UNESCO doc. ED.95/WS.30.)

Dimensions of migration

Throughout history there have been periods when migration has been an important economic and social safety valve, allowing labour to relocate to areas where it was more scarce. Usually the cost and difficulty of travel were a serious limitation, but a major break occurred in the twentieth century, when lower transportation costs made possible a sharp increase in labour mobility, even as the rise of the nation-state increased controls on migration. Today the number of both sending and receiving nations has increased – at least 125 million people now live outside their country of origin. Migrants today increasingly come from poor countries, and their stay in the host countries is becoming shorter. The number of highly skilled workers on the move has increased as well. There has also been a sharp rise in the number of refugees, a consequence of regional conflicts and the breakup of the old East–West order.

More than half the global flow of migrants is now between developing countries – examples include South Asians going to oil-rich countries in the Middle East and newly industrializing economies in East Asia, and relatively successful countries in Sub-Saharan Africa attracting workers from their poorer neighbours. Côte d'Ivoire, Nigeria and South Africa have received about half of Africa's large migratory flow.

[. . .]

Most recently there has been a rising demand for temporary workers in the successful Asian economies, particularly Japan, the Republic of Korea, and Malaysia. Fears of massive population movement following the dissolution of the Soviet Union have not materialized, either within the region or from East to West.

The flow of migrants to industrial countries has risen, and its composition has shifted to developing-country sources. In Australia, Canada and the United States inflows from developing countries have risen slowly, reaching about 900,000 a year by 1993. In Western Europe large-scale labour recruitment began during the boom years of the 1960s. After the oil shock of 1973 and the ensuing recession, foreign workers were encouraged to return home. A dip in the early 1980s was soon followed by a rise in the growth of the foreign population to about 180,000 a year. Unlike that of the 1960s, however, this latest burst of growth is occurring in an environment of rising unemployment that is exacerbating social tensions and increasing xenophobia – both in the United States and across Europe.

Source: World Development Report 1995. Workers in an Integrating World, op. cit., pp. 64–5.

receptiveness to what is 'foreign' can be measured.

Another facet of the problems of the future is the multiplicity of languages, an expression of humanity's cultural diversity. There are an estimated 6,000 languages in the world, of which a dozen are spoken by over 100 million people. The increased population movements of recent years have created new language situations that underscore this diversity, especially in the big cities. At the same time, widely spoken languages – those that enable people to communicate both internationally and within nations – are gaining in importance with the increase in population mobility and the development of the media. The complexity of linguistic situations from country to country makes it very difficult to put forward any recommendation that would apply in all circumstances. What is certain, however, is that the study of widely used languages should be combined with the study of local languages in bilingual or even trilingual curricula which are already the norm in some regions of the world. In multilingual societies, acquisition of mother-tongue literacy skills, where feasible, is often considered desirable for a child's academic development, to be followed by a gradual transition to the common language.

Generally speaking, linguistic diversity cannot be viewed merely as an obstacle to communication between the various groups; rather, it should be regarded as a source of enrichment, which is an argument in favour of strengthening language teaching. The requirements of globalization and cultural identity should be seen as complementary rather than contradictory.

An uncertain world

Although the collapse of the Soviet empire in 1989 turned a new page of history, paradoxically, the end of the Cold War which had marked the preceding decades has produced a more complex, uncertain and perhaps more dangerous world. It may be that the Cold War had for a long time masked latent tensions between nations, ethnic groups and religious communities: these are now resurfacing to create countless areas of unrest or causes of overt conflict. The entry into what is, or is felt to be, a world fraught with danger, many elements of which are still impossible to decipher, is one of the characteristic features of the late twentieth century that profoundly disturbs and challenges the conscience of the world.

The failure of certain totalitarian regimes may rightly be hailed as a step forward on the road to freedom and democracy, but there is still a long way to go, and the discovery of the host of dangers that the world will have to face in the future brings the observer face to face with many paradoxes: totalitarian power has been shown to be fragile, but its effects have endured; we are witnessing, at one and the same time, the decline of the nation-state and the rise of one form or another of nationalism; and while peace now seems less impossible than during the Cold War, war seems less unlikely.[6]

Uncertainty about where humanity is heading is taking on a new, many-faceted form. The stockpiling of weapons, including nuclear weapons, is no longer simply a deterrent intended as insurance against the risk of war between two blocs: it is now the product of widespread competition for the possession of sophisticated weaponry.[7]

The arms race no longer involves only a few states; it now involves non-institutional entities such as political groups and terrorist organizations. Even if the world resolves the issue of nuclear non-proliferation, it is at risk from new state-of-the-art chemical and biological weapons. Hence, over and above the

6. See Pierre Hassner, *La violence et la paix*, Paris, Éditions Esprit, 1995.

7. *Our Global Neighbourhood, the Report of the Commission on Global Governance*, p. 13, Oxford, Oxford University Press, 1995.

risk of conflicts between nations, there is now the risk of civil war and widespread violence which leaves the major international organizations, in particular the United Nations, and national governments powerless.

Beyond the uncertainty about the future felt by all the people in the world, none of whom is safe from violence, the general impression is an unclear one, since although the sense of solidarity has never been so keen, never have there been so many opportunities for division and conflict.

Even though the fear of these dangers is universally shared, especially because of the wide dissemination of information on the effects of violence, it is not felt so acutely by those who are benefiting from the changing situation as by those who are experiencing only the disadvantages. People are upset by the rapid changes and feel obliged to protect themselves against them, or at least to manage them so as to minimize them, but some people, for economic or political reasons, are powerless to control them. The danger for the world as a whole is that they may become the hostages, and then possibly the mercenaries, of those who are ready to use violence in order to gain power.

The local and the global

The uneasiness engendered by the indecipherable nature of the future is combined with ever sharper awareness of the huge disparities existing in the world and the myriad resulting tensions between the local and the 'global'.

Growing interdependence has served to highlight a multiplicity of disparities: the imbalance between rich and poor countries; the social cleavage between the affluent and society's outcasts within each country; and the reckless use of natural resources which is hastening the degradation of the environment. Inequalities in levels of development have in some cases got worse, as most international reports stress, and the very poorest countries can be seen to be really adrift. These blatant inequalities are more and more keenly felt as the information and communication media reach a wider audience. The often smug picture of the lifestyles and consumption patterns of the affluent presented by the media arouses rancour and frustration among the very poor, if not outright hostility and rejection. It is increasingly difficult for the wealthier countries to shut their eyes to the pressing need for active international solidarity in order to guarantee the shared future by progressively building a juster world.

Furthermore, as we approach the turn of the century, the rapid changes we are witnessing in human societies operate at two levels: as we have already seen, there is growing internationalization but at the same time a search in many quarters for specific roots. Such changes are thus creating, for those who experience them or must endeavour to direct them, a mass of contradictory tensions against a background of upheaval.

Beset on all sides by a modern society in which they are often ill-equipped to play a meaningful part and which may conflict to some extent with their personal allegiance to a variety of local communities, people feel somehow dazed by the complexity of the modern world, which blurs their familiar landmarks. That sense of bewilderment is compounded by a number of factors: fear of disasters and conflicts that could place people's very integrity in jeopardy; a feeling of vulnerability to such hazards as unemployment caused by a change in employment structures; or a more general impotence when confronted by a globalization in which only a privileged few seem able to participate. Shaken by this undermining of the very pillars of their existence, people are likely to perceive the trends occurring outside the confines of their immediate group as threats, and be tempted, somewhat paradoxically, by the illusory sense of security offered by withdrawal into their own group and the rejection of 'the other' which this sometimes entails.

Key decision-makers, on the other hand, are falling prey to a perplexity of a different kind, though of identical origin, at a time when nation-states' organizational structures are, as it were, subjected to upward pressures created by the imperatives of globalization and to downward pressures generated by the demands of local communities. Rendered helpless by the rapid succession of events which often seem to outstrip or confound analysis and deprived of reliable criteria for action for lack of the necessary perspective, political decision-makers at times appear to swing between contradictory positions in order to justify the twists and turns that in fact betray their disarray.

In the final analysis, the difficulty, for public authorities, societies and individuals alike, lies in successfully overcoming the conflicting tensions that are to be found today at the heart of a great many human activities.

Understanding the world and understanding others

One of education's essential tasks is to help to transform de facto interdependence into a solidarity freely entered into. To that end, it must enable people to understand themselves and to understand others through better understanding of the world.

The first step towards grasping the growing complexity of world events and combating the feeling of uncertainty it engenders is to acquire a body of knowledge and then learn to put the facts in perspective and adopt a critical approach to the flow of information. Here, more than ever, education shows itself to be irreplaceable in developing judgement. It fosters a genuine understanding of events, going beyond the media's sometimes over-simplified and distorted portrayal. Ideally, it should help everyone to become, to some extent, a citizen of the turbulent and changing world that is being born before our very eyes.

There is obviously no way of understanding the world without understanding the relationship between human beings and their environment. This does not call for a new subject to be added to the already crowded curricula but for existing subjects to be reorganized around a comprehensive view of the ties that bind men and women to their environment, involving both the natural and the social sciences. This type of training could also be offered to everyone as part of life-long education.

Worldwide solidarity also means overriding the inward-looking tendency to focus on one's own identity in favour of an understanding of others based on respect for diversity. Here, the responsibility of education is both essential and problematic, in that the concept of identity can be interpreted in two ways: to assert one's difference, rediscover one's cultural roots and reinforce group solidarity can be a positive and liberating experience for every individual, but if misunderstood it can also make contact and dialogue with others difficult or well-nigh impossible.

Education should therefore seek to make individuals aware of their roots so as to give them points of reference that enable them to determine their place in the world, but it should also teach them respect for other cultures. Some subjects are of crucial importance in this regard. History, for instance, has often served to bolster a sense of national identity by highlighting differences and extolling a sense of superiority, essentially because history teaching was based on a non-scientific outlook. Insistence on the truth, on the other hand, which obliges one to admit that 'human groups, peoples, nations and continents are not all alike, forces us by this simple fact to look beyond our immediate experience, to accept and recognize people's differences and discover that other peoples also have a history that is rich and instructive'.[8] Knowledge of other cultures leads, then, to an awareness of the uniqueness of one's own culture but also an awareness of a heritage common to all humanity.

Understanding others thus makes possible a better knowledge of oneself: any form of identity is complex, for individuals are defined in relation to other people – both individually and collectively – and to the various groups to which they owe allegiance, in a constantly shifting pattern. The realization that there are many such allegiances, over and above such relatively restricted groups as the family, the local community or even the national community, informs the search for common values that can serve as the foundation for the 'intellectual and moral solidarity of mankind' proclaimed in UNESCO's Constitution.

Education thus has a special responsibility to exercise in the building of a more mutually supportive world, and the Commission takes the view that educational policies should forcefully reflect that responsibility. Education must help to engender a new humanism, one that contains an essential ethical component and sets considerable store by knowledge of, and respect for, the cultures and spiritual values of different civilizations, as a much-needed counterweight to a globalization that would otherwise be seen only in economic or technological terms. The sense of shared values and a common destiny is in fact the basis on which any scheme for international co-operation must be founded.

Young people and World Heritage

In order to sensitize young people to the need to protect the world's cultural and natural heritage, seriously threatened by pollution, population pressure, wars and poverty, UNESCO launched in 1994 the interregional project 'Young People's Participation in World Heritage Preservation and Promotion' with funding from the Rhône-Poulenc Foundation and NORAD. Its aims are to make students aware of their own culture and history, to help them learn about and respect other cultures and feel a common responsibility for the world heritage in the future.

Students and teachers from about fifty countries participating in the project have been acquainted with the spirit and the practical implications of the international Convention for the Protection of the World Cultural and Natural Heritage. Adopted in 1972, the Convention covers 469 outstanding cultural and natural sites in 104 countries, including the Great Wall of China, the Pyramids of Egypt and the Galapagos Islands.

Having learnt about the sites in their own countries and elsewhere in the context of different study areas, such as history, geography and languages, the students have gone on field visits to them or carried out information campaigns about them. Some classes have learnt the traditional craft skills that are needed for restoration work. Students and teachers were also able to exchange experiences gained at the first World Heritage Youth Forum, held in Bergen, Norway in June 1995. The ultimate aim is to find ways to integrate heritage education into the curriculum in schools all over the world.

8. Statement by René Rémond to the Commission.

Pointers and recommendations

• Worldwide interdependence and globalization are major forces in contemporary life. They are already at work and will leave a deep imprint on the twenty-first century. They require that overall consideration, extending well beyond the fields of education and culture, be given, as of now, to the roles and structures of international organizations.

• The major danger is that of a gulf opening up between a minority of people who are capable of finding their way successfully about this new world that is coming into being and the majority who feel that they are at the mercy of events and have no say in the future of society, with the dangers that entails of a setback to democracy and widespread revolt.

• We must be guided by the Utopian aim of steering the world towards greater mutual understanding, a greater sense of responsibility and greater solidarity, through acceptance of our spiritual and cultural differences. Education, by providing access to knowledge for all, has precisely this universal task of helping people to understand the world and to understand others.

Chapter 2

From social cohesion to democratic participation

The cohesion of any society is predicated on shared activities and purposes, but also on shared values, which represent different aspects of the desire to live together. In the course of time, these material and spiritual links enhance each other and become, in the individual and collective memory, a cultural heritage, in the broad sense of the term, on which the sense of belonging and the feeling of solidarity are based.

Throughout the world, one purpose of education, in its many forms, is to create social links between individuals on the basis of shared references. The means used are as varied as the cultures and circumstances, but in every case the central aim of education is the fulfilment of the individual as a social being. Education serves as a vehicle for cultures and values, creates an environment where socialization can take place and is the melting-pot in which a common purpose takes shape.

Today, these different forms of socialization are being sorely tested in societies that are themselves threatened by the disorganization and breakdown of social ties. Education systems are consequently subject to a whole set of tensions since they have, among other things, to show regard for individual and group differences while upholding the principle of homogeneity implicit in the need to observe common rules. In this respect, education has to face considerable challenges and finds itself on the horns of a seemingly insuperable dilemma: on the one hand, it is accused of being the cause of many different forms of exclusion and of making the rents in the social fabric worse, while on the other, it is under pressure to help in restoring some of those 'similarities essential to life in society', of which the French sociologist, Émile Durkheim, spoke at the end of the last century.

Faced with the breakdown of social ties, education has to take on the difficult task of turning diversity into a constructive contributory factor of mutual understanding between individuals and groups. Its highest aim will then be to give everyone the means of playing an informed and active part as a citizen, which is something that cannot be fully achieved except within the framework of democratic societies.

Education and the crisis of social cohesion

Throughout history, societies have been racked by conflicts that in extreme cases have threatened their cohesion. There is no getting away from the fact that, in most countries today, a whole set of phenomena point to an acute crisis in social cohesion.

The first point to note is the growing inequality due to rising poverty and exclusion. It is not just a question of the disparities between nations or regions of the world, but of deep divides between social groups in both developed and developing countries. The World Summit for Social Development painted an alarming picture of the present social situation, stating in particular that more than 1 billion people in the world live in abject poverty and most of them go hungry every day, and that over 120 million people worldwide are officially unemployed and many more are underemployed.

While population growth in developing countries is jeopardizing the chances of better standards of living, other factors are reinforcing the sense of a social crisis affecting most countries. The uprooting that goes with migration or the rural exodus, the breakdown of family life, uncontrolled urbanization and the collapse of traditional neighbourhood solidarity are condemning many groups and individuals to isolation and marginalization in both developing and underdeveloped countries. The social crisis throughout the present-day world is compounded by a moral crisis and the spread of violence and crime. The collapse of neighbourhood ties can be seen in the alarming increase in the number of inter-ethnic conflicts, which seems to be one of the characteristic features of the end of the twentieth century. Everywhere the values that promote cohesion are in one way or another being challenged. Particularly serious is the fact that the concepts of the nation and of democracy, which may be considered the cornerstones of cohesion in modern societies, are also now being challenged. The nation-state, as it came to be defined in Europe in the nineteenth century, is no longer in some cases the sole frame of reference, and other allegiances, closer to individuals in that they function on a smaller scale, are tending to develop. Concomitantly, whole regions of the world are moving towards vast transnational groupings that are the beginnings of new areas with which people can identify, even though in many cases they are still limited to economic activities.

In some nations, centrifugal forces are stretching to breaking point the customary relationships between communities and individuals. In the countries of the former Soviet Union, for example, with the collapse of the Soviet system came a fragmentation of national territories. Again, the association of the idea of the nation-state with that of strong state centralization may explain the rise of a bias against it, exacerbated by civil society's need to participate and the demand for broader decentralization.

The concept of democracy, on the other hand, is being questioned in a way that seems paradoxical: in so far as it reflects a political system that seeks to safeguard, by means of the social contract, compatibility between individual freedoms and the shared organization of society, it is unquestionably gaining ground and fully accords with the demand for individual autonomy that is spreading throughout the world; but its application, in the form of representative democracy, is at the same time coming up against a whole series of problems in the countries that initially promoted the idea. The system of political representation and its characteristic model for the exercise of power are in some places facing a crisis: the widening gap between those who govern and those who are governed, the surfeit of short-lived emotional reactions fuelled by the media, the image of politics as entertainment made possible by the media presentation of debates or even the image of the corruption of the political world – all these things are placing some countries in danger of 'government by the judiciary' and leading ordinary people to feel increasing disaffection for public affairs. Many countries are also experiencing a crisis in social policies which is undermining the very foundations of a system of solidarity that had appeared able to reconcile, in a democratic way, the economic, political and social aspects of society under the aegis of the Welfare State.

As a result, the democratic ideal needs as it were to be reinvented or at least revitalized. It must at all events remain at the top of our list of priorities, since there is no other system of organization for the body politic or for civil society that can claim to replace democracy and at the same time carry through joint action in favour of freedom, peace, genuine pluralism and social justice. Awareness of the difficulties that exist should in no way be a cause of discouragement nor an excuse for deviating from the path that leads to democracy. The process is one of continuous creation and calls for a contribution from everyone. This contribution will be all the more valuable if education has fostered in everyone both the ideal and the practice of democracy.

At issue here is the capacity of the individual to behave as a true citizen, aware of the collective interest and anxious to play a part in democratic life. This is a challenge for the policy-makers but also for the education system, whose role in the workings of society should therefore be defined.

Education versus exclusion

Education can promote cohesion if it strives to take the diversity of individuals and groups into consideration while taking care that it does not itself contribute to social exclusion.

To show regard for diversity and individuality is a fundamental principle that should rule out any kind of standardized teaching. Formal education systems are often rightly accused of stunting personal fulfilment by forcing all children into the same cultural and intellectual mould, without taking sufficient account of the variety of individual talents. They tend to emphasize, for example, the development of abstract knowledge to the detriment of other qualities such as imagination, the ability to communicate, leadership, a sense of beauty or the spiritual dimension of existence, or manual skills. Depending on their aptitudes and natural inclinations, which are different from the moment they are born, children do not therefore benefit in exactly the same way from the educational resources of the community. They may even be left stranded if the school is not suited to their talents and ambitions.

As well as the great variety of individual talents, education has to face the wide range of cultural backgrounds of the groups making up a society. Respect for pluralism is one of the basic principles of the Commission's thinking. Although the situation differs greatly from one country to another, a considerable variety of cultural and linguistic roots is characteristic of most countries. In former colonies such as the countries of sub-Saharan Africa, where cultures and traditional forms of education had superimposed on them the language and educational model of the former colonial power, the search for a form of education that reflects and reinforces their own identity, above and beyond the ancestral form of education and the one imported by the colonial powers, is reflected in the revival of the use of local languages for teaching. The question of cultural and linguistic pluralism also arises in the case of indigenous peoples or migrant groups who have the problem of finding a balance between wanting to integrate successfully and not losing their cultural roots. Any education policy must therefore be able to meet the challenge of how to turn this legitimate wish into something that makes for social cohesion. It is, in particular, important that everyone should be enabled to find their place in the community, in most cases local, to which they primarily belong, and at the same time be given the means to open out to other communities. In that respect, it is important to establish a form of intercultural education that will genuinely contribute to social cohesion and peace.

Furthermore, education systems must not themselves lead to exclusion. Competition, which is in certain cases favourable to intellectual development, can also take the form of undue selection by academic results. Academic underachievement then becomes irreversible and frequently leads to social marginalization and exclusion. Many countries, especially in the developed world, are now experiencing a problem that is very disconcerting for educational policy-makers, in that the lengthening of compulsory education has, paradoxically, aggravated rather than improved the situation of the most socially disadvantaged young people and/or of those who have failed at school. Even in countries where expenditure on education is among the highest in the world, underachievement and dropping out affect a large percentage of young people. This is causing a divide between two kinds of young people, a divide that is all the more serious in that it extends into the world of work. Young people without formal qualifications have a disadvantage that is almost impossible to overcome when they apply for a job. Some of them, regarded by firms as 'unemployable', find themselves shut out once and for all from employment and deprived of any possibility of becoming socially integrated.

Because it generates exclusion, academic failure is in many instances the cause of certain forms of violence or individual maladjustment that tear the social fabric. As a result, schools are both criticized for causing social exclusion and at the same time much in demand for their key role in integration or re-integration. The problems that these processes raise for educational policy-makers are particularly difficult: countering academic failure has to be seen as a social necessity (see the proposals in Chapter 6).

Education and the forces at work in society: some principles for action

The first thing to be done to restore to education its central place among the forces at work in society should be to safeguard its function as a melting-pot by combating all forms of exclusion. An effort must therefore be made to attract or attract back to the education system those who have been kept out of it or who have turned their backs on it because the teaching given was not suited to their particular needs. Among other things this implies that parents should be given a say in their children's schooling and that the poorest families should be given assistance so that they will not regard their children's schooling as an insuperable opportunity cost.

Teaching should also be individualized, striving to promote originality by offering introductory courses in as wide a range of disciplines, activities or arts as possible and by entrusting such courses to specialists who are able to communicate their enthusiasm and explain the choices they themselves have made in life.

To create possibilities for recognizing latent aptitudes and skills, and hence for social recognition, teaching systems should be diversified as far as possible, while families and people and

Community and schooling in East Harlem: a successful initiative

Community involvement is an essential characteristic of New York City's Central Park East Schools. The schools, located in East Harlem and working with predominantly low-income Hispanic and African-American populations, were established in the 1970s by a group of dedicated elementary-school teachers who believed that involvement of families, community members and community organizations is an important aspect of quality schooling.

These teachers designed and implemented an interdisciplinary curriculum infused with cultural relevance and based on local, national and international politics. Using themes and projects as organizing tools, the curriculum was designed to be both fluid and dynamic. As part of this curriculum, community representatives, union members, researchers, counsellors, and artists and poets in residence spend time in the schools, helping the students think of the world in different ways and understand it from numerous perspectives. In addition, the students are given the opportunity to put what they learn into practice; they are required to spend one morning each week working in the community, usually through internships with community-based organizations.

Parents, who are encouraged to visit the school at all times, are required to have a conference with their child and his/her teacher twice per year. Parents are also given the opportunity to participate in school decision-making.

In a time when school districts like New York have drop-out rates for minority students of 30 and 40 per cent, the Central Park East Schools have proven highly successful: 100 per cent of the students graduating from the elementary schools completed high school and half have gone on to college.

Sources: M. Fine, *Framing Dropouts*, New York, State University of New York Press, 1990; D. Meier, 'Central Park East: An Alternative Story', *Phi-Delta-Kappan*, Vol. 68, No. 10, 1987, pp. 753–7.

institutions active in society should be involved in educational partnerships.

It is important, moreover, to learn to accept diversity and multiple loyalties as a valuable asset. *Education for pluralism* is not just a safeguard against violence but an active principle for the enrichment of the cultural and civic life of present-day societies. Between the extremes of abstract and over-simplifying universalism and a relativism which makes no higher demand going beyond the horizon of each particular culture,[1] one needs to assert both the right to be different and receptiveness to universal values.

In that context, devising a form of education suited to the different minority groups is a matter of priority. The goal of such education should be to enable the various minorities to take control of their own future. This principle was unanimously approved by the Commission, but further, highly complex problems nevertheless arise in that connection, particularly regarding the language of instruction. When the necessary conditions are met, bilingual education beginning in the first years of schooling with instruction in the mother tongue, followed later by instruction in a more widely spoken language, is to be recommended. However, the danger that minorities might become isolated should constantly be borne in mind: what must be avoided is a misplaced inter-

Souleymane Bachir Diagne, *Pour une éducation philosophique au pluralisme*, paper presented at the International Study Days on 'Philosophy and Democracy in the World', organized by UNESCO, Paris, 15 and 16 February 1995.

cultural egalitarianism that would imprison some minorities in linguistic and cultural, thus economic, ghettos.

Education in tolerance and respect for other people, a prerequisite for democracy, should be regarded as a general and ongoing enterprise. Values in general and tolerance in particular cannot be taught in the strict sense: the desire to impose from the outside predetermined values comes down in the end to negating them, since values only have meaning when they are freely chosen by the individual. At the very most, therefore, schools may facilitate the daily practice of tolerance by helping pupils to allow for the point of view of others and by encouraging the discussion of moral dilemmas or cases involving ethical choices,[2] for example.

It should, however, be the school's role to explain to young people the historical, cultural or religious background to the various ideologies competing for their attention in the society around them or in the school and classroom. This task of explanation – which could possibly be carried out with the help of outsiders – is a delicate one, since it must avoid giving offence and can bring politics and religion, generally banned from the classroom, into schools. Adolescents can thus be helped to build their system of thought and values freely and in full knowledge of facts, without succumbing blindly to dominant influences, and thuswise acquiring greater maturity and openmindedness. One can, in this way, lay the foundations of future harmony and peace, by encouraging democratic dialogue.

These recommendations are chiefly concerned with what can be done in school, but education should promote cultural pluralism throughout a person's lifetime by presenting it as a source of human enrichment: racial prejudice, which breeds violence and exclusion, should be combated by exchanges of information about the history and values of different cultures.

The democratic spirit, however, cannot be satisfied with a minimalist form of tolerance that consists merely of putting up with otherness. This attitude, though ostensibly simply neutral, is at the mercy of circumstances, which may undermine it when the economic or sociological situation at a particular moment makes the cohabitation of several cultures especially conflict-prone. The simple notion of tolerance must therefore be transcended in favour of an education for pluralism based on respect for, and appreciation of, other cultures.

But it is not merely a matter of acquiring the democratic

2. International Commission on Education for the Twenty-first Century, Fifth Session, Santiago, Chile, 26–28 September 1994, *Report*, Paris, UNESCO, 1994. (UNESCO doc. EDC/7.) The report also gives an account of a number of original experiments, particularly in Portugal where a Secretariat for Intercultural Education has been set up and where individual and social training is regarded as a transdisciplinary activity in primary and secondary education.

spirit. At a more fundamental level, it is a question of helping pupils to acquire, as they embark on life, the ability to interpret those things that mainly affect their personal future and the future of society as a whole. From this point of view, support from the social and human sciences is essential, insofar as they relate both to life itself and to social phenomena. Needless to say, history and philosophy should also occupy an important place in such multidisciplinary research: philosophy because of its role in forming that critical outlook which is indispensable to the functioning of democracy and history because of its irreplaceable role in broadening the individual's horizons and raising awareness of collective identities. The teaching of history should, however, transcend the national context and should encompass a social and cultural dimension, in order that knowledge about the past may lead to a better understanding and a truer appreciation of the present. There is new territory here to be worked both by those who decide the main lines of emphasis of education policy and by those who draw up curricula. The aim would be to integrate the achievements of the social sciences into a global approach whereby a broad understanding of past and present could be attained.

Democratic participation

Civic education and the practice of citizenship

Education cannot be satisfied with bringing individuals together by getting them to accept common values shaped in the past. It must also answer the question as to *what for and why we live together* and give everyone, throughout life, the ability to play an active part in envisioning the future of society.

The education system has therefore the explicit or implicit task of preparing everyone for this social role. In the complex societies of today, participation in the common enterprise far transcends strictly political considerations. Every day, in fact, in their work, in cultural activities, in associations or as consumers, all members of the community must individually accept their responsibilities towards others. Schools must therefore prepare people for this role by instructing them in their rights and duties, and also by developing their social skills by encouraging teamwork.

Preparation for active participation in the life of the

community has become, for education, a more and more widely recognized task as democratic principles have spread throughout the world. There are, in that respect, several levels of action which, in a modern democracy, should complement one another.

From an initial, minimalist viewpoint, the objective is simply learning to perform one's social role in accordance with established sets of rules. This job is one for basic education, where the need is for civic instruction viewed as elementary 'political literacy'. As in the case of tolerance, such instruction cannot be regarded as a straightforward classroom subject among others. The aim is not to teach precepts as rigid rules, which could slide towards indoctrination, but to make school a model of democratic practice so that children can understand, on the basis of practical problems, what their rights and duties are and how their freedom is limited by the exercise of the rights and freedom of other people. Learning democracy in school could be reinforced by practices that have already been tried out, including drawing up charters for the school community, setting up pupil parliaments, role-play simulating the functioning of democratic institutions, school newspapers and exercises in non-violent conflict-resolution. As education for citizenship and democracy is *par excellence* an education that is not restricted to the space and time of formal education, it is also important for families and other members of the community to be directly involved.

For pupils, however, civic education is a complex matter covering acceptance of values, acquiring knowledge and learning how to take part in public life. It cannot therefore be considered as ideologically neutral: the pupil's conscience is necessarily challenged by it. To safeguard independence of conscience, education in general, from childhood throughout life, must also build up a critical sense that makes for free thought and independent action. When pupils become citizens, education will be their constant guide along a difficult path where they will have to reconcile the exercise of individual rights based on public freedoms with the fulfilment of duties and responsibilities towards others and to their communities. It is thus education in general, as a process for constructing the faculty of judgement, that is being called into action. The problem that then arises concerns the balance between individual freedom and the principle of authority that is present in all teaching. This highlights the role of teachers in fostering that independence of judgement that is vital for those who are going to participate in public life.

uilding and living in a civil society:
n experiment in Hungary

e programme entitled 'Education for
emocracy' has been gradually
established since 1990, when the Maxwell
hool of Citizenship and Public Affairs
ccepted the invitation of the Rákoczi
mnázium of Budapest and the
ungarian Institute for Educational
search to join them to study ways and
eans of improving civic education and
e responsible exercise of citizenship in
ungary. Founded on the conviction that
ucation can and must be at the
efront of any effort to enable
mocracy to be established in Central
d Eastern Europe during the current
riod of transition, it proposes to
achers and students a number of
inciples for the renewal of approaches
education:

A new approach to *history and
cial sciences* stresses the teaching of
cts, concepts and general ideas about

social phenomena, based on the principle
that mastering those disciplines will
enable citizens to understand problems of
civic life better when they arise.
* *Introduction to legal issues* stresses
the preponderance of law in a democracy
and the importance of teaching the
fundamental principles that regulate
legal procedures.
* The aim of *critical reasoning* is to
develop in citizens the intellectual ability
to assess the quality and validity of
different types of reasoning and value
judgements.
* *Ethics and moral instruction* can be
taught through concrete examples: the
pupils are given moral dilemmas and
questions of conscience and are asked to
discuss among themselves the reasons
why the solution which is right from a
moral point of view is indeed right.
* *Understanding the global dimension*

emphasizes the fact that mastering the
art of being a citizen must be based on a
reasoned knowledge of different ways of
life in other cultures, and the way world
problems are connected with the lives of
communities large and small and have
repercussions on them.
* *Pluralism and multicultural
education* take account of the growing
interest in Hungarian schools in studies
relating to the ethnic heritage. They
invite pupils to assess the value of the
principles of religious freedom applicable
to peoples of all denominations.

Lastly, this new approach stresses the
need to *reform the school* since it is
clearly contradictory to teach democracy
in authoritarian institutions.

Source: taken from Patrice Meyer-Bisch (ed.),
Culture of Democracy: A Challenge for Schools,
Paris, UNESCO, 1995. (Cultures of Peace Series.)

Lastly, if there is to be a synergetic relationship between education and the practice of participatory democracy, not only should everyone be trained to exercise their rights and fulfil their duties, but use should be made of lifelong education in order to build an active civil society which, occupying the middle ground between scattered individuals and a distant political authority, would enable each person to shoulder his or her share of responsibility in the community, with a view to achieving true solidarity. Thus, the education of each citizen must continue throughout his or her life and become part of the basic framework of civil society and living democracy. It even becomes indistinguishable from democracy when everyone plays a part in constructing a responsible and mutually supportive society that upholds the fundamental rights of all.

Information societies and learning societies

This essential democratic requirement, which must lie at the heart of all plans for education, is highlighted by the dramatic emergence of 'information societies', without doubt carrying great implications for the future. The digitization of information has led to a tremendous revolution in communications in the shape of multimedia systems and the spectacular expansion of information technology networks. The Internet, for example, has doubled the number of its users and networks as well as its volume of traffic each year since 1988. More than 5 million computers are currently linked up to it and the number of users is estimated at around 20 million. Even though the impact of the expansion of these networks is still limited owing to the relatively small number of people with the necessary technology and know-how, everything suggests that an unstoppable revolution is in progress, a revolution that will make it possible to transmit an ever-increasing mass of information in an ever shorter space of time. At the same time, these new technologies are steadily finding their way into every area of life, thanks to the falling cost of equipment, which makes them more and more accessible.

This technological revolution is clearly vital for an understanding of our modern world as it is creating new forms of socialization and even new types of individual and collective identity. The expansion of information technologies and networks is tending both to encourage communication with other people, sometimes right across the world, and to reinforce trends towards withdrawal and isolation. The development of teleworking, for example, can upset the companionship of the workplace and we are witnessing an increasing number of recreational activities that isolate people in front of their computer screens. Some fears have been voiced about those developments. Some people think that access to this virtual world may lead to a diminishing sense of reality, and it has been said that the learning process and access to knowledge are, in a manner of speaking, slipping away from the formal education systems, with potentially serious consequences for the socialization of young children and adolescents. On the basis of what is known today,

Learning in the electronic age

At the end of the 1970s the personal computer appeared. It was, so to speak, the bicycle of information technology, creative but local in the way it was used. Today we have information superhighways and the bicycle has become a mountain bike. The impact on our ways of learning will be inevitable and massive. It is important to understand the nature of these new technologies, which is relatively simple, but what is really essential is to ask the right questions about future developments. What contents, what interactivity, what enrichment of the cognitive activities previously described, what relationship between converging needs to find information and the diverging search required by the network architecture, what new forms for the functioning of society, what new balance between increased contact among individuals and greater protection for privacy, what new tensions between easier access to technology and exclusion resulting from their use, between controls and freedoms? We are just at the beginning. It is time to take a practical interest in these questions and think them through.

Source: G. Delacôte, *Savoir apprendre. Les nouvelles méthodes*, Paris, Odile Jacob, 1996.

the Commission cannot presume to undertake a definitive analysis of the influence of virtual reality on individual and interpersonal behaviour or on societal relationships. The question will, however, become a more and more pressing one.

To return to education and culture, it would seem that the main danger of the new technologies is the creation of divides and disparities. The new disparities may appear between different societies, that is to say between societies which have managed to adjust to these technologies and societies which have not been able to do so for lack of funds or political will. The biggest danger, however, is not necessarily a widening gap between the developed and developing countries, as steps have already been taken to provide developing countries with basic infrastructures and there is every possibility that technological breakthroughs will enable developing countries to equip themselves with advanced technology from the start. The rapid progress of technology may even offer new prospects for development by opening up a large number of isolated regions and enabling people to communicate with the whole world. In the vital field of scientific research, it may facilitate access to international databases and permit the establishment of 'virtual laboratories' that would enable researchers from developing countries to work in their own countries and thus reduce the brain drain. Furthermore, the problems encountered in introducing the new technologies because of the cost of the necessary infrastructures are tending to disappear as a result of the general fall in equipment costs. In conclusion, it seems that the differences will be chiefly between societies that will be capable of producing the content and those that will merely receive the information without taking a real part in the exchanges.

In fact, the greatest cleavages are likely to occur within given societies, between those who can use the new tools and those with no possibility of using them: there is a real danger of societies with fast and slow tracks, depending on individuals' access to technology. That is why the Commission considers that the emergence of information societies is a challenge to both democracy and education, and that the two aspects are closely interrelated. Education systems have a major responsibility: it is their job to give everyone the means of coming to grips with the proliferation of information, that is, of displaying a critical spirit in sorting and ordering information. It is also their job to help people to stand back from the society of media and information that could tend to be nothing more than a society of the ephemeral and the immediate. The tyranny of 'real time' is in conflict with after-the-event time, the time needed for ripening, which is the time of culture and assimilation of knowledge. The use of technology in the school environment can, of course, take different forms, which will be considered in Chapter 8 of this report. In all cases, however, the principle must continue to be that of equality of opportunity, the aim being to ensure that those who have the greatest need, because they are the most disadvantaged, can benefit from the new aids to understanding the world. Thus, as well as providing vital modes of socialization, education systems are going to have to lay the very foundations for citizenship in an information society.

Thus, information and communication technologies can no doubt represent for everyone a real means of contact with non-formal education, becoming one of the most important delivery systems of a learning society in which the various stages of the learning process will be radically rethought. In particular, the development of those technologies, the skilled use of which makes possible a continuous broadening of knowledge, should lead to a reconsideration of the role and function of education systems in the context of an education that extends throughout life. The communication and exchange of knowledge will no longer be simply one of the main growth centres of human activities but something that contributes to personal fulfilment within the context of new modes of social life.

The Commission therefore recommends that the full potential of the new information and communication technologies should be harnessed to serve education and training. Most of the specialists it has consulted are optimistic about the prospects opened up by the new technologies for developing countries, and consider that it would be particularly harmful for these countries not to be able to seize the opportunity they offer in order to narrow the gap that separates them from developed countries. It also notes that the scene in information societies is changing very rapidly before our very eyes as a result of technological progress and competition between major corporations. Believing that UNESCO could take such an initiative, the Commission therefore suggests the establishment of a high-level working group with a widely representative international membership, whose task would be to report on current developments and make certain suggestions concerning standardization (see Chapter 9). This is because, although governments do not appear to have a large measure of responsibility for recreation and culture, the situation is totally different in the field of education, where it is important to ensure that all educational products meet specific quality standards.

Pointers and recommendations

• Education policy must be sufficiently diversified and must be so designed as not to become another contributory cause of social exclusion.

• The socialization of individuals must not conflict with personal development. It is therefore necessary to work towards a system that strives to combine the virtues of integration with respect for individual rights.

• Education cannot, on its own, solve the problems raised by the severance (when this happens) of social ties. It can, however, be expected to help to foster the desire to live together, which is a basic component of social cohesion and national identity.

• Schools cannot succeed in this task unless they make their own contribution to the advancement and integration of minority groups by mobilizing those concerned while showing due regard for their personality.

• Democracy appears to be progressing, taking forms and passing through stages that fit the situation in each country. Its vitality is nevertheless constantly threatened. Education for conscious and active citizenship must begin at school.

• Democratic participation is, so to say, a matter of good citizenship, but it can be encouraged or stimulated by instruction and practices adapted to a media and information society. What is needed is to provide reference points and aids to interpretation, so as to strengthen the faculties of understanding and judgement.

• It is the role of education to provide children and adults with the cultural background that will enable them, as far as possible, to make sense of the changes taking place. This presupposes that they are capable of sorting the mass of information so as to interpret it more effectively and place events in a historical perspective.

Chapter 3

From economic growth to human development

During the past half-century, the world has experienced unprecedented economic expansion, particularly as a result of increasingly rapid technological progress and more intense international competition. While the Commission does not intend to give a complete overview of that period, which would be outside its terms of reference, it would like, from its own particular standpoint, to point out that this progress is due above all to the capacity of humanity to control and organize its environment in accordance with its needs, in other words, to science and education, the main driving forces of economic progress. Being aware, however, that the present growth model has obvious limits because of the inequalities it provokes and the human and ecological cost it entails, the Commission wishes to define education not, as hitherto, solely from the point of view of its impact on economic growth, but from the broader perspective of human development.

Highly inequitable economic growth

Through the combined effects of the second industrial revolution, rising productivity and technological progress, the world's wealth has grown considerably since 1950. The world's aggregate GDP has risen from $4,000 billion to $23,000 billion, and average per capita income has more than trebled during that time. Technological progress has spread apace. A case in point is information technology, which has gone through more than four successive phases of development in the space of a lifetime: world sales of computer terminals exceeded 12 million in 1993.[1] Lifestyles and consumer habits have changed radically, and the idea of improving human well-being by economic progress has taken hold virtually throughout the world.

This type of development, founded on economic growth alone, is nevertheless still profoundly inegalitarian, and growth rates vary considerably from country to country and from region to region. Over 75 per cent of the world's population are estimated to live in the developing countries yet partake of only 16 per cent of the world's wealth. Even more disturbing, studies carried out for the United Nations Conference on Trade and Development (UNCTAD) reveal that the average annual per capita income of the least-developed countries, with a total population of 560 million, is currently falling: it has been reckoned at $300 as against $906 for the other developing countries and $21,598 for the industrialized countries.

What is more, the disparities have been exacerbated by competition among nations and among various groups: the inequitable distribution of the surpluses created by higher productivity, both between countries and within certain countries regarded as being rich, shows that growth is widening the gulf between the most dynamic and the rest. Certain countries would thus appear to be lagging behind in the race for competitivity. Such disparities can be partly explained by dysfunctional markets and by the intrinsically inegalitarian nature of the world political system; they are also closely linked to contemporary forces behind development, which give pride of place to brainpower and innovation.

The demand for education for economic purposes

Under the pressure of technological progress and modernization, the demand for education for economic purposes has been constantly on the rise in most countries during the period under consideration. International comparisons have for some time highlighted the importance, for increased productivity, of

1. For an overview, see *Human Development Report 1995* (published for UNDP), New York/Oxford, Oxford University Press, 1995.

human resources and hence of investment in education.[2] The link between the rate of technical progress and the quality of human intervention has become increasingly evident, as has the need for those active in the economy to be trained to use the new technologies to innovate. New skills are needed and education systems are required to meet that need by providing not only the minimum of schooling or vocational training, but also training for scientists, innovators and high-level specialists.

Developments in recent years in continuing education, especially designed to speed up economic growth, may also be seen from this same angle. The sheer pace of technological change has convinced business communities and nations alike of the need for flexibility in the quality of the labour force. Keeping up with, and even ahead of, the technological changes that continuously influence the nature and organization of labour has become a matter of paramount importance. Every sector, including agriculture, has need of evolutive skills tied in with knowledge and know-how. This irreversible development is a blow to practices and qualifications acquired by repetition or by imitation, and there is evidence of the growing importance of investment 'intangibles', such as education, as the effects of the 'intelligence revolution' make themselves felt.[3] In that case, the continuing education of the workforce also becomes something of a strategic investment requiring the involvement of people and institutions of various kinds: in addition to the education systems, private instructors, employers and employees' representatives are in particular demand. In many industrialized countries, funds for continuing education are thus being increased substantially.

There is every indication that this trend will gather strength as work continues to change in contemporary societies. The nature of work has already changed considerably in recent years, with a distinct increase in the tertiary sector, which today employs a quarter of the labour force of the developing countries and more than two-thirds in the industrialized world. The emergence and development of 'information societies' and continued technological progress, which is a marked trend of the late twentieth century, emphasize the increasingly intangible dimension of work and accentuate the role played by intellectual and social skills. Education systems can therefore no longer be expected to train a labour force for stable industrial jobs; they must instead train individuals to be innovative, capable of evolving, adapting to a rapidly changing world and assimilating change.

Edward F.
ison, *Why*
wth Rates
er: Postwar
erience in
e Western
ntries,
hington,
, Brookings
itution,
.

Olivier
rand,
ation and
k (study
ared for the
mission),
, UNESCO,
. (UNESCO
EDC/IV/1.)

The uneven distribution of knowledge

As the twenty-first century dawns, the activity of education and training of all kinds has become one of the prime movers of development. It also contributes to scientific and technological progress, and to the widespread advance of knowledge, which are the most decisive factors of economic growth.

Many developing countries are particularly disadvantaged in this regard and suffer from a serious shortage of knowledge. Admittedly, literacy teaching and school enrolment are increasing among the populations of the South, which will, perhaps, eventually make it possible to redress the balance of the world's economic relations (see Chapter 6). None the less, where science and research and development capacity is concerned, the inequalities are still pronounced: in 1990, 42.8 per cent of R&D spending was in North America and 23.2 per cent in Europe, as against 0.2 per cent in sub-Saharan Africa and 0.7 per cent in the Arab States.[4] The brain drain to the rich countries is accentuating this state of affairs.

As things stand at present, the developing countries do not on the whole possess the funds needed to make any effective investment in research, and the absence of a sufficiently large scientific community is a severe handicap. Knowledge, which produces considerable economies of scale in fundamental research, only becomes effective in this field when a critical threshold of substantial investment has been exceeded. The same applies to R&D, which calls for massive, risky investments and presupposes the existence of an environment already adequately provided with scientific resources – an environment of that kind is needed in order to give a significant return on investment in research and to allow of external savings in the short and long term. That is doubtless one of the reasons for the failure of transfers of technology from the industrialized to the developing countries. It is quite clear that such transfers require a favourable environment that marshals and makes the most of local knowledge, enabling genuine assimilation of the technologies to take place in the context of endogenous development. It is therefore important that the poorest countries should be able to set up their own research and study capabilities, particularly through the establishment of centres of excellence at regional level. The situation is different in the so-called emerging countries, particularly in

4. *World Education Report 19.* Paris, UNE. 1993.

The brain drain from poor countries to rich

eloping countries lose thousands of ed people each year – engineers, tors, scientists, technicians. Frustrated ow pay and limited opportunities at ne, they head for richer countries re their talents can be better applied nd better rewarded.

The problem is partly overproduction. cation systems in developing ntries are often modelled on the uirements of industrial countries, and n too many high-level graduates. alia produces around five times more luates than the country can employ. in Côte d'Ivoire, up to 50 per cent of luates are unemployed.

Industrial countries certainly profit n immigrants' skills. Between 1960 and 0, the US and Canada accepted more

than 1 million professional and technical immigrants from developing countries. The US education system is particularly dependent on them. In engineering institutions in 1985, an estimated half of the assistant professors under 35 were foreign. Japan and Australia, too, have tried to attract skilled migrants.

This loss of skilled workers represents a severe haemorrhage of capital. The US Congressional Research Service estimated that in 1971–72 the developing countries as a whole lost an investment of $20,000 in each skilled migrant – $646 million in total. Some of this returns as remittances but not on a scale to compensate for the losses.

Some countries may have more educated people than they can use, but

others are losing desperately needed skills. In Ghana, 60 per cent of doctors trained in the early 1980s are now abroad – leaving critical shortages in the health service. And Africa as a whole is estimated to have lost up to 60,000 middle- and high-level managers between 1985 and 1990.

The major responsibility for reducing such losses lies with the developing countries. They need to tailor their education systems more closely to their practical needs and improve the management of their economies. But for that, they also need better access to international markets.

Source: Human Development Report 1992 (published for UNDP), p. 57, New York/Oxford, Oxford University Press, 1992.

Asia, where there is a marked growth in private investments. Such investments normally go together with transfers of technology and can form the basis of rapid economic development if they are also accompanied by a genuine policy for training the local labour force, as is usually the case.

One initial conclusion seems to be self-evident, namely, that the developing countries cannot afford to disregard anything that may give them the necessary entrée into the world of science and technology and all that this entails in terms of cultural adaptation and the development of a modern outlook. Seen in that light, investment in research and education is a necessity. One of the international community's primary causes of concern must be the risk of total marginalization facing those who are excluded from progress in a rapidly changing world economy. Unless a vigorous effort is made to obviate this risk, some countries that lack the wherewithal to join in international technological competition are liable to become enclaves of poverty, despair or violence that cannot be eliminated by aid and humanitarian action. Even within the developed countries, entire social groups are in danger of exclusion from the process of socialization represented until recently by an industrial-type organization of labour. In both cases, the core problem is still the uneven distribution of knowledge and skills.

We might mention here a fact which, though well known, has implications for education that are perhaps not given sufficient weight, namely, that the difference between North and South is much less sharply defined than it was some years ago. The former communist countries, now in transition, are experiencing specific problems reflected, in varying degrees, in the difficulties they are encountering in the thoroughgoing rebuilding of their education systems. Moreover, the emerging countries have moved out of underdevelopment, and it is they, on the whole, that have made the greatest investments in the development of education, in ways appropriate to their particular cultural, social and economic situations. While there is no model to follow in that respect, the example of the newly industrialized countries in Asia deserves to be considered when educational reforms are being planned in other parts of the world.

It is, however, impossible to think in terms of education as the prime mover of truly equitable development without first considering ways of averting the accelerating downward spiral of certain countries into poverty. The most disturbing example here is that of the countries of sub-Saharan Africa, where GDP is at a standstill and the population is soaring. As their average standards of living fall, those countries, with very young populations, can today no longer devote as large a share of GDP to education as they did in the early 1980s. The current state of affairs is a serious threat to the future development of the region: it calls for increased attention from the international community, and even more for the galvanizing of local resources.

Education for women, an essential means of promoting development

In this brief outline of the most important disparities in access to knowledge and know-how, the Commission feels bound to say something about a disquieting fact, observable throughout the world but perhaps more especially in the developing countries, namely, the inequality between men and women in the field of education. To be sure, some progress has been made in recent years: UNESCO statistics show, for instance, that the female literacy ratio has increased in virtually all countries for which

Africa on the eve of the twenty-first century

- Real per capita income for sub-Saharan Africa declined from $563 in 1980 to $485 in 1992.
- Over 215 million Africans were living in poverty in 1990.
- The burden of poverty is most severe among women, in both rural and urban areas.
- The number of Africans unable to obtain the minimum daily requirements of 1,600–1,700 calories increased from 99 million in 1980 to 168 million in 1990–91.
- The spread of the AIDS pandemic in Africa has reached catastrophic proportions.
- Diarrhoea claims the lives of 1.5 million children annually.
- In 1989 alone, malaria killed 1.5 million children under 5 years of age.
- Over 20 million Africans are today refugees and displaced persons owing to deprivation of their basic human requirements, civil wars, ethnic and religious conflicts, political repression, human rights violations and lack of security.
- Only two out of three men, and one out of three women, are literate in sub-Saharan Africa.
- By the early 1990s, growth in enrolment (in education) at all levels represented less than one half of that in the 1970s, with primary education recording the sharpest decline.
- While the need for high-level human resources has become increasingly crucial to rapid socio-economic, cultural and technological advancement, higher education institutions throughout Africa are fast deteriorating both in quality and quantity.
- Millions of African children, women and men need protection from disease, human rights abuse, ethnic conflicts and political repression. They want to acquire knowledge and skills, and stand on their own feet as responsible and productive citizens. They want to participate in decision-making issues relating to their daily lives and well-being, and the governance of their society. They do not want to be mere recipients of foreign relief assistance. It is against this background that Africa's human development priorities and the strategies for realizing them must be formulated.

Source: Audience Africa: An Introductory Note by the Director-General of UNESCO, pp. 3–4, Paris, UNESCO, 1995.

data are available. The disparities are nevertheless still blatant: two-thirds of the illiterate adults in the world, or 565 million people, are women, most of whom live in the developing regions of Africa, Asia and Latin America.[5] Worldwide, fewer girls attend school than boys: one primary-school-aged girl out of four is not in school (24.5 per cent or 85 million), whereas this is the case for one boy out of six (16.4 per cent or 60 million). These disparities can be explained chiefly by the situation in the least-developed regions. In sub-Saharan Africa, for example, fewer than half the girls aged 6 to 11 attend school, and the rates drop very noticeably in the higher age-brackets.

A respect for equity demands a special effort to do away with all inequality between the sexes in the field of education. Gender inequality lies at the root of the lasting situations of inferiority that affect women at every stage of their lives. And yet, the strategic importance of women's education for development is today acknowledged by all experts. A very clear correlation has been established between the educational level of women and the overall improvement in the population's health and nutrition and the drop in fertility rates. UNESCO's *World Education*

5. *World Education Report 1995*, Paris, UNESCO, 1995.

Report 1995 examines the different aspects of the question and states that, in the poorest regions of the world, 'women and girls are locked into a circle [. . .] with illiterate mothers bringing up illiterate daughters who are married off too early into yet another cycle of poverty, illiteracy, high fertility and early mortality'. The vicious circle linking poverty to inequality between men and women has to be broken. In more general terms, the education of girls and women would appear, from what a minority of them has already accomplished, to be the basic precondition for active participation by the population at large in development activities.

Estimated net enrolment ratios for the age-groups 6–11, 12–17 and 18–23 years,* by region, 1995

	6–11		12–17		18–23	
	M	F	M	F	M	F
Sub-Saharan Africa	55.2	47.4	46.0	35.3	9.7	4.9
Arab States	83.9	71.6	59.2	47.1	24.5	16.3
Latin America/ Caribbean	88.5	87.5	68.4	67.4	26.1	26.3
Eastern Asia/ Oceania	88.6	85.5	54.7	51.4	19.5	13.6
Southern Asia	84.3	65.6	50.5	32.2	12.4	6.6
Developed countries	92.3	91.7	87.1	88.5	40.8	42.7

* Percentage ratio of the number of enrolled pupils/students in each age-group to the total population in the age-group.

Source: World Education Report 1995, p. 36, Paris, UNESCO, 1995.

Counting the cost of progress

As an objective, economic growth alone is not enough to ensure human development. It has been criticized on two fronts, so to speak, not just for its inegalitarian nature but also for the high toll it takes, particularly on the environment and employment.

At present rates of production, the so-called non-renewable resources, whether of energy or arable land, are liable to become more and more scarce, while industries deriving from the physical, chemical and biological sciences generate pollution which destroys or interferes with nature. More generally, living conditions on our planet are under threat. The growing scarcity of drinking water, deforestation, the 'greenhouse effect' and the use of the oceans as a giant rubbish dump are all disturbing manifestations of the present century's lack of concern for future generations, the seriousness of which was stressed at the 1992 United Nations Conference on Environment and Development.

In many respects, the rapid spread of unemployment in recent years in a great many countries represents a structural phenomenon bound up with technological progress. The

Gender bias

Women perform the lion's share of work in subsistence economies, toiling longer hours and contributing more to family income than their male relatives. Gender bias is thus a primary cause of poverty, because in its various forms it prevents hundreds of millions of women from obtaining the education, training, health services, child care, and legal status needed to escape from poverty. In developing countries, women work an average of 12 to 18 hours per day – producing food, managing and harvesting resources, and working at a variety of paid and unpaid activities – compared to 8 to 12 hours for men. Estimates indicate that women are the sole breadwinners in one-fourth to one-third of the world's households. And at least one-fourth of all other households rely on female earnings for more than 50 per cent of total income. Female-headed families are very often below the poverty line.

Indications are that the position of women within subsistence economies is growing increasingly insecure. The growing time constraints imposed on women by the longer hours they must work to make ends meet simultaneously lowers their status and keeps birth rates high. When they can no longer increase their own labour burdens, women lean heavily on the contributions of their children – especially girls – to alleviate time constraints. In fact, the increasing tendency in many areas to keep girls out of school to help with their mothers' work virtually ensures that another generation of females will grow up with lesser prospects than their brothers.

Source: taken from J. L. Jacobson, *Gender Bias: Roadblock to Sustainable Development*, Washington, D.C., Worldwatch Institute, 1992.

systematic replacement of human labour by innovative technology contributes to the underemployment of a portion of the workforce. First felt in production, this is something that is now affecting jobs in design or computation and is likely to move higher up the ladder of skills as artificial intelligence is progressively introduced. The question is less one of excluding groups of poorly trained people from employment, or even from society, than one of an evolution that could change the place, indeed the very nature, of labour in the societies of tomorrow. As things stand, it is difficult to make a confident diagnosis, but the question should nevertheless be addressed.

It should be said, however, that in industrial societies, held together by the integrating value of labour, this problem is now a source of inequality, since some people have work while others, who cannot find jobs, live on welfare or become social rejects. These societies are in crisis as a result of their failure to find a new way of structuring people's time: work is becoming a scarce commodity which nations fight to get their hands on, introducing every kind of protectionist practice and social 'dumping'. The danger is everywhere: hordes of jobless young people, left to fend for themselves in the big cities, are exposed to all the dangers inherent in social exclusion. This development is proving very costly in social terms and, at worst, could jeopardize national solidarity. It is therefore possible to say, in deliberately cautious terms, that technological progress is outstripping our capacity to think up solutions to the new problems it raises for individuals and modern societies.

This unavoidable development must lead to a rethinking of the organization of society.

Economic growth and human development

It is doubtless this sort of quandary, the inevitable outcome of a purely production-driven model, that has over the years led the relevant United Nations bodies to assign a broader meaning to the concept of development, transcending economics and encompassing its ethical, cultural and ecological dimensions as well.

Thus, UNDP, in its first *Human Development Report* in 1990, while stressing the seriousness and the extent of poverty the world over, proposed that human welfare should be considered the goal of development. Development indicators should not be restricted to per capita income, but should also embrace data on health (including infant mortality rates), diet and nutrition, access to drinking water, education and the environment. Equity and equality between the various social groups and between the sexes, and the degree of democratic participation are also to be taken into account. The notion of sustainability further complements that of human development, stress being placed on the long-term viability of the development process, on improving the standard of living of future generations and on showing regard for the natural environments on which all life depends. Strong criticism is being voiced about the tendency to step up military spending, in developing and developed countries alike, inasmuch as this increase is taking place at the expense of other types of spending more likely to generate human well-being.

It is this broader definition of development that forms the context for the Commission's thoughts on education for the twenty-first century. Education must now be viewed as part of a new approach to problems in which it is not simply one of many means towards development, but one of its constituent elements and one of its essential goals.

Education for human development

One of education's principal functions is therefore that of fitting humanity to take control of its own development. It must

he state of human development

man development is a process of
arging people's choices. In principle,
se choices can be infinite and can
inge over time. But at all levels of
elopment, the three essential ones are
people to lead a long and healthy life,
acquire knowledge and to have access
:he resources needed for a decent
ndard of living. If these essential
ices are not available, many other
ortunities remain inaccessible.
: human development does not end
re. Additional choices, highly valued
many people, range from political,
nomic and social freedom to
ortunities for being creative and
ductive and enjoying personal self-
pect and guaranteed human rights.

[. . .]
   The concept of human development
is much broader than the conventional
theories of economic development.
Economic growth models deal with
expanding GNP rather than enhancing
the quality of human lives. Human
resource development treats human
beings primarily as an input in the
production process – a means rather
than an end. Welfare approaches look at
human beings as beneficiaries and not as
agents of change in the development
process. The basic-needs approach
focuses on providing material goods and
services to deprived population groups
rather than on enlarging human choices
in all fields.

Human development, by contrast,
brings together the production and
distribution of commodities and the
expansion and use of human capabilities.
Encompassing these earlier concerns,
human development goes beyond them.
It analyses all issues in society – whether
economic growth, trade, employment,
political freedom or cultural values –
from the perspective of people. It thus
focuses on enlarging human choices –
and it applies equally to developing and
industrial countries.

Source: Human Development Report 1995
(published for UNDP), pp. 11–12, New
York/Oxford, Oxford University Press, 1995.

enable all people without exception to take their destiny into their
own hands so that they can contribute to the progress of the society in
which they live, founding development upon the responsible participation of individuals and communities.

   Seen from the standpoint adopted here, every part of education
contributes to human development, but responsible development
cannot mobilize people's energies unless it first provides them at the
earliest opportunity with a 'passport to life' that will enable them to
better understand themselves and others, and thus to share in collective undertakings and in the life of society. Basic education for all is
absolutely vital (see Chapter 6). Since the purpose of development is
the full flowering of the human being as such and not as a means of
production, basic education should clearly encompass all the elements of knowledge needed for ultimate access to other educational
levels. In this connection, emphasis should be placed on the formative role of science teaching and, accordingly, a type of education
needs to be outlined that – through what are often very simple
means such as the traditional 'touch and learn' general science
lesson – is able, from a very early age, to arouse the curiosity of
children, develop their powers of observation and introduce them
to the experimental approach. Basic education must also – and
most importantly – in the context of lifelong education give
everyone the means to shape their lives as they will and to

contribute to the development of society. The Commission's position is here fully in line with the deliberations and resolutions of the 1990 Jomtien Conference. Its aim is to give the fullest possible sense to the notion of 'basic education',[6] by including in it a body of knowledge and skills that is essential with a view to human development: environmental, health and nutrition education, in particular, should have their place therein.

From this point of view of development based on responsible participation by all members of society, the general principle of action that seems to be called for is one that encourages initiative, teamwork and synergies as well as self-employment and entrepreneurship: human resources in every country must be activated and local knowledge and local people and institutions mobilized to create new activities that will make it possible to ward off the evil spell of technological unemployment. This is the best way of initiating and sustaining processes of endogenous development in the developing countries. The various elements of educational strategy must therefore be seen as being co-ordinated and complementary, underpinned by the quest for an education in each case suited to local circumstances.

Above all, however, the Commission wishes to emphasize that the view of human development outlined above leads beyond any narrowly utilitarian idea of education. Education has other purposes than to provide a skilled workforce for the economy: it should serve to make human beings not the means but the justification of development. Bringing out the talents and aptitudes latent in everyone fulfils, at one and the same time, the fundamentally humanist mission of education, the requirement of equity that should inform all educational policy and the genuine need for an endogenous development that shows regard for the human and natural environment and the diversity of traditions and cultures. More particularly, while it is true that lifelong learning is still an essential idea at the end of the twentieth century, it is important that it should move beyond mere adaptation to work, to become part of the broader concept of an education pursued throughout life, seen as the precondition for the harmonious and continuous development of the individual.

In that respect, the Commission's thoughts echo the remarks made by the Director-General of UNESCO, Federico Mayor, speaking at the international symposium 'What Happened to Development?' (UNESCO, Paris, 18–19 June 1994), when he said that the process of development 'must first and foremost make room for

6.   The text of the World Declaration on Education for All adopted at Jomtien defines basic learning needs and the term 'basic education' was selected to describe the concept as it is understood in this report. (See Chapter

akar Recommendations

To diversify the education provided by ersifying (a) its content, in order to oid having a monolithic model, the use of rivalry and frequently of istration (developing the teaching of s and craft trades can be a positive y of making school attractive); (b) the ies and paths of education, as regards tems and structures, while preserving erall cohesion (use of the media; itribution of informal education; ucational partnerships; organizing ucational paths so that they spread tually throughout the life of each ividual); (c) the methods and places of rning, notably for practical tasks mber of years of schooling; on-the- learning; sandwich courses).

To set up regional centres of research d expertise: to teach the sciences in a

systemic way using the 'touch and learn' approach whereby knowledge can be gained by observing the natural or artificial environment; to draw on the ingrained knowledge of everybody, including that of the oldest generations (crop rotation methods, problems of soil erosion, natural hazards, etc.); to mobilize international scientific knowledge in multidisciplinary projects that involve the social sciences – for example history, sociology, ethnology, economic geography – and which can deal with local specifics (many agricultural projects have failed not because of any professional shortcomings in the agricultural engineers involved but because their knowledge of local social and cultural conditions was inadequate).
• To encourage the development of

creativity and domestic entrepreneurial capabilities. Observation of the informal economy in developing countries and of technological innovation in developed countries proves that the most creative people are not necessarily those who do well in formal schooling. Creation is in itself a process of education in terms of problems to be resolved. Therefore without stamping out initiative and originality, action must be taken to ensure that the development potential of the personality is not wasted – for example in illegal activities – or discouraged.

Source: taken from International Commission on Education for the Twenty-first Century, Dakar, Senegal, 18–21 September 1993, *Report*, Paris, UNESCO, 1994. (UNESCO doc. EDC/3.)

an awakening of the potential of the beings who are both its initial protagonists and its ultimate targets: human beings – and not only those who live today but also those who live on earth tomorrow'.

Pointers and recommendations

• Further reflection on the theme of a new model of development, showing more respect for nature and the structuring of people's time.

• A future-oriented study of the place of work in society, taking into account the effects of technical progress and change on both private and community life.

• A fuller assessment of development, taking all its aspects into account, along the lines of the work done by UNDP.

• The establishment of new links between educational policy and development policy, with a view to strengthening the bases of knowledge and skills in the countries concerned: encouragement of initiative, teamwork, realistic synergies taking local resources into account, self-employment and the spirit of enterprise.

• The necessary improvement and general availability of basic education (importance of the Jomtien Declaration).

Part Two

Principles

Chapter 4

The four
pillars
of education

Because the next century will provide unprecedented means for communication and for the circulation and storage of information, it will impose on education two demands which at first sight may appear contradictory. Education must transmit, efficiently and on a massive scale, an increasing amount of constantly evolving knowledge and know-how adapted to a knowledge-driven civilization, because this forms the basis of the skills of the future. At the same time, it must find and mark the reference points that will make it possible, on the one hand, for people not to be overwhelmed by the flows of information, much of it ephemeral, that are invading the public and private domains and, on the other, to keep the development of individuals and communities as its end in view. Education must, as it were, simultaneously provide maps of a complex world in constant turmoil and the compass that will enable people to find their way in it.

In this view of the future, traditional responses to the demand for education that are essentially quantitative and knowledge-based are no longer appropriate. It is not enough to supply each child early in life with a store of knowledge to be drawn on from then on. Each individual must be equipped to seize learning opportunities throughout life, both to broaden her or his knowledge, skills and attitudes, and to adapt to a changing, complex and interdependent world.

If it is to succeed in its tasks, education must be organized around four fundamental types of learning which, throughout a person's life, will in a way be the pillars of knowledge: *learning to know*, that is acquiring the instruments of understanding; *learning to do*, so as to be able to act creatively on one's environment; *learning to live together*, so as to participate and co-operate with other people in all human activities; and *learning to be*, an essential progression which proceeds from the previous three. Of course, these four paths of knowledge all form a whole, because there are many points of contact, intersection and exchange among them.

Yet formal education has traditionally focused mainly, if not exclusively, on *learning to know* and to a lesser extent on *learning to do*. The two others are to a large extent left to chance, or assumed to be the natural product of the two former. The Commission believes that equal attention should be paid in all organized learning to each of these four pillars, so that education is regarded as a total experience throughout life, dealing with both understanding and application, and focusing on both the individual and the individual's place in society.

Right from the beginning, the Commission felt that meeting the challenges of the coming century would necessarily entail changing the aims of education and the expectations people have of what education can provide. A broad, encompassing view of learning should aim to enable each individual to discover, unearth and enrich his or her creative potential, to reveal the treasure within each of us. This means going beyond an instrumental view of education, as a process one submits to in order to achieve specific aims (in terms of skills, capacities or economic potential), to one that emphasizes the development of the complete person, in short, *learning to be*.

Learning to know

This type of learning is less a matter of acquiring itemized, codified information than of mastering the instruments of knowledge themselves, and it can be regarded as both a means and an end in life. As a means it serves to enable each individual to understand at the very least enough about his or her environment to be able to live in dignity, to develop occupational skills and to communicate. As an end, its basis is the pleasure of understanding, knowing and discovering. Although studying to no immediately useful purpose is becoming less common, since applicable knowledge is so important in life today, the trend towards a longer period of education and more free time should lead to an increasing number of adults being able to appreciate the pleasures of personal research. The widening of the field of knowledge which enables people to understand the various aspects of their environment better arouses intellectual curiosity, stimulates the critical faculty and enables people to make sense of reality by acquiring independence of judgement. From this point of view, it is vital that all children, wherever they may be, should be able to acquire a knowledge of the scientific method in some appropriate form and become 'friends of science'[1] for life. In secondary and higher education, the initial training must provide all pupils and students with the instruments, concepts and references that scientific progress and contemporary paradigms make available.

As knowledge is manifold and constantly changing, however, it is increasingly futile to try to know everything – after basic education, omnidisciplinarity is an illusion – but specialization, even for future researchers, must not exclude general knowledge. 'Today, a really well-trained mind needs a broad background and the opportunity to study a small number of subjects in depth. Both need to be encouraged during the whole of a person's education.'[2] A general education brings a person into contact with other languages and areas of knowledge, and in the first instance makes communication possible. Specialists shut away in their own fields are in danger of losing interest in what other people are doing. Whatever the circumstances, they will find it difficult to co-operate. In addition, general education bonds societies together in time and space, and fosters receptiveness to other areas of knowledge, enabling fruitful synergies to develop between disciplines. Some significant advances in knowledge, particularly in research, are made on the boundaries between disciplines.

Learning to know presupposes learning to learn, calling upon the power of concentration, memory and thought. From childhood, especially in societies dominated by television, young people must learn to concentrate their attention on things and people. The very rapid succession of items of information broadcast through the media and the widespread habit of 'channel surfing' are harmful to the process of discovery, which takes time and involves going more deeply into the message received. Learning to concentrate

1. Third meeting of the Commission, Paris, 12–15 January 1994.

2. See Laurent Schwartz, 'L'enseignement scientifique', in: Institut de France, *Réflexions sur l'enseignement*, Paris, Flammarion, 1993.

can take many forms and make use of many different situations (games, periods of training in industry, travel, practical scientific work, etc.).

Using the memory is a necessary antidote to being swamped by the instant information put out by the media. It would be dangerous to imagine that memory has become unnecessary because of the incredible capacity to store and circulate information now at our disposal. We must certainly be selective about what we learn 'by heart', but the specifically human faculty of memory by association, which cannot be reduced to a form of automatic functioning, must be carefully cultivated. All specialists agree that the memory must be trained from childhood and that it is inappropriate to eliminate from schools certain traditional, supposedly boring, exercises.

Exercise of the faculty of thought, to which children are first introduced by their parents and then by their teachers, must entail a two-way traffic between the concrete and the abstract. In teaching and in research it is therefore important to combine two methods often regarded as conflicting: the deductive and the inductive. One may be more relevant than the other in particular disciplines, but in most cases, coherent thinking requires a combination of the two.

Acquiring knowledge is a never-ending process and can be enriched by all forms of experience. In this sense, it is increasingly interwoven with the experience of work, as work becomes less routine in nature. Initial education can be regarded as successful if it has provided the impetus and foundation that will make it possible to continue to learn throughout life, while working but also outside work.

Learning to do

Learning to know and learning to do are to a great extent indissociable, but learning to do is more closely linked to the question of vocational training: how can children be taught to put what they have learned into practice and how can education be adapted to future work when it is impossible to foresee exactly how that work will evolve? The Commission addressed itself in particular to this latter question.

In this connection, it is necessary to distinguish between the industrial economies, dominated by wage-earning occupations, and other economies still broadly dominated by independent and informal work. In the wage-earning societies, in which development followed the industrial pattern throughout this century, the substitution of machines for human labour is having the effect of making human labour increasingly immaterial. It is accentuating the knowledge-related nature of work, even in industry, and the importance of the service sector. The future of industrial economies depends on their ability to transform advances in knowledge into innovations that generate new businesses and new jobs. Learning to do can therefore no longer have the simple meaning it had when it was a matter of preparing someone for a clearly defined practical task in order to contribute to the manufacture of something. Learning must change accordingly and can no longer be regarded as the simple transmission of a more or less routine practice.

From skill to competence

In industry, especially for machine operators and technicians, the ascendancy of knowledge and information as factors in production systems is making the idea of occupational skills obsolete and is bringing personal competence to the fore. Technical progress is ineluctably changing the skills required by new production processes. Purely physical tasks are being replaced by more intellectual, more mental work, such as controlling, maintaining and monitoring machines, and by the work of design, study and organization, as machines themselves become more 'intelligent' and the physical labour required for work diminishes.

The demand for higher skills at all levels has a number of causes. As far as workers are concerned, the juxtaposition of prescribed tasks and individual operations is frequently being replaced by organization into 'work teams' or 'project groups', as in Japanese companies, while employee interchangeability is being superseded by the personalization of assignments. Instead of requiring a skill, which they see as still too narrowly linked to the idea of practical know-how, employers are seeking competence, a mix, specific to each individual, of skill in the strict sense of the term, acquired through technical and vocational training, of social behaviour, of an aptitude for teamwork, and of initiative and a readiness to take risks.

If we add to those new demands the requirement for personal commitment on the part of the worker, regarded as an agent of change, it becomes clear that highly subjective qualities, innate or acquired, that company heads often call 'life skills', combine with knowledge and know-how to make up the competence required – which provides a good illustration of the link that education must maintain with the various aspects of learning, as the Commission has emphasized. Among those qualities, the ability to communicate, work with others, and manage and resolve conflicts is becoming increasingly important. This trend is being accentuated by the development of service activities.

The 'dematerialization' of work and the rise of the service sector

The consequences for education of the 'dematerialization' of the advanced economies are particularly striking if one looks at the qualitative and quantitative changes in services. Services, which form a very varied category, can best be defined by what they are not: they are neither industrial nor agricultural and, despite their variety, have in common the fact that they do not produce material goods.

Many services are defined principally in terms of the interpersonal relationships they involve. Examples can be found both in the market sector, which is proliferating as a result of the increasing complexity of economies (experts of all types, technological monitoring and consultancy services, financial, accounting and management services) and in the more traditional non-market sector (social services, education, health, etc.). In both cases information and communication are of the utmost importance, in that emphasis is placed on the personalized capture and processing of specific information for a specific purpose. In these types of services, the quality of the relationship between provider and user is also very dependent on the user. It is therefore understandable that it is no longer possible to train for this work in the same way as when it was a question of ploughing the land or sheet-metal working. The relationship with the material and the technology is secondary to the interpersonal relationship. The development of services therefore makes it essential to cultivate human qualities that are not necessarily inculcated by traditional training and which amount to the ability to establish stable, effective relationships between individuals.

It can be imagined that, in the high-tech organizations of the future, relational difficulties might create serious dysfunctions calling for new types of skill, more behavioural than intellectual. This may provide opportunities for people with few or no formal qualifications. Intuition, flair, judgement and the ability to hold a team together are not necessarily abilities peculiar to those with the highest paper qualifications. How and where are these qualities, innate in varying degrees, to be taught? It is not easy to imagine the content of training programmes that will produce the required abilities and aptitudes. The same problem arises in connection with vocational training in the developing countries.

Work in the informal economy

In developing economies where wage-earning occupations are not the rule, the nature of work is very different. In many countries of sub-Saharan Africa and some Latin American and Asian countries, only a small proportion of the population is formally employed, the great majority being involved in the traditional subsistence economy. There is no formal definition of work skills; know-how is often traditional. In addition, the function of learning is not limited to work but must respond to the broader objective of formal or informal participation in development. It is often as much a matter of social as of occupational skills.

In other developing countries, side-by-side with agriculture and a small formal sector, there is also a sector based on trade and finance, which is both modern and informal and is sometimes quite dynamic, and which indicates there is an entrepreneurial potential well adapted to local conditions.

In both cases, the Commission's consultations in developing countries indicated that these countries see the acquisition of a scientific culture which will give them access to modern technology as the way to the future, without, however, ignoring the specific capacities for innovation and creativity to be found within the local context.

This brings us back to a question that faces both developed and developing countries: how can people learn to cope effectively with uncertainty and to play a part in creating the future?

Learning to live together, learning to live with others

This type of learning is probably one of the major issues in education today. The contemporary world is too often a world of violence that belies the hope some people placed in human progress. There has always been conflict throughout history, but new factors are accentuating the risk, in particular the extraordinary capacity for self-destruction humanity has created in the course of the twentieth century. Through the media, the general public is becoming the impotent observer, even the hostage, of those who create or maintain conflicts. Education has up to now not been able to do much to alleviate that state of affairs. Is it possible to devise a form of education which might make it possible to avoid conflicts or resolve them peacefully by developing respect for other people, their cultures and their spiritual values?

The idea of teaching non-violence in schools is laudable even if it is only one means among many for combating the prejudices that lead to conflict. It is a difficult task, since people very naturally tend to overvalue their own qualities and those of their group and to harbour prejudices against others. Furthermore, the general climate of competition that is at present characteristic of economic activity, within and above all between nations, tends to give priority to the competitive spirit and individual success. Such competition now amounts to ruthless economic warfare and to a tension between rich and poor that is dividing nations and the world, and exacerbating historic rivalries. It is regrettable that education sometimes helps maintain this climate by its misinterpretation of the idea of emulation.

How can we do better? Experience shows that, to reduce this risk, it is not enough to organize contact and communication between members of different groups (in schools shared by several ethnic groups or religions, for example). If the different groups are in competition or have unequal status in the environment they share, such contact can, on the contrary, inflame latent tensions and degenerate into conflict. On the other hand, if contact takes place in an egalitarian context, and there are common objectives and shared purpose, prejudices and latent hostility can dwindle and give way to more relaxed co-operation or even friendship.

It would seem, therefore, that education must take two complementary paths: on one level, gradual discovery of others and, on another, experience of shared purposes throughout life, which seems to be an effective way of avoiding or resolving latent conflicts.

Discovering others

The task of education is to teach, at one and the same time, the diversity of the human race and an awareness of the similarities between, and the interdependence of, all humans. From early childhood, schools must therefore take every opportunity to teach these two things. Some subjects are particularly well suited for this task: human geography beginning with basic education, and foreign languages and literature slightly later on, for example.

If one is to understand others, one must first know oneself. To give children and young people an accurate view of the world, education, whether in the family, the community or at school, must first help them discover who they are. Only then will they genuinely be able to put themselves in other people's shoes and understand their reactions. Developing such empathy at school bears fruit in terms of social behaviour throughout life. For example, by teaching young people to adopt the point of view of other ethnic or religious groups, the lack of understanding that leads to hatred and violence among adults can be avoided. The teaching of the history of religions and customs can thus serve as a useful benchmark for future behaviour.[3]

Finally, the actual form that teaching takes must not run counter to this acknowledgement of others. Teachers whose dogmatic approach stifles pupils' curiosity or critical spirit instead of inculcating those qualities in them can do more harm than good. If teachers forget they are role models, their attitude may forever weaken their pupils' ability to be receptive to others and face the inevitable tensions between people, groups and nations. Encountering others through dialogue and debate is one of the tools needed by twenty-first-century education.

Working towards common objectives

When people work together on rewarding projects which take them out of their usual routine, differences and even conflicts between individuals tend to fade into the background and sometimes disappear. People derive a new identity from such projects, so that it is possible to go beyond individual routines and highlight what people have in common rather than the differences between them. In many cases, tensions between social classes and nationalities have in the end been transformed into unity by the common effort involved, in sport for example. Similarly, where work is concerned, many ventures would never have been successfully completed had the conflicts commonly found in hierarchical organizations not been transcended by a shared purpose.

Formal education must therefore provide enough time and

. David A. lamburg, *'ducation for 'onflict 'esolution* eprinted from ne *Annual 'eport 1994* of ne Carnegie orporation of lew York).

opportunity in its programmes to introduce the young, from childhood, to co-operative undertakings through participation in sport or in cultural activities, and also through participation in social activities such as neighbourhood renovation, helping the underprivileged, humanitarian work, inter-generational assistance, etc. Other educational organizations and voluntary bodies must take over where schools leave off. In addition, in everyday school life, the involvement of teachers and pupils in joint undertakings could provide an initiation into a way of resolving conflicts and a benchmark for pupils to refer to in the future, while at the same time enhancing the teacher–pupil relationship.

Learning to be

At its very first meeting, the Commission firmly restated the fundamental principle that education must contribute to the all-round development of each individual – mind and body, intelligence, sensitivity, aesthetic sense, personal responsibility and spiritual values. All human beings must be enabled to develop independent, critical thinking and form their own judgement, in order to determine for themselves what they believe they should do in the different circumstances of life.

The Preamble of the report *Learning to Be* expressed the fear that the world would be dehumanized as a result of technical change,[4] one of its essential messages being that education must enable every person 'to solve his own problems, make his own decisions and shoulder his own responsibilities'. All the changes in society since then, and particularly the fantastic development of the power of the media, have accentuated this fear and given even greater legitimacy to the imperative that stems from it. In the twenty-first century, these phenomena may loom even larger. The problem will then no longer be so much to prepare children for a given society as to continuously provide everyone with the powers and intellectual reference points they need for understanding the world around them and behaving responsibly and fairly. More than ever, education's essential role seems to be to give people the freedom of thought, judgement, feeling and imagination they need in order to develop their talents and remain as much as possible in control of their lives.

This is not simply an individualistic imperative: recent experience shows that what might appear to be only an indi-

4. [. . .] the risk of personality-alienation involved in the more obsessive forms of propaganda and publicity, and in the behavioural conformity which may be imposed on him from the outside, to the detriment of his genuine needs and his intellectual and emotional identity. Meanwhile, machines [. . .] are ousting him from a certain number of areas in which he used to feel able, at least, to move freely and pursue his ends after his own fashion' – Edgar Faure et al., *Learning to Be: The World of Education Today and Tomorrow*, p. xxiv, Paris, UNESCO, 1972.

vidual's way of defending himself or herself against an alienating system, or one that is perceived as hostile, sometimes offers societies too the best chance of progress. The diversity of people's personalities, their independence and initiative, and even the desire to provoke – these are all safeguards of creativity and innovation. To reduce violence and combat the various ills afflicting society, new methods born of experience have shown themselves to be effective.

In an ever-changing world in which social and economic innovation seems to be one of the main driving forces, a special place should doubtless be given to the qualities of imagination and creativity, the clearest manifestations of human freedom, which may be at risk from a certain standardization of individual behaviour. The twenty-first century needs this variety of talents and personalities; it also needs the exceptional individuals who are also essential in any civilization. It is therefore important to provide children and young people with every possible opportunity for discovery and experiment – aesthetic, artistic, sporting, scientific, cultural and social – as well as appealing introductions to the creation of their contemporaries or earlier generations. Art and poetry, too often taught in a way that has become more utilitarian than cultural, should again be given more importance in schools than is commonly the case in many countries. The desire to develop the imagination and creativity should also result in higher regard being paid to oral culture and knowledge derived from the child's or adult's experience.

The Commission fully endorses the principle set out in the report *Learning to Be*: 'the aim of development is the complete fulfilment of man, in all the richness of his personality, the complexity of his forms of expression and his various commitments – as individual, member of a family and of a community, citizen and producer, inventor of techniques and creative dreamer'.[5] Individual development, which begins at birth and continues throughout life, is a dialectical process which starts with knowing oneself and then opens out to relationships with others. In that sense, education is above all an inner journey whose stages correspond to those of the continuous maturing of the personality. Education as a means to the end of a successful working life is thus a very individualized process and at the same time a process of constructing social interaction.

Ibid., p. vi.

It goes without saying that the four pillars of education described in this chapter cannot relate exclusively to one phase of life or to a single place. As will be seen in the next chapter, the phases and areas of education must be rethought and must complement and interpenetrate one another, so that all can derive the greatest benefit, throughout their lives, from an ever-broadening educational environment.

Pointers and recommendations

• Education throughout life is based on four pillars: learning to know, learning to do, learning to live together and learning to be.

• **Learning to know**, by combining a sufficiently broad general knowledge with the opportunity to work in depth on a small number of subjects. This also means learning to learn, so as to benefit from the opportunities education provides throughout life.

• **Learning to do**, in order to acquire not only an occupational skill but also, more broadly, the competence to deal with many situations and work in teams. It also means learning to do in the context of young peoples' various social and work experiences which may be informal, as a result of the local or national context, or formal, involving courses, alternating study and work.

• **Learning to live together**, by developing an understanding of other people and an appreciation of interdependence – carrying out joint projects and learning to manage conflicts – in a spirit of respect for the values of pluralism, mutual understanding and peace.

• **Learning to be**, so as better to develop one's personality and be able to act with ever greater autonomy, judgement and personal responsibility. In that connection, education must not disregard any aspect of a person's potential: memory, reasoning, aesthetic sense, physical capacities and communication skills.

• Formal education systems tend to emphasize the acquisition of knowledge to the detriment of other types of learning; but it is vital now to conceive education in a more encompassing fashion. Such a vision should inform and guide future educational reforms and policy, in relation both to contents and to methods.

Chapter 5

Learning Throughout Life

Education is coming to occupy an ever larger place in people's lives as its role among the forces at work in modern societies increases. There are several reasons for this. The traditional division of life into separate periods – childhood and youth devoted to schooling, adulthood and working life, and retirement – no longer corresponds to things as they are today and corresponds still less to the demands of the future. Today, no one can hope to amass during his or her youth an initial fund of knowledge which will serve for a lifetime. The swift changes taking place in the world call for knowledge to be continuously updated, and at the same time, the initial education of young people is tending to become more protracted. A shorter working life, shorter working hours and a longer expectancy of life after retirement are also increasing the time available for other activities.

Education, too, is changing fast. More and more opportunities for learning out of school are occurring in all fields, while skills, in the traditional sense of the term, are giving way in many modern sectors of activity to the ideas of developing competence and adaptability (see Chapter 4).

The traditional distinction between initial education and continuing education therefore needs to be reconsidered. Continuing education that is really in harmony with the needs of modern societies can no longer be defined in relation to a particular time of life (adult education as opposed to the education of the young, for instance) or to too specific a purpose (vocational as opposed to general). The time to learn is now the whole lifetime, and each field of knowledge spreads into and enriches the others. As the twenty-first century approaches, education is so varied in its tasks and forms that it covers all the activities that enable people, from childhood to old age, to acquire a living knowledge of the world, of other people and themselves. It quite naturally combines the four basic types of learning described in the preceding chapter. It is this educational continuum, coextensive with life and widened to take in the whole of society, that the Commission has chosen to refer to in this report as 'learning throughout life'. A key to the twenty-first century, learning throughout life will be essential for adapting to the evolving requirements of the labour market and for better mastery of the changing time-frames and rhythms of individual existence.

An imperative for democracy

Learning throughout life is not a remote ideal, but a reality which is tending more and more to take shape in a complex educational scene marked by a series of changes that are accentuating the need for it. In order to organize it, we must stop regarding the different forms of teaching and learning as independent from one another and, in a sense, as superimposable or even competing; we must try, on the contrary, to enhance the complementary character of the stages of modern education and the environments where it is provided.

First of all, as indicated earlier, advances in science and technology and the transformation of industrial processes to make them more competitive are rapidly making the learning and know-how that people have acquired in their initial education obsolete and call for the development of continuing vocational education. This continuing education is in large measure a response to an economic demand. It enables firms to acquire the greater skills needed to maintain employment and gain a competitive edge. At the same time it provides people with opportunities for updating their knowledge and improving their earning power.

Learning throughout life as understood by the Commission goes further than that: in a world in which the accelerated rate of change and rapid globalization are transforming each individual's relationship with both time and space, learning throughout life is essential for people to retain mastery of their own destinies. Major transformations in the nature of employment are taking place in some parts of the world, undoubtedly to spread, that will involve a reorganization of individuals' use of time. Learning throughout life can become, then, the means for each of us to establish an equilibrium between learning and working, continued adaptation for a number of occupations and for the exercise of active citizenship.

Basic education, if it achieves what it sets out to do, arouses a desire to carry on learning. This leads to the continuation of education within the formal system, but those who so wish must also be able to go further. In fact, surveys conducted in different countries show that adults' further participation in educational and cultural activities is related to the level of schooling already received. There is, very clearly, a cumulative effect: the more education you have, the more education you want, as may be observed in both developed and developing countries. The rise in school enrolment figures and literacy rates, and the fresh impetus given to basic education, thus herald an increased demand for adult education in the societies of the future.

This issue is closely bound up with that of equality of opportunity. The general increase in the desire to learn – holding out the promise of increased personal fulfilment – must not conceal the increased risk of inequality that goes with it, since having a limited initial education – or no initial education at all – can jeopardize the continuation of learning throughout life. The risk is apparent in the gap between developed and developing countries but also, within each society, in the inequality of educational opportunity. Illiteracy in the developing countries, functional illiteracy in the developed countries and inadequate further education provision are major barriers to the establishment of genuine learning societies.

If these inequalities are recognized and energetic measures are taken to correct them, learning throughout life should offer new opportunities to those who, for one reason or another, have been unable to complete their schooling or who have dropped out. Educational inequalities need not be reproduced either completely or automatically, provided that, for example, school enrolment is increased among disadvantaged populations or non-formal education for young people who left school too early is developed. Various strategies for correcting certain inequalities have been

implemented with success, such as the popular education programmes in Sweden, adult literacy campaigns or missions in
Nicaragua, Ecuador and India, paid study-leave policies in Denmark, France and Germany, and decentralized public non-formal
basic education services in Thailand and Viet Nam.[1]

Generally speaking, equality of opportunity is an essential
principle for all who are trying gradually to put into place the different components of learning throughout life. As democracy
requires, that principle should be embodied in flexible types of education whereby society would, as it were, guarantee from the outset
the equality of the opportunities for schooling and further education
offered to all people throughout their lives, whatever twists and turns
their educational careers may take. Various approaches are possible:
in Chapter 8, in connection with the financing of education, the
Commission proposes the creation of a study-time entitlement.

A multidimensional education

Learning throughout life is a continuous process for each human
being of adding to and adapting his or her knowledge and skills, and
his or her judgement and capacities for action. It must enable people
to become aware of themselves and their environment, and to play a
social role at work and in the community at large. Knowledge, know-
how, knowing how to live with other people and 'life skills' constitute
four intimately linked aspects of the same reality. Learning throughout life is a day-to-day experience punctuated by periods of intense
effort to understand complex data and facts, and is the product of a
multidimensional dialectic. Although it involves the repetition or imitation of actions and practices, it is also a very special way of learning and of achieving something personal and creative. It combines
non-formal with formal learning, and the development of innate
abilities with the acquisition of new competencies. It requires effort
but also brings the joy of discovery. It is an experience particular to
each individual but also the most complex of social relationships
in that it comes, at one and the same time, within the fields of
culture, work and citizenship.

Does this make it a fundamentally new human experience? In
traditional societies, the stability of the way in which production,
society and political life were organized guaranteed a relatively
unchanging educational and social environment, punctuated by

1.   Paul
Bélanger, *Des
sociétés
éducatives en
gestation*, Paris
UNESCO, 199
(UNESCO doc.
EDC/S/8.)

initiation rites that followed a prearranged pattern. Modern times have disturbed the traditional educational environments – religious institutions, family and neighbourhood. In addition, the rationalist illusion that school could by itself meet all educational needs has been punctured by the changes in social life and by the progress of science and technology, with its implications for people's work and their environment. The need to adjust and to retrain, first apparent in employment in the industrial societies, has gradually spread to other countries and other fields of activity. The relevance of the education systems, both formal and non-formal, built up in the course of time is being challenged and their ability to adapt is being questioned. Despite the spectacular development of school enrolments, education systems seem to suffer from an inherent lack of flexibility and they are at the mercy of the slightest forecasting error, especially when it comes to training people in the skills of the future.

The reason why the idea of a multidimensional education extending over a lifetime, which links up with the basic ideas intuited by the principal educational thinkers of the past in different cultures, is being taken up again today is that it seems more and more necessary to put it into practice. At the same time, however, it is proving increasingly complex. The individual's natural and human environment is expanding, to become global: how can it be made a place for education and action, and how can people be educated in the universal and the particular, so that they profit both from the variety of the world cultural heritage and from the specific features of their own history?

New times, fresh fields

The substantial increase in the demand for adult education, so great that it has sometimes been referred to as a veritable explosion, has often been stressed. Adult education takes on many different forms, such as basic education in a non-formal setting, part-time enrolment in higher education, language courses, vocational training and retraining, courses organized by various associations or trade unions, open learning systems and distance teaching.[2] In some countries, Sweden and Japan for instance, around 50 per cent of the population are at present involved in adult education, and there is every reason to think that all over the world the development of adult education represents a strong and sustained

Bélanger,
. cit.

A nation of adult learners – Sweden

Adult education in Sweden is widespread and based on a long tradition. It is provided in many different forms and under many different auspices. The level of participation in formal and non-formal education activities is high. More than 50 per cent of the adult population takes part in some form of organized learning in the course of a year.

Swedish *municipal adult (formal) education* aims at bridging education gaps in society and satisfying individual desires for broader study, through preparing adult students for further study, work and community participation. It is free of charge and gives adults a chance to make up for deficiencies in their previous schooling by supplementing the nine-year compulsory basic school and upper secondary school. During the period 1979–91, every third student in universities and colleges came via municipal adult education.

Education is organized in the form of separate courses, and the students themselves decide on the number and combination of subjects to be taken and the rate of progress. Studies can be thus combined with employment.

The objective of Swedish *popular adult (non-formal) education* is to develop basic democratic values in society by giving all citizens the opportunity to develop their general knowledge and skills, strengthen their self-confidence and increase their understanding and respect for other people's opinions. Education is based on the active participation of the students in the planning and implementation of the work. The ability to co-operate with others is considered essential. Popular education activities are to a large extent state-subsidized, but organizers (political, trade-union and popular movements as well as local authorities) are at complete liberty to decide their activities themselves.

Popular adult education comprises studies in residential colleges for adults *(folk high schools)* or in *study circles* under the aegis of voluntary education associations. The study circles are small groups of people who meet and carry on planned studies or cultural activities together over a period of time. There are no formal qualifications for joining or leading a study circle. The study circles reach more than 25 per cent of the adult population in Sweden.

Sources: Swedish Ministry of Education and Science, *Coherence between Compulsory Education, Initial and Continuing Training and Adult Education in Sweden*, Stockholm, 1994; Swedish National Federation of Adult Education, *Non-formal Adult Education in Sweden*, Stockholm, 1995.

trend that may cause education as a whole to reorient itself in the direction of lifelong education.

In addition to all this, the place of work in society is being profoundly affected by change in the industrialized countries. What if people were no longer to be identified mainly by the work they do? This is a question that has to be asked in view of the reduction in the amount of time devoted to work, with the later arrival of young people on the labour market, the lowering of the age of retirement, the lengthening of annual holidays, the reduction of the working week and the spread of part-time employment. What is more, it is possible that, if full employment is not achieved, we could be moving towards a great variety of work situations and contracts – part-time employment, fixed-term or casual employment, indeterminate employment, self-employment.

At all events, the increase in spare time should be accompanied by an increase in time given over to education, whether initial education or further education. The responsibility that falls to society in the field of education is correspondingly greater, the more so as education is now a multidimensional process which is not limited to the acquisition of knowledge and which is not the province of education systems alone.

owards a policy of choosing
ne's own time

the future, new ideas about working
he need to be devised which take more
count of people's individual
eferences and of the needs of
sinesses for flexibility. These
hovations must go beyond a mere
duction in the length of the working
ek and must touch on the whole of a
rson's active life. This also concerns the
e of retirement. Why should people
ve to stop work between the ages of
 and 65 when they often want to carry
 working? Side by side with the right
 receive a pension from the age of 60,
 example, provision should be made

for a flexible retirement age so that
people could continue to work after 60.
Again, why should people between the
ages of 25 and 35 necessarily have to
work full time since it is precisely at that
time of life that they have to shoulder
many different obligations, and
arrangements like shorter hours, parental
leave, sabbaticals or study leave would be
particularly welcome. A working-hours
policy that took account of these needs
would go a long way to help reconcile
family life and work and bridge the
traditional gap between the roles played
by men and women. As long ago as the

early 1980s, André Gorz was arguing for
a substantial reduction in the length of a
person's working life. The proposal made
by the former President of the European
Commission, Jacques Delors, that by the
year 2010 a person's working life should
be one of 40,000 hours, underlines the
topicality and relevance of this view.

Source: European Trade Union Institute, 'Pour
une politique novatrice du temps de travail en
vue de sauvegarder l'emploi et d'améliorer la
qualité de la vie', in: R. Hoffman and J. Lapeyre
(eds.), *Le temps de travail en Europe.
Organisation et réduction,* pp. 285–6, Paris,
Syros, 1995.

In the same way that the period of education is becoming a whole lifetime, so the facilities and opportunities for learning are tending to become more numerous. Our educational environment is becoming more varied; education is reaching out from formal systems to benefit from the contributions of other people and institutions active in society.

Different societies may of course approach the sharing of roles and functions among the various people and institutions differently, but still it seems that, all over the world, the educational dimensions of society are being organized around the same cardinal points.

Education at the heart of society

All education begins at home, and the family thus provides the link between the emotions and the intellect, and passes on values and standards. Its relationship with the education system is often felt to be antagonistic. In some developing countries, what is taught at school may indeed conflict with traditional family values. Disadvantaged families often see the school as an alien world whose codes and practices they do not understand. A real dialogue between parents and teachers is thus essential, for the harmonious development of children depends on whether the education given by the school is backed up by the education given at home. In that connection, pre-school education projects for disadvantaged groups of the population have shown that their effectiveness was largely due to better understanding of the school system and greater respect for it that families derived from them.

Individuals also learn, throughout life, from the social milieu formed by the community to which they belong. That community naturally varies, not only from one person to another, but also in the course of the same person's life. Here, education proceeds from the will to live together and to base the group's cohesion on a number of shared undertakings such as membership of voluntary movements, of a religious denomination or of a political party, which all contribute to this form of education. The school does not merge with the community but, while retaining its specific character, it must avoid cutting itself off in any way from the social environment. The community to which a person belongs is a powerful educational influence, if only because of the opportunity it affords of learning co-operation with, and concern for, others or, perhaps at a deeper level, of gaining active experience of citizenship. The community as a whole should feel responsibility for the education of its members, expressed either by means of constant dialogue with the school or, if there is no school, by taking partial charge of their education in a non-formal setting. From that viewpoint, the education of women and girls is the precondition for the genuine equal participation of women in community life.

The workplace, too, can provide an excellent educational environment. To begin with, work involves the learning of a whole series of skills and, in that connection, the formative value of work ought to receive greater recognition in most societies, particularly within the education system. Recognition of that fact implies that universities in particular should also take account of the experience gained in employment. In that context, the systematic establishment of bridges between university and working life should help those who so wish to both continue general learning and complete their formal training. More partnerships should be developed between the education system and firms, so as to promote the necessary link between initial and further training. Courses for young people alternating study with work can supplement or correct

mproving the quality of life hrough community action in Jordan

e Noor Al Hussein Foundation (NHF), a ominent non-governmental ganization in Jordan, has adopted the nilosophy of comprehensive socio-onomic development for low-income pulations, with special emphasis on omen and on interdisciplinary action. Quality of Life Project addresses all e development needs of the community cluding health, nutrition, the nvironment and education. The project troduces programmes of human sources development that empower ommunities with knowledge, education nd skills, and that involve parents and ommunity leaders as partners in the rovision of formal and non-formal ducation.

The Quality of Life Project is nplemented in rural areas and follows a pecific strategy that focuses primarily on ne training of villagers in various areas:

to assume a greater share of responsibility – previously taken largely by government employees – in the mechanisms of consultation, consensus building, and mutual decision-making; in the use of appropriate local technologies; in problem identification, planning, specifying types of support needed, implementation and evaluation of their own development projects – where priority is given to projects that ensure maximum participation of women; in the management and auditing of their own finances; and training in the continuous collection, analysis and evaluation of information to be utilized in decision-making.

Quality of Life Project objectives are achieved by encouraging and training local communities to form their own Village Development Councils (VDC) in order to promote self-reliance and set up

their own Village Development Funds (VDF) to encourage self-financing.

Through community participation in VDC and VDF, an increased sense of self-worth and achievement is established as the villagers increasingly become an educated, productive community able to depend on their own human resources and on their own income-generating activities, and capable of meeting their development needs and social obligations in a self-reliant manner. It is inherent in the strategy of the project to nurture a sense of community and social cohesion. This is achieved by focusing on the active participation of the entire community in the development process, by their continuous training and by the provision of education, formal and non-formal, to all its members.

In'am Al Mufti

initial training and, by reconciling theory and practice, facilitate entry into employment. They can be very helpful in enabling adolescents to become aware of the restrictions and opportunities of working life, to know themselves better and to find their bearings. Finally, they can be an asset in the maturation process, and a powerful force for socialization.

With more free time, people can focus on leisure activities and self-fulfilment. Two related trends can be seen: cultural institutions such as museums or libraries are tending to develop their educational role, no longer confining themselves to research or conservation; and the education system is tending to co-operate with cultural institutions more than it did formerly. The success of 'cultural heritage classes' is a relevant example; in some countries, such classes are enabling pupils to become familiar with a monument or site, thanks to genuine co-operation between teachers and the cultural authorities. The school should, taking advantage of television when possible, increase pupils' receptivity to museums, theatres, libraries, cinemas and, more generally, the whole of the country's cultural life, so as to give the adult public of the future an experience of aesthetic feeling and the desire to keep abreast of cultural developments. Lastly, it is important to reduce the antagonism, often represented as implacable, existing between education and the media. Educationists frequently criticize the media, and more especially television, for imposing a kind of lowest cultural common denominator, cutting down the time devoted to reading and thought, forcing scenes of violence on people and, more generally, playing on emotions. The advocates of the media, for their part, readily accuse schools of conservatism and of resorting to outmoded methods to pass on obsolete knowledge, boring pupils and students, and making them lose interest in learning.

The media are an integral part of our cultural environment, in the broadest sense of the term. Their aims are not necessarily educational, but their very real power of attraction has to be taken into account. Schools and universities are thus well advised to use them for their own purposes by making educational radio or television programmes for schools. In Japan, 90 per cent of schools already use television as a teaching aid. Schools have a specific responsibility with regard to the media, above all television, if only because television is assuming increasing prominence in pupils' lives, judging by the time they devote to it – 1,200 hours a year in Western Europe and about double that in the United States, as compared with only about 1,000 hours a year spent in school by the same children. Teachers need, therefore, to develop in pupils a critical approach to television that will enable them to use it as a learning aid, sifting and arranging in order of importance the huge volume of information it conveys. We

Learning at work and at school - sandwich courses in Germany

The German system of vocational education, known as the 'dual system', or sandwich education, has aroused increasing interest around the world in recent years. This system is often regarded as one of the factors in the relatively low rate of unemployment among young people in Germany as compared with other countries. It is thought to make for a successful transition from school to employment and to enable firms to adapt more easily to new circumstances.

On leaving the various streams of general education, more than two-thirds of young people go into vocational education in the dual system. Most of them enter at the age of 16 or 17, after nine or ten years of schooling. There is no particular requirement except a minimum age level of 15.

In the dual system, two places of learning complement one another – the firm and the school. The young people learn the skills of a particular job in a factory, workshop, laboratory, office or shop and, at the same time, attend a vocational school one or two days a week. The firm plays a decisive role, because it decides how many apprentices to take – and signs contracts with them –

and it is in the firm that the young people spend most of their training tim To ensure that the theoretical and practical instruction given in the two different places is complementary, the two types of education are co-ordinate

At the institutional level, the dual system depends on a co-ordinating bod the Federal Institute for Vocational Training, which decides on the courses collaboration with the employers' organizations and trade unions. The system is designed in such a way as to evolve and adapt to the changing needs of the economy.

Sandwich education enables young people to obtain a qualification corresponding to the level of skilled manual or office worker after two to three and a half years. This form of education currently concerns about 380 recognized occupations. Many young people find a job in the firm in which they were trained.

Sources: Vocational Training in the Dual Syste in the Federal Republic of Germany, Bonn, Federal Ministry of Education, Science, Research and Technology, 1994; *Bildung und Wissenschaft* [Education and Science] (Bonn), Nos. 5–6, pp. 7 et seq., 1992.

must keep in mind the essential purpose of education, which is to enable everyone to develop the ability to form judgements and act therefrom.

The media are also widely recognized as an effective means of providing non-formal education and adult education. Open university and distance education projects, for instance, have shown the importance of working out for the future an educational strategy that incorporates information and communication technologies (see Chapter 8).

Seeking out educational synergies

One or other of the various learning environments will have priority in each time of life, but the complementarity between them should be enhanced and the transitions from one type of education to another should be made easier. The aim is to achieve a genuinely coherent education, as has been imagined in other forms in many traditional societies.

It is with this in mind that we should, for example, seek out possible synergies between theory and practice, and between 'life skills' and knowing how to live with others, and hence the complementarity of the corresponding types of education and educational environments. In addition, by developing very broadly outside the formal system, the supply of education is responding to the demand for diversity expressed in all societies and is making a variety of educational careers possible. Accordingly, there should be a dynamic relationship between school or university and these different alternative types of learning, a relationship involving complementarity and partnership but also a process of change and a questioning of traditional educational practice.

Education thus concerns all citizens, who should all be active participants in, and not just passive consumers of, the education provided by institutions. Everyone may learn in a variety of educational situations and, ideally, become alternately learner and teacher in the learning society. With the integration of the non-formal in the formal, education is embedded in society, which is wholly responsible for it and renewed through it.

Thus, broadening the initial concept of lifelong education beyond the immediate requirements of retraining provides a response to the new and crucially important demand for active self-reliance in a swiftly changing society. As many of the points of reference provided in the past by tradition have disappeared, people must continually use what they know and their own judgement to find their bearings, to think and to act. All periods of life and all fields of activity should contribute, so that personal fulfilment coincides with participation in society. Education, no longer temporally and spatially segmented, can thus become a dimension of life itself.

Pointers and recommendations

- The concept of learning throughout life is the key that gives access to the twenty-first century. It goes beyond the traditional distinction between initial and continuing education. It links up with another concept often put forward, that of the learning society, in which everything affords an opportunity of learning and fulfilling one's potential.

- In its new guise, continuing education is seen as going far beyond what is already practised, particularly in the developed countries, i.e. upgrading, with refresher training, retraining and conversion or promotion courses for adults. It should open up opportunities for learning for all, for many different purposes – offering them a second or third chance, satisfying their desire for knowledge and beauty or their desire to surpass themselves, or making it possible to broaden and deepen strictly vocational forms of training, including practical training.

- In short, 'learning throughout life' must take advantage of all the opportunities offered by society.

Part Three

Directions

Chapter 6

From basic education to university

The idea of learning throughout life has not misled the Commission into overlooking the importance of formal, as against non-formal or informal, education. On the contrary, it believes it is within formal education systems that the skills and aptitudes individuals will need in order to carry on learning are acquired. The role of formal and informal education, far from being in opposition one to the other, is therefore to cross-fertilize each other. For this purpose, however, education systems need to adapt themselves to these new requirements: accordingly, the various sequences of education have to be reconsidered, linked together and re-arranged, possibilities of transference between them have to be provided and a variety of pathways through the system has to be offered. This would be a way out of the dilemma that has plagued education policies: whether to be selective, thus increasing the number of academic failures, or to be egalitarian, providing the same schooling for all, as against promoting individual talents.

Attitudes towards the sort of learning that will continue throughout life are formed in the family but also, more broadly, at the stage of basic education (which includes, in particular, pre-primary and primary schooling): it is there that the spark of creativity may either spring into life or be extinguished, and that access to knowledge may or may not become a reality. This is the time when we all acquire the instruments for the future development of our faculties of reason and imagination, our judgement and sense of responsibility, when we learn to be inquisitive about the world around us. The Commission is fully aware of the intolerable disparities that still exist between different social groups, countries or parts of the world: making good-quality basic education generally available remains one of the great challenges for the end of the twentieth century. This is indeed the end to which the international community pledged itself at the 1990 Jomtien Conference. The need throughout the world – for the question is not one that concerns the developing countries alone – is for everyone to be in command of the knowledge they require in order to understand the world in which they live. This pledge should be renewed and the efforts already undertaken should be pursued.

The Commission considers, however, that a similar commitment, to secondary education in this case, should be written into the agenda of the major international conferences for the next century. Secondary education must be seen as a crucial point in the life of individuals: it is at this stage that young people should be able to decide their own futures, in the light of their own tastes and aptitudes, and that they can acquire the abilities that will make for a fully successful adult life. Education at that level should thus be adapted to take account both of the different processes whereby adolescents attain maturity – processes that differ from one individual and one country to another – and of economic and social needs. Pupils should be offered a choice of educational pathways so as to cater for the diversity of their talents and there should be a greater emphasis on guidance, with opportunities for remedial teaching or changes of direction. The Commission also makes a strong plea for the development of 'sandwich' courses, alternating study with work. The point here is not only to bring schools into a closer relationship with the working environment but also to bring young people face to face with social realities and the realities of the workplace, thus making them aware of their weaknesses and strengths, which will undeniably help them to grow in maturity.

Higher education, finally, must continue to play its part in creating, preserving and passing on knowledge at the highest levels. Institutions of higher education also play a decisive part in rethinking education, as regards both where and when it takes place. Although the number of places in higher education is everywhere limited, it is important for higher education to be conceived in such a fashion as to unite equity with excellence, within institutions that are wide open to people from every social and economic group, whatever their previous education. Universities, in particular, must lead the way by trying out new methods of reaching new groups of learners, recognizing skills and knowledge acquired outside formal systems, and promulgating, through the training of teachers and teacher trainers, new approaches to learning.

In seeking to move towards a society where each individual can and will learn throughout life, we must rethink the relationship between educational institutions and society, and the sequencing of the various levels of education. Educational – as well as occupational – careers will of necessity be less linear in the future, with periods of study interspersed with periods of work, both paid and unpaid. These comings and goings between work and study must increasingly be accommodated through recognition of skills and aptitudes acquired in a variety of settings, through easier passage from one type or level of education to another and through less strict separations between education and work.

A passport to life: basic education

The record of the twentieth century in expanding educational opportunities is a source both of pride and of shame. Since 1960, enrolment in the world's primary and secondary schools has risen from an estimated 250 million children in 1960 to more than 1,000 million today. The number of literate adults has nearly tripled in that period, from approximately 1,000 million in 1960 to over 2,700 million today. Even so, there are still 885 million adult illiterates in the world, some two out of five women and one out of five men. Access to basic education, let alone the expectation of completing primary education, is far from universal: 130 million children have no access to primary education and another 100 million enrol in school but do not complete the four years considered a minimum to ensure they do not forget what they have learned, reading and writing for example. The gender gap, although it is narrowing, is still shockingly high, in spite of overwhelming evidence of the benefits to the whole of society of educating girls and women.[1]

. See the Beijing Declaration and the Platform for Action adopted on 15 September 1995 by the Fourth World Conference on Women, in Beijing, China, in the *Report of the Fourth World Conference on Women (Beijing, 4–15 September 1995)*, New York, United Nations, 1995 (UN doc. A/Conf. 177/20) and Elizabeth M. King and M. Anne Hill (eds.), *Women's Education in Developing Countries*, Washington, D.C., The World Bank, 1993.

Reaching those still out of reach does not mean merely expanding existing education systems: it will mean designing and
developing new models and delivery systems, tailored to specific
groups, in a concerted effort to ensure relevant, high-quality basic
education for every child and adult.

Basic education for children can be defined as an initial education (formal or non-formal) extending in principle from around the
age of 3 to at least age 12. Basic education is an indispensable
'passport to life' that will enable people to choose what they do, to
share in building the collective future and to continue to learn. Basic
education is essential if inequality, both between the sexes and
within and between countries, is to be successfully challenged:

Education is a human right and an essential tool for achieving the goals of
equality, development and peace. Non-discriminatory education benefits both
girls and boys, and thus ultimately contributes to more equal relationships
between women and men. Equality of access to and attainment of educational
qualifications is necessary if more women are to become agents of change.
Literacy of women is an important key to improving health, nutrition and
education in the family and to empowering women to participate in decision-
making in society. Investing in formal and non-formal education and training
for girls and women, with its exceptionally high social and economic return,
has proved to be one of the best means of achieving sustainable development
and economic growth. (Platform for Action adopted at Beijing in 1995, para-
graph 69.)

Basic education is the first step in attempting to attenuate the enormous disparities affecting many groups – women, rural populations,
the urban poor, marginalized ethnic minorities and the millions of
children not attending school and working.

Education is at the same time both universal and specific. It must
provide the common factors uniting all humankind, whilst at the
same time it must deal with the specific challenges of very different
worlds. In order to escape from the educational segregation that
today divides the world, with high-level education, knowledge and
skills available to many in industrialized countries and to very few
in developing countries, it is necessary to see how to make good
the 'knowledge deficit' that is so closely linked with underdevelopment. By defining the cognitive and affective skills that need to
be developed as well as the body of essential knowledge that
must be transmitted through basic education, it is possible for
educationists to ensure that all children, whether in industrial-

Child labour in the world today

fficial estimates put the number of orking children between the ages of ve and fourteen at 78.5 million today. hese estimates, made by the ILO, are ased on the answers to a questionnaire at 40 per cent of countries did not nswer. Thus the actual numbers are ithout doubt much higher. Furthermore, he can assume that many of the 128 illion primary school age children out school in the world and of the 50 per nt of secondary school age children not ceiving any education are in fact hgaged in some form of economic tivity.

There exist in addition various forms f child slavery all over the world, either y a link being established between an dult's work contract and the availability of a child or by the exchange of a child for a sum of money. The ILO estimates that there are tens of millions of child slaves in agriculture, domestic help, the carpet and textile industries, quarrying and brick-making, as in the sex 'industry'.

In absolute terms it is Asia, as the most populous region of the world, that has the most child workers (probably over half of the total number). But in relative terms Africa comes first, with an average of one child out of three engaged in some form of economic activity. In the industrialized countries, although child labour is much less common than in the Third World, the phenomenon has been re-emerging.

The most wide-spread risk to children caused by excessive working hours is the inability to benefit from education. Fatigue is a major cause of accident and can impair intellectual development. Girls are especially at risk: almost everywhere girls work even longer hours than boys, often engaged in both economic and household tasks.

Child workers are exposed to extreme risk of long-term disease or disability, like wounds, infections and skeleton deformities, by poorly controlled and dangerous working environments. Psychological problems are common among children working as domestic aids, who suffer from long working hours and isolation from family and friends.

Source: taken from *Child Labour*, Geneva, ILO, 1995.

ized or in developing countries, attain minimum levels of competence in the main areas of cognitive skills:

Every person – child, youth and adult – shall be able to benefit from educational opportunities designed to meet their basic learning needs. These needs comprise both essential learning tools (such as literacy, oral expression, numeracy, and problem solving) and the basic learning content (such as knowledge, skills, values, and attitudes) required by human beings to be able to survive, to develop their full capacities, to live and work in dignity, to participate fully in development, to improve the quality of their lives, to make informed decisions, and to continue learning. (World Declaration on Education for All, Art. 1, para. 1.)

The basic learning needs of which the Jomtien Declaration speaks pertain to 'every person – child, youth and adult'. Any tendency to view basic education as a kind of emergency educational package for poor people and poor countries would, in our view, be an error. The broad definition of the function of basic education is not only applicable to all societies, but should lead to a review of educational practice and policies at the initial level in all countries. What the world community endorsed at Jomtien was the universal provision of an education worthy of all, an education that provides both a solid basis for future learning and the essential skills for living a constructive life within society. The fact that much education, in both the industrialized and the developing countries, falls far short of that standard does not suggest that we should settle for less, but rather that we should strive for more.

Pursuing the right to education, equal access and a second chance for all requires the involvement of various categories of participants at several levels. Public authorities must not only ensure provision of basic education but must also attempt to remove obstacles to school attendance, in particular for girls, by examining some of the following possibilities:

• careful school mapping, to try to ensure that children (girls included) do not have to travel too far;

• establishing single-sex schools or special facilities for girls, in cultures where parents keep girls out of school to prevent them from mixing with boys;

• hiring more women teachers when the majority of teachers are men;

Female and male school life expectancy (years) in selected countries, 1992

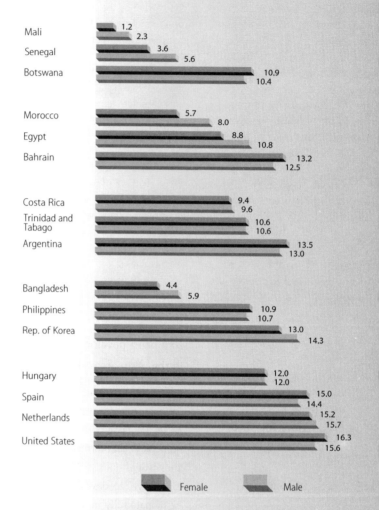

School life expectancy in this table is the number of years of formal education a child of 5 enrolled in school in 1992 could expect to receive. The countries used in this table are examples from their region, not chosen for any particular reason. More details can be found in Table 2.2 and Appendix I of UNESCO's *World Education Report 1995*.

• providing school meals;

• adapting school timetables to take into account children's family duties;

• supporting non-formal programmes that involve parents and local organizations; and

• improving basic infrastructure, in particular access to clean water, so as to release girls from some domestic chores and thus free time for education.

Furthermore, a greater focus on quality is desirable everywhere, even in countries where all children are enrolled in basic education. Basic education is both a preparation for life and the

best time for learning how to learn. In countries where professional teachers and supervisors are still scarce, basic education is
the key to self-teaching. In countries that offer pupils a choice of
educational courses, it both consolidates the bases of knowledge
and constitutes the first stage of guidance.

After the availability of school books, one of the most important factors in learning at all levels and thus in basic education is
time spent in a learning environment. Every interruption, every
incident that reduces the time available for learning, lowers the
quality of the outcome; in policy-making, greater attention should
be paid to ensuring that the school year runs according to schedule
in most cases. As teaching often gives considerable weight to performance in examinations, it is up to the authorities to make sure that
examinations test the knowledge and skills they want pupils to
acquire. Furthermore, careful review of the content of the curriculum
and of teaching methods is necessary when attempting to broaden the
scope of education so as to encompass not only knowledge and skills
but also the ability to live with others and individual fulfilment.

Early childhood education

The Commission wishes to emphasize the importance of early childhood education. Apart from the socialization process that early childhood centres and programmes allow to begin, there is evidence that
children who receive early childhood education are more favourably
disposed towards school and less likely to drop out prematurely than
those who do not. Early schooling can contribute to equality of
opportunity by helping overcome the initial handicaps of poverty or a
disadvantaged social or cultural environment. It can help greatly in
the integration into the school environment of children of immigrant
families and those who come from minority cultural and linguistic
groups. In addition, the availability of educational facilities for children of pre-school age makes it easier for women to participate in
social and economic life.

Regrettably, early childhood education is still very poorly
developed in most countries of the world, and although in the
highly industrialized countries most children attend pre-primary
school, there is much progress to be made there also. Where a
child-development component can be integrated into a multi-
purpose community service, very low-cost programmes can be
set up. Early childhood education can also be integrated

into community education programmes for parents, particularly in developing countries where the high cost of institutional pre-school education makes it available only to the privileged. It is to be hoped that efforts will be launched or continued to extend early childhood learning opportunities all over the world, as part of the push to make universal basic education a reality.

Children with special needs

The family home is the child's first school. But, when the family environment is deficient or lacking, it is up to the school to ensure that each child's potential is realized. Special attention must be paid to all aspects of educational provision for children from disad-vantaged backgrounds; street children, orphans, victims of war and other catastrophes must be the focus of concerted efforts on the part of educators. When children have special needs that cannot be diagnosed or met exclusively in the family environment, it is the responsibility of schools to provide the professional help and guidance to ensure that the talents of children with learning difficulties or physical handicaps do not go to waste.

Adult basic education and literacy

For adults, basic education and literacy programmes tend to be more appealing if they are linked to the acquisition of useful skills related to agriculture, crafts and other forms of economic activity. Adult edu-cation also provides an excellent opportunity for dealing with envi-ronmental and health issues, population education, and education for understanding different values and cultures. The use of mass media for educational purposes can introduce people to a world beyond that of narrow individual experience, in particular to the science and technology that pervade the modern world but are not yet widely available to the citizens of developing countries.

Community participation and responsibility

The success of schooling depends in very large measure upon the value that communities attach to education. Where education is highly valued and actively sought, the mission and goals of the school are shared and supported by the community. Thus, the increasing focus on the role of local communities needs to be encouraged and supported. Education needs to be seen by the

Estimated number (millions) of adult illiterates by region, 1980–2010

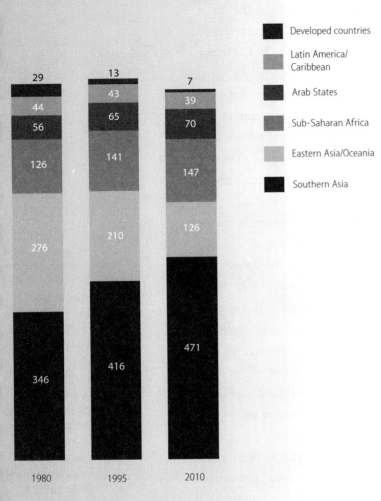

Developed countries

Latin America/ Caribbean

Arab States

Sub-Saharan Africa

Eastern Asia/Oceania

Southern Asia

Figures compiled by UNESCO's Division of Statistics. The regions correspond to UNESCO's nomenclature. The countries of the former Soviet Union are considered as developed countries, and those that are in Asia are also included here.

community as applicable to their real-life situations, needs and aspirations. Specific characteristics of life in both rural and urban environments should be taken into account, through decisions about the language of instruction and a careful analysis of what needs to be adapted in the curriculum, course content, teacher training and materials. Where there is reluctance on the part of parents to send their children to school, involving the local community in the assessment of needs – through a dialogue with the authorities and other interested groups within society, and a continuation of that dialogue through use of the media, community discussions, parental education and training, and in-service teacher training – can result in the community assuming greater responsibility for its own welfare and development. State subsidies in support of local communities' efforts at self-help, self-improvement and self-organization have proved to be more efficacious than efforts to impose progress from the top down.

Local leaders' initiatives should be encouraged, and their managerial and technical skills, in the area of financial control in particular, should be improved. Women's groups, in particular those involving mothers, can play a pivotal role in ensuring that basic education programmes are successfully implemented and sustained.

Community involvement may include the use or establishment of community centres where all sorts of educational activities can take place, including parent education, education for social development (such as primary health care or family planning) and education to improve economic capacities through both technical and financial inputs. For example, there are a number of experiments, supported by United Nations agencies or non-governmental organizations, that successfully link literacy training and information about how to obtain loans with programmes targeting women.[2] Community centres can serve a wide variety of purposes, offering programmes on food, programmes for senior citizens, youth programmes, social and cultural events, and income-generating programmes. In the end, closer community involvement should lead both to greater demand for services and a better understanding of what those services can provide.

Using members of the community as auxiliary teachers or para-professionals within the school system can also be a form of community participation. This use of a teacher recruited from the community to work alongside a government-appointed teacher has proved to be very successful in Guinea's recent educational reform. Training programmes to upgrade such community personnel to higher levels of educational theory and practice have been much appreciated and strongly supported by the community itself in the case of educational programmes for Mozambican refugees in Zimbabwe. These community teachers were able to achieve full teachers' certificates after a ten-year period of service alternating with periods of full-time study.

Despite the many advantages, there are also drawbacks to the participation and empowerment of communities: it is very difficult to repeat experiments elsewhere; with decentralized decision-making, power can become concentrated in the hands of factions that do not represent the community as a whole; maintaining standards and imposing quality control can become more difficult; but, in favourable conditions, with appropriate support from government, participatory approaches can have positive results.[3]

Community participation in education, particularly at the basic education level, must go hand-in-hand with commitment and strong action on the part of the state, which has an important role to play in ensuring that the children of all communities have the chance to receive a good education and that adults are given learning opportunities relevant both to their work and to their quality of life.

2. For a description of the pioneer experiment in credit for poor people see, for example, Rahnuma Shehabuddin, *The Impact of Grameen Bank in Bangladesh*, Bangladesh, Grameen Bank, 1992. One of the achievements of the Beijing Conference was the linking of banking and literacy activities through an agreement signed by Mohammed Yunis, founder of the Grameen Bank, and Federico Mayor, Director-General of UNESCO.

3. See Sheldon Shaeffer (ed.), *Collaborating for Educational Change: The Role of Teachers, Parents and the Community in School Improvement*, Paris, International Institute for Educational Planning, 1992. (Increasing and Improving the Quality of Basic Education Series.)

Secondary education: the crossroads of life

Many of the hopes and criticisms aroused by formal systems seem to focus on secondary education. On the one hand, it is often regarded as the gateway to social and economic advancement. It is accused, on the other hand, of being inegalitarian and not suffi- . ciently open to the outside world and, generally, failing to prepare adolescents not only for higher education but also for the world of work. In addition, it is also argued that the subjects taught are irrelevant and that not enough attention is paid to the acquisition of attitudes and values. It is now generally recognized that, for economic growth to take place, a high proportion of the population has to have received secondary education.[4] It would thus be useful to clarify what secondary education needs to do to prepare young people for adulthood.

The view of learning as a process that continues throughout life leads us to reconsider both the content and the organization of secondary education. The requirements of the labour market create a pressure owing to which the number of years of schooling tends to increase. Taken worldwide, in terms of enrolment ratios, secondary education is the fastest-expanding sector of formal education.

In many countries, though, rising enrolments are accompanied by an increase in academic failure, as evidenced by high rates of repeating and drop-out: for example, every year up to 30 per cent of pupils in Latin America repeat a grade, wasting precious human and financial resources. The Commission feels that wherever there are high repeating and drop-out rates, energetic measures are needed to analyse the causes and to attempt to find remedies. Such measures can range from the reform of teacher training to financial assistance, innovative experiments in group work, team teaching and the use of technologies enabling up-to-date teaching materials to be employed.

At the same time, the principle of lifelong education should open up wider possibilities of self-fulfilment and training after basic education, for example allowing adults to return to the formal system. Clearly, serious consideration of secondary education cannot be separated from thinking about the educational opportunities afforded to adults. The idea of 'education-time

. Luis Crouch, miliana Vegas and onald Johnson, *Policy Dialogue and Reform in the Education Sector: Necessary Steps and Conditions*, Washington, D.C., Research Triangle Institute, USAID, 1993.

entitlements' that can be used throughout life can help focus policy-making on the practicalities of further educational opportunities for people who interrupted schooling in youth: possibilities include study leave, recognition of skills already acquired, certification of non-formal learning experience and bridges between various educational streams.

Secondary education can thus be linked in the context of lifelong education to three major principles: diversity of courses, increased emphasis on the alternating of study and professional or social work, and attempts to improve quality.

Diversity in secondary education

While basic education, whatever its duration, should aim to meet the common needs of the population as a whole, secondary education should be the time when the most varied talents are revealed and flourish. Common core elements (languages, science, general knowledge) should be enriched and brought up to date, so as to reflect the increasing globalization of phenomena, the need for intercultural understanding and the use of science to foster sustainable human development. In other words, greater attention has to be paid to quality and to preparation for life in a rapidly changing, often technology-dominated world. Everywhere it met, the Commission heard the hope expressed that formal education, and secondary education in particular, could play a larger part in helping develop the qualities of character that would enable young people to anticipate and adapt to major changes. Schooling should help pupils acquire, on the one hand, the tools for dealing with the new technologies and, on the other, the aptitudes for managing conflict and violence. They need to develop the creativity and empathy necessary for them to become actively participating and creative citizens of tomorrow.

Academic courses at the secondary level today most often serve principally to prepare young people for higher education, leaving under-achievers and those who drop out or do not get a place in higher education by the wayside and inadequately equipped for work and life. Diversifying the course structure and paying closer attention to preparation for working life as well as content should be among the aims of any reform. The dedication and competence of the teaching profession, as much as the specific content of the curriculum, determines the quality and relevance of education; curriculum reform without the participation and full support of teachers would therefore be fruitless.

Technical and vocational education and training which prepare middle-level technicians and craftspeople are of particular importance in developing countries and need to be developed. The scarcity of resources and the relatively higher cost of good-quality technical training, however, render the development of this sector problematic in the very countries where it is most needed. Vocational training has to reconcile two divergent goals: preparation for jobs that exist at the present time and the capacity to adapt to jobs as yet not even imagined. Pragmatic approaches to making technical and vocational education and training available can be found in developing countries, and imaginative solutions have been devised in some East Asian countries such as Singapore, Thailand and Hong Kong. Some of these courses are relatively inexpensive and are well adapted to the application of intermediate technologies that will improve economic productivity. For example, many of the methods for updating agricultural skills are not expensive and can be introduced at both basic and secondary-school levels. Industrial-type training needs to be closely linked to the employment sector, to aim for relevance.

Educational programmes take a long time to set up, particularly when they involve teacher training, and a new programme can take ten years to impact on the labour market. More attention might well be given to strengthening existing informal arrangements and on-the-job training by developing partnership arrangements with employers in all sectors[5] and by making more use of new delivery systems for training. As in other types of education, policies should aim at reducing male/female disparities and at encouraging the participation of girls in all types of technical training.

The length of courses should also be diversified, favouring learning throughout life. In many cases, alternating periods of school and work may be better suited to youngsters' way of learning, but it is incumbent on the authorities to ensure that the doors to further study remain open to them and that official recognition is given to the technical and vocational courses they have followed and to their periods of apprenticeship. The organization of short- or longer-term sandwich courses, combining work with studies at secondary level, can only be of interest in the long run if this makes it possible to return to continuing education after several

See Claude air, *Vocational* *aining* *esterday, Today* *d Tomorrow,* aris, UNESCO,)94. (UNESCO)c. EDC/III/3 :v. 1.)

months or years spent working. Thus, authorities will need to provide financial support and incentives to employers to offer in-service training to all employees, above all to young people, and to grant study leave to employees wishing to continue in post-compulsory education. More generally, the guiding principles of an 'education throughout life' should lead to the establishment of new educational itineraries (making use of both time and money credits) that can enable people to alternate periods of professional activity with periods of study.

In pluri-ethnic societies, attention is now being paid to the development of teaching in the mother tongue and, increasingly, policies tend towards providing at least basic education in the child's first language wherever possible, but not enough consideration is given to the teaching of second and third languages everywhere. The Commission feels that more emphasis should be placed on language teaching, so as to enable the widest possible number of young people to learn both a national language and another widely spoken language. Knowledge of an international language will be essential in the global village and global market of the twenty-first century. Bilingualism for everyone is not an impossible goal; indeed, the ability to speak several languages has historically been the norm in many parts of the world. Knowledge of an international language may be essential in many contexts for the acquisition of up-to-date knowledge in science and technology that can help a country to attain modern levels of economic development. Encouraging children and young people to learn more than one language is a way of providing them with the assets they need to live in the world of tomorrow.

In the global village of tomorrow, lack of access to the latest information technology can have a negative impact on every level of scientific and technological education, from teacher training through to the education system and including higher education. Thus, in keeping with the Commission's conviction that learning about science and technology must be an integral part of education for everyone, a particular effort must be made to bridge the gap between the industrialized and non-industrialized countries in science and technology education. Innovative ways to introduce computer and industrial technology, both for educational purposes and, perhaps more importantly, to ensure high quality teacher education and communication between teachers all over the world, need to be found. Equipping and staffing central schools with information and computer capacity, so that they can serve satellite schools, could be a first step, even in countries where cost is a problem. The creation of science museums, co-operation from the employment sector and mobile teaching units, for example, can also help enlarge exposure of learners to up-to-date knowledge in science and technology, and thus enhance learning. The lack of good-quality science teaching at secondary levels compromises the development of national scientific capacity in a number of countries and urgent measures must be found, both within countries and through inter-country co-operation, to remedy these problems.

Vocational guidance

Secondary education is normally the time when young people choose the path by which they are going to enter into adult, working life. Vocational guidance, which allows pupils to choose among various streams, should not close the door to other, later possibilities. Education systems should be sufficiently flexible to accommodate individual differences in organizing study modules, building bridges between courses and, as stated above, making arrangements for a possible return to formal education after periods of time in work.

The choice of a particular stream of vocational or general education should be based on careful assessment of a pupil's strong and weak points. Academic evaluations, which are part of the general assessment, should not result in selection by failure or by stereotypes, shunting the weaker pupils systematically in the direction of manual work, or girls systematically away from technology and science.

In other words, guidance entails evaluation based on a subtle mix of educational criteria and a forecast of the adolescent's future personality. The school must be able to form a clear picture of the capacity of each of its pupils. Thus, as far as possible, professional guidance counsellors should be available to help with the choice of appropriate courses of study (taking into account the needs of the labour market), to diagnose learning difficulties and assist with social problems when necessary. The responsibility of secondary education is vast indeed, for it is very often within the walls of the school that the future life of each pupil takes shape. Secondary education must be more open to the outside world, enabling pupils to adjust their itineraries according to their cultural and educational development.

Higher education and education throughout life

Higher education is at one and the same time one of the driving forces of economic development and the focal point of learning in a society. It is both repository and creator of knowledge. Moreover, it is the principal instrument for passing on the accumulated experience, cultural and scientific, of humanity. In a world where resources of knowledge will increasingly predominate over material resources as factors in development, the importance of higher education and of higher education institutions can only grow. Moreover, the effect of innovation and technological progress means that economies will increasingly demand competencies that require high-level studies.

Pressure is everywhere being put on institutions of higher education to expand enrolments. Worldwide, they have more than doubled in twenty years, from 28 million students in 1970 to more than 60 million today, yet considerable inequalities persist, in access and in the quality of teaching and research. In sub-Saharan Africa in particular, the number of students enrolled in higher education is 1 per 1,000 inhabitants, whereas in North America it is 1 per 50. Expenditure per student in real terms is ten times higher in the industrialized countries than in the least-developed countries, yet even these relatively low levels of expenditure impose a very heavy burden on some of the poorest countries.

In much of the developing world, higher education has been in crisis for the past decade. Structural adjustment policies and political instability have taken their toll on the institutions' budgets. Moreover, confidence in higher education has been eroded by graduate unemployment and the brain drain. The overwhelming bias towards the social sciences has led to imbalances in the categories of graduates coming on to the labour market, leading to disenchantment on the part of graduates and employers alike as to the quality of what is being taught in higher education institutions.

Social pressures and the specific requirements of the labour market have resulted in an extraordinary diversification in institutions and in courses of study. Higher education has not been exempt from the 'force and urgency with which educational reform is politically advocated to respond to the economic imperative.'[6] Universities no longer have the monopoly of

6. George S. Papadopoulos, *Learning for the Twenty-first Century*, Paris, UNESCO, 1994. (UNESCO doc. EDC/III/1.)

higher learning; indeed, national higher education systems have now become so varied and complex in terms of structures, programmes, student populations and funding that it has become difficult to categorize them.[7]

The expansion in enrolments and in the number of institutions has entailed increased expenditure on higher education, which is faced with the formidable problems of the development of mass higher education. The challenge of mass higher education has still not been met adequately, making it necessary to re-examine the role of higher education.

The functions of higher education

It is primarily the universities that unite all the traditional functions associated with the advancement and transmission of knowledge: research, innovation, teaching and training, and continuing education. To these one can add another function that has been growing in importance in recent years; international co-operation.

These functions can all contribute to sustainable development. As autonomous centres for research and the creation of knowledge, universities can address some of the developmental issues facing society. They educate the intellectual and political leaders and company heads of tomorrow, as well as many of the teachers. In their social role, universities can use their autonomy in the service of debate on the great ethical and scientific issues facing the society of the future, and serve as links with the rest of the education system by providing further learning opportunities for adults and acting as a centre for the study, enrichment and preservation of culture. There is increasing pressure on higher education to respond to social concerns, while the other precious and indispensable features of universities, their academic freedom and institutional autonomy, have also been the focus of attention. Those features, although no guarantee of excellence, are a prerequisite for it.

Nowhere is the universities' responsibility for the development of society as a whole more acute than in developing countries, where research done in institutions of higher learning plays a pivotal role in providing the basis for development programmes, policy formulation and the training of middle- and higher-level human resources. The importance of local and national institutions in raising the developmental levels of their countries cannot be overemphasized. Much of the responsibility for

7. *Policy Paper for Change and Development in Higher Education*, Paris, UNESCO, 1995. (UNESCO doc. ED.94/WS/30.)

building bridges between the developed, industrialized countries and the developing, non-industrialized countries rests with them. They can also be instrumental in the reform and renewal of education.

A place for learning and a source of knowledge

With the growing role of scientific and technological knowledge in society, in industry and trade, and in the application of research to the problems of human development, institutions of higher education have an extremely important duty to maintain their capacities for high-level research in their fields of competence. Today, they are in competition for research funds with a wide variety of operators, some in the private sector. On the other hand, they are uniquely well-placed to play their traditional and necessary role of advancing knowledge by virtue of the intellectual freedom, freedom of debate and the guarantee of independent evaluation they offer to researchers.

Research, in both the social and natural sciences, must indeed be independent and free from political and ideological pressures, but must nevertheless contribute to the long-term development of society. Science teaching must avoid the pitfalls of a sterile academic approach and an ivory tower mentality, particularly in countries which especially need to make progress in technological fields. Conversely, however, the quality of science should not be sacrificed in the interests of immediate productivity, since what is at stake is universal, like science itself, and long range.

At a time when the sheer quantity of knowledge and information is expanding exponentially and when higher education institutions are confidently expected to be able to meet the learning needs of a constantly growing and increasingly varied student population, the quality of training for teachers and the quality of teaching in higher education institutions takes on ever greater importance. Higher education institutions have a key responsibility in training teachers, in establishing links with non-higher-education teacher-training institutions and in training teacher educators. They must open themselves up to bring in teachers from the economic and other social sectors to facilitate interchange between them and the education sector.

Thus, everyone should be able to count more or less directly on higher education for access to the common heritage of knowledge and the most recent research findings. The university must accept a kind of moral contract with society in exchange for the resources assigned to it by society.

Higher education and the changing labour market

Employment structures are changing as societies progress and machines replace human beings: the number of manual workers is declining, whereas supervisory, managerial and organizational tasks are expanding, thus increasing the need for intellectual abilities in employees at all levels.

Qualification requirements are constantly rising. In industry and agriculture, the pressure of modern technologies puts a premium on those capable of understanding and coping with them. The ability to solve new problems and to take initiative is increasingly demanded by employers. In addition, the service sector, which is coming to pre-dominate in the long-industrialized countries, often calls for a general education and an understanding of the human environment that makes new demands on education. Innovative forms of development call for perceptiveness and imagination.

Universities have come to place more emphasis on training in science and technology in response to the demand for specialists familiar with the most recent technologies, capable of running increasingly complex systems. As there is no reason to think there will be any reversal of this trend, universities must continue to be in a position to meet the demand and thus must constantly adapt specialized courses of study to the needs of society.

The difficulty of the task must not, however, be underestimated. There is often rivalry between research and teaching. The division of subject-matter into separate disciplines may be just what the labour market does not need and the most successful institutions are those that have evolved flexible, co-operative forms of cross-disciplinary teaching. Although many scientific universities face the question of whether to steer the best students towards research or towards industry, flexibility dictates that, wherever possible, the multi-dimensional character of higher education must be protected to ensure that graduates receive an appropriate preparation for the labour market.

The university as a place of culture and learning open to all

In addition to preparing large numbers of young people either for research or for specialized occupations, the university must continue to be the fountainhead at which the growing numbers of people who find in their own sense of curiosity a way of giving meaning to their lives may slake their thirst for knowledge. Culture should here be considered in its widest sense, ranging from the most mathematical of sciences to poetry, by way of all the fields of the mind and the imagination.

In that respect, universities have specific features that make them especially favoured environments. They constitute the living repository of the human heritage, a heritage continually revitalized by the use made of it by teachers and researchers. Universities are usually multidisciplinary, making it possible for each individual to escape the confines of his or her initial cultural environment. They are usually more in touch with the international world than are other educational structures.

Each university should become an 'open' university, offering possibilities for distance learning and learning at various points in time. Experience in distance teaching has shown that, for people studying at the higher education level, a judicious mix of media, correspondence courses, computer communications technology and personal contact can broaden the options on offer at relatively low cost. These should include both vocational training and personal development courses. Furthermore, in keeping with the idea that each person should be both learner and teacher, greater use should be made of specialists other than faculty members: teamwork, co-operation with the surrounding community and community service by students are some of the factors that can enrich the cultural role of higher education institutions.

By calling upon universities to be places of culture and of learning open to all, the Commission intends not only to reinforce its central theme, that is, learning throughout life. It also wishes to contribute to affirmation of a major task of the university – even a moral obligation – to participate in the major debates concerning the direction and the future of society.

Higher education and international co-operation

Institutions of higher education are ideally placed to use globalization as a tool for bridging the knowledge gap and in order to enrich the dialogue between peoples and between cultures. Co-operation among scientists working in the same discipline transcends national boundaries and is a powerful tool for the internationalization of research, technology, ideas, attitudes and activities. However, the concentration of research and research facilities in the countries belonging to the Organisation for Economic Co-operation and Development (OECD) constitutes a challenge to sustainable development in economically less-advanced countries.

The networks that have been developed amongst the wealthier countries, in the European Union and the OECD countries, have produced enormous scientific and cultural benefits, but networks, useful and powerful though they are, can exacerbate the differences between the countries which participate in them and those which are left outside, unless there is a concomitant strengthening of North–South and South–South co-operation. In the medium term at least, the exodus of highly qualified personnel seeking research posts in the main centres will continue to impoverish the poorer regions of the world still further. The hopeful sign is that, as soon as opportunities arise, however modest, some graduates and researchers are beginning to return to their countries of origin. One of the urgent tasks facing the university community in the wealthier regions is to devise ways to accelerate co-operation and to help build up research capacity in the less-developed countries.

The twinning of research institutions in industrialized countries with their counterparts in developing countries will benefit both sides, as greater understanding of developmental problems is essential in solving problems in the global village. South–South co-operation also holds out great promise: work done in Asia or Latin America has enormous relevance to Africa and vice versa.

The economic sector also needs to set up partnerships with universities in both the developed and the developing world to carry out research on problems related to development in the different regions. International donors can also give a fresh impetus to these kinds of partnerships.

The advent of new possibilities for communication, through

computers in particular, has created a potential for the internationalization of research and co-operation in general. In spite of some scepticism as to whether previously announced revolutions in the styles and methods of teaching and learning have really taken place, the possibilities for interactive on-line research, documentation and teaching may very well bring about as yet unforeseeable changes in the educational processes, especially at the higher levels.

The free movement of persons and the sharing of scientific knowledge are important principles, endorsed by the Commission. While paying due respect to intellectual property, the universities and governments of 'knowledge-wealthy' countries should employ every means whereby the potential of the poorest regions of the world may be enhanced and their access to information improved. These include exchanges of students and teachers, assistance in the development of communication systems, particularly on-line systems, the pooling of research findings, inter-university networking and the establishment of regional centres of excellence.

The vital need to combat under-achievement

Present throughout the Commission's proceedings were its apprehensions concerning under-achievement and the increasing incidence of that problem. Although young people from disadvantaged backgrounds are particularly at risk, it affects every social category. It takes many forms – the repeating of one grade after another, dropping out, relegation to streams that offer no real prospects and, at the end, pupils who leave school without formal qualifications or recognized skills. In all cases it represents a waste, devastating in its effect on morale and in its human and social effects, and often leading to some form or other of exclusion that will mark its victims throughout their adult lives.

The primary aim of education systems must be to make children from marginal or disadvantaged backgrounds less socially vulnerable, so as to break the vicious circle of poverty and exclusion. The handicaps that schoolchildren are suffering from must be identified, handicaps that are often linked to their family backgrounds, and policies of positive discrimination towards those who are having the most difficulties are needed. Extra

The experience of 'accelerated schools' in the United States

success story in the USA, 'accelerated schools' constitute one of the best solutions Americans have found to the crisis faced by their education system, confronted with under-achievement by almost one third of primary and secondary pupils.

Such under-achievers, or 'pupils at risk', are usually two years behind the others; over half of them leave school without any paper qualifications; most of them are from deprived and poor areas and belong to ethnic minorities not speaking English; many of them also come from single-parent families.

These accelerated schools are based on the conviction that all pupils in the same age group are capable of reaching the same level of academic achievement by the time they are of school-leaving age. This means that under-achievers have to be made to work at an accelerated pace as compared to better-off pupils, which is done by providing schools of excellence for the former.

The concept underlying these schools is that the teaching provided for 'gifted' children is also suitable for all children. This means not viewing under-achievers as slow on the uptake and incapable of learning within the usual time-frames, but – on the contrary – setting them ambitious objectives to be achieved within firmly fixed periods.

Every pupil, each parent, every teacher must be convinced that failure is not inevitable. Those involved are called on to work together, in co-operation with teaching staff, as a responsible community which has taken full possession of all rights and powers. After drawing up a common vision of what the school should be like, this school community sets out to build an accelerated school, firmly resolved to respond, on its own, to any problems as and when they arise.

Such a community needs to be founded on the generally under-used talents everyone has. The process of transforming the school changes attitudes and creates a new culture.

Source: European Commission, *Teaching and Learning. Towards the Learning Society*, p. 89, Luxembourg, Office for Official Publications of the European Communities, 1996.

resources must therefore be made available and special teaching methods put in place, as is already being done in many countries, for the benefit of target groups and schools in the inner cities or on deprived outer housing estates. Care should, however, be taken to avoid creating educational ghettos and hence to avoid any kind of segregation from children whose schooling follows traditional lines. Supporting measures could well be organized within all schools: more adaptable, flexible pathways would accordingly be devised for children who are less well adapted to the school system but who often show aptitudes for other types of activity. This will require specially adapted teaching rhythms and small classes. Opportunities for switching back and forth between school and business or industry are, furthermore, conducive to better integration into a working environment. Taken together, these measures should, among other things, at least limit the number of children who drop out or leave school without qualifications, if not eliminate these phenomena altogether.

Re-integration measures or remedial action must likewise be devised to enable young people starting work without qualifications to acquire the occupational skills they need. Subsequently, arrangements should be systematically developed to offer marginalized young people or adults a fresh chance in the shape of access to further courses of training. In more general terms, it may be said that learning throughout life offers outstanding opportunities for acquiring new qualifications in keeping with societies' evolving needs.

Recognizing subsequently acquired skills by means of new methods of certification

In order for individuals to be able to build up their own qualifications on an ongoing basis, the Commission considers that certification procedures should be thoroughly re-examined, bearing in mind the specific conditions prevailing in each country, so that skills acquired beyond the stage of initial education may be taken into account.

The fact is that a certificate obtained at the end of formal education is still, all too often, the only means of gaining access to skilled employment, and young people who leave school without any qualifications and without any recognized skills not only suffer a personal sense of failure but are placed at a disadvantage, in most cases a long-term disadvantage, in relation to the job market. It is therefore important to make it possible for acquired skills, especially those acquired in the course of people's working lives, to be recognized not only in the workplace but also within the formal education system, including universities. Schemes of this kind are at present being studied in some parts of the world; thus, the European Commission, in a recent *White Paper*,[8] envisaged the creation of 'personal skills cards' enabling individuals to obtain recognition of their knowledge and skills as and when they acquire them. It does seem that the worldwide implementation, in various forms, of such certification systems, taken together with the formal qualifications obtained during initial education, would allow due credit to be given to the totality of a person's skills and would make for greater possibilities of movement between education and the working environment. These proposals apply, incidentally, just as much to those with as to those without formal qualifications.

8.   European Commission, *Teaching and Learning: Towards the Learning Society*, Luxembourg, Office for Official Publications of the European Communities, 1995.

Pointers and recommendations

- A requirement valid for all countries, albeit in various forms and with different types of content – the **strengthening of basic education:** hence the emphasis on **primary education** and its traditional basic programmes – reading, writing, arithmetic – but also on the ability to express oneself in a language that lends itself to dialogue and understanding.

- The need, which will be still greater tomorrow, for receptivity to science and the world of science, which opens the door to the twenty-first century and its scientific and technological upheavals.

- The adaptation of **basic education** to specific contexts, the most deprived countries as well as the most deprived section of the population, starting out with the facts of everyday life, which affords opportunities for understanding natural phenomena and for different forms of socialization.

- The pressing needs of literacy work and basic education for adults are to be kept in mind.

- In all cases, emphasis is to be placed on pupil–teacher relations, since the most advanced technologies can be no more than a back-up to the relationship (transmission, dialogue and confrontation) between teacher and pupil.

- Secondary education must be rethought in this general context of learning throughout life. The key principle is to arrange for a variety of individual paths through schooling, without ever closing the door on the possibility of a subsequent return to the education system.

- Debates on selection and guidance would be greatly clarified if this principle were fully applied. Everyone would then feel that whatever the choices made or the courses followed in adolescence, no doors would ever be closed in the future, including the doors of the school itself. Equality of opportunity would then mean what it says.

- **Universities** should be central to the higher level of the system, even if, as is the case in many countries, there are other, non-university establishments of higher education.

- Universities would have vested in them four key functions:
1. To prepare students for research and teaching.
2. To provide highly specialized training courses adapted to the needs of economic and social life.
3. To be open to all, so as to cater for the many aspects of lifelong education in the widest sense.
4. International co-operation.

- The universities should also be able to speak out on ethical and social problems as entirely independent and fully responsible institutions exercising a kind of intellectual authority that society needs to help it to reflect, understand and act.

- The diversity of secondary schooling and the possibilities afforded by universities should provide a valid answer to the challenges of mass education by dispelling the obsession with a one-and-only educational 'king's highway'. Combined with more widespread application of the practice of alternating periods of education with periods of work, these approaches can provide effective tools for fighting against school failure. The extension of learning throughout life will require consideration of new procedures for certification that take account of acquired competences.

Chapter 7

Teachers in search of new perspectives

The previous chapters have shown that we set education an ambitious task in individual and social development. Our vision of the coming century is of one in which the pursuit of learning is valued by individuals and by authorities all over the world not only as a means to an end, but also as an end in itself. Each person will be encouraged and enabled to take up learning opportunities throughout life. Hence, much will be expected, and much demanded, of teachers, for it largely depends on them whether this vision can come true. Teachers have crucial roles to play in preparing young people not only to face the future with confidence but to build it with purpose and responsibility. The new challenges facing education – to contribute to development, to help people understand and to some extent come to terms with the phenomenon of globalization, and to foster social cohesion – must be met from primary and secondary school onwards. Teachers are instrumental in the development of attitudes – positive or negative – to learning. Teachers can awaken curiosity, stimulate independence, encourage intellectual rigour and create the conditions for success in formal and continuing education.

The importance of the role of the teacher as an agent of change, promoting understanding and tolerance, has never been more obvious than today. It is likely to become even more critical in the twenty-first century. The need for change, from narrow nationalism to universalism, from ethnic and cultural prejudice to tolerance, understanding and pluralism, from autocracy to democracy in its various manifestations, and from a technologically divided world where high technology is the privilege of the few to a technologically united world, places enormous responsibilities on teachers who participate in the moulding of the characters and minds of the new generation. The stakes are high, and the moral values formed in childhood and throughout life become of particular importance.

Improving the quality of education depends on first improving the recruitment, training, social status and conditions of work of teachers; they need the appropriate knowledge and skills, personal characteristics, professional prospects and motivation if they are to meet the expectations placed upon them.[1] This chapter will focus mainly on these questions in relation to primary and secondary education and on possible measures for improving teaching at those levels.

What can society reasonably expect of its teachers? What are the realistic demands that must be met? What are teachers entitled to in return, in terms of working conditions, rights and status? What type of people can become good teachers, how can they be recruited and trained, and how can their motivation and the quality of their teaching be maintained?

The world comes into the classroom

In recent years, the sources and distribution of information have developed in a spectacular fashion almost everywhere. Increasingly, children come to school bearing the imprint of a world – real or fictitious – far beyond the boundaries of the family and the immediate community. The entertainment, news and advertising put out by the media convey messages that compete with or contradict what children learn at school. The organization of all those messages in brief sequences by the media has in many parts of the world detrimentally affected pupils' attention spans and, consequently, relationships within the classroom. When pupils spend less time in school than in front of a television set, the effortless and instant gratification offered by the media contrast starkly, in their minds, with what is required to succeed at school.

1. See A. R. Thompson, *The Utilization and Professional Development of Teachers: Issues and Strategies*, Paris, International Institute for Educational Planning, 1995. (The Manageme of Teachers Series.)

Teachers and schools, having thus to a large extent lost their leading place in the learning experience, face the new tasks of making school more appealing to children while implicitly providing them with a 'users' guide' to the media.

Furthermore, the problems of the social environment can no longer be left behind at the school gates: poverty, hunger, violence and drugs enter classrooms with the children, whereas in the not so distant past they were kept outside with the unschooled. Teachers are expected not only to cope with those problems and to help develop understanding of a whole range of social topics, from promoting tolerance to birth control, but also to succeed where parents and the religious or secular authorities tend to fail. Moreover, they must find appropriate balances between tradition and modernity, and between the ideas and attitudes the child brings to school and the content of the curriculum. Thus, as the separation between the classroom and the outside world becomes less rigid, teachers also need to make efforts to take the learning process outside the classroom: physically, by practical learning experiences at sites outside schools, and from the content point of view by linking subject-matter to daily life.

A look at the roles of teachers, both traditional and recent, should not be based on false premises. In particular, it is important not to lend credence to those who would ascribe all the ills of our societies to what some people consider to be ill-advised educational policies. It is up to society itself to find the remedies for its malfunctions and to find the elements with which to rebuild its social fabric and the interpersonal relationships that make it up.

In the past, pupils were generally obliged to accept whatever was offered by the school, in terms of language of instruction, content, and organization. Today, communities increasingly expect to have a say in decisions concerning the organization of schooling. Such decisions have a direct influence on teachers' working conditions and the demands made on them, and are responsible for another contradiction inherent in modern teaching: on the one hand, for children to learn properly, teachers must use the knowledge children bring to school with them as the starting-point; this applies not only to the language of instruction but also to science, mathematics or history; on the other hand, if children are to acquire the qualities of independence, creativity and inquisitiveness that must complement their acquisition of knowledge, teachers must at all costs maintain a certain distance between school and the social environment, so as to give children and young people the opportunity to exercise their critical judgement. Teachers must adapt their relationship with learners, switching roles from 'soloist' to 'accompanist', and shifting the emphasis from dispensing information to helping learners seek, organize and manage knowledge, guiding them rather than moulding them.[2] On the other hand, they need to display great firmness in relation to the fundamental values that should guide each individual's life.

Expectations and responsibilities

The demands on teachers' competence, professionalism and dedication impose on them an enormous responsibility. Expectations are high and needs are seemingly limitless. In many countries, quantitative expansion has often resulted in a shortage of teachers and increases in class size, with consequent pressures on the education system. Stabilization measures, euphemistically called 'structural adjustment policies', have taken a heavy toll on education budgets and therefore on teachers' salaries.

The teaching profession is one of the most highly organized in the world and teachers' organizations can and do play powerful roles in a variety of fields. Most of the more than 50 million teachers in the world belong to, or consider themselves represented by, unions. These organizations, which are concerned with conditions of employment, can bring considerable weight to bear on the share-out of financial allocations for education; they also have in many cases a deep knowledge and experience of almost every aspect of the educational process, including the training of teachers. Teachers' organizations are, in many countries, essential participants in the dialogue between school and society. It is possible and desirable to improve the dialogue between teachers' organizations and educational authorities, and to broaden the discussion beyond the concerns of pay and conditions to cover the central role that teachers must play in planning and carrying out reform. Teachers' organizations can be instrumental in establishing a climate of confidence in the profession and a positive attitude to new approaches to education. In all instances, they are a means of communication with practitioners throughout the education system. The planning and implementation of reform should be an opportunity for seeking a

2. General Union of Educational Personnel (ABOP), National Institute for Curriculum Development (SLO) (Netherlands), *Teaching in the Information Age: Problems and New Perspectives* (paper submitted to the Commission), Amsterdam, ABOP/SLO, 1994. (In Dutch.)

consensus on its ends and means. No reform has succeeded against teachers or without their participation.

Teaching: an art and a science

The powerful relationship between teacher and learner is central to the teaching process. Knowledge can, of course, be acquired in a variety of ways, and the use of both distance learning and the new technologies in classrooms has proved to be effective. Yet, for the vast majority of learners, particularly those who have not yet mastered the skills of thinking and learning, the teacher remains an essential catalyst. Whilst the capacity for independent learning and research is the key to continued individual growth, this capacity is only possible after some period of interaction with a teacher or intellectual mentor. Doesn't everyone still recall a particular teacher who knew how to make them stop and think, who made them want to work a little harder in order to get to the bottom of some question? Is there anyone who, when having at some point in their lives had major decisions to take, was not at least to some extent influenced by what they learned under the guidance of a teacher?

The teacher's work is not confined simply to transmitting information or even knowledge; it also entails presenting that knowledge in the form of a statement of problems within a certain context and putting the problems into perspective, so that the learner can link their solution to broader issues. The teacher–pupil relationship aims at the full development of the pupil's personality, with emphasis on self-reliance; from this point of view the authority vested in teachers is always paradoxical, since it is not based on the assertion of their power but on the free recognition of the legitimacy of knowledge. This function of the teacher as a figure of authority will probably evolve, yet it remains essential as a source of the answers to questions raised by the pupil about the world and as a key prerequisite for the full success of the learning process. Besides, it is becoming increasingly necessary in modern societies for teaching to help form individual judgement and a sense of individual responsibility, so as to enable pupils to develop the ability to foresee changes and to adjust to them, in other words to continue learning throughout their lives. It is through working under, and through dialogue with, the teacher that a pupil's critical faculty is helped to develop.

Teachers' great strength lies in the example they set, of curiosity, open-mindedness, willingness to put their assumptions to the test and to acknowledge mistakes; most of all, they must transmit a love of learning. The Commission believes that a rethinking of teacher education is necessary, in order for it to bring out in future teachers precisely those human and intellectual qualities that will facilitate a fresh approach to teaching along the lines set out in this report.

The quality of teachers

Teachers have been recruited in large numbers to cope with the rapid increase in the world school population. Recruitment has frequently had to be carried out with limited financial resources, and it has not always been possible to find qualified candidates. Teachers' working conditions have in many cases deteriorated greatly owing to the shortage of financial resources and suitable teaching materials, and to overcrowded classrooms. Catering for pupils who have serious social or family difficulties implies new tasks, for which teachers are often ill-prepared.

The importance of the quality of teaching, and therefore of teachers, cannot be overemphasized. It is at an early stage of basic education that the principal attitudes toward learning as well as the self-image of the learner are formed. The role of the teacher at this stage is crucial. The greater the handicaps the children coming to school have to overcome – in terms of poverty, difficult social environment or physical impairments – the greater the demands on the teacher. He or she, to be effective, must draw upon a broad range of teaching skills, as well as on the human qualities of empathy, patience and humility, as a complement to authority. When a child's or adult's first teacher is poorly trained and poorly motivated, the very foundations on which all subsequent learning will be built will be unsound. The Commission feels that reasserting the importance of teachers in basic education and improving teachers' qualifications are tasks to which all governments must address themselves. The measures needed to recruit future teachers from among the most motivated students, improve their training and encourage the best among them to take on the most difficult posts need to be determined in relation to the specific circumstances of each country; but such measures must be taken, since, without them,

Number of teachers (all levels) per 1,000 population in the age-group 15–64 by region, 1980 and 1992

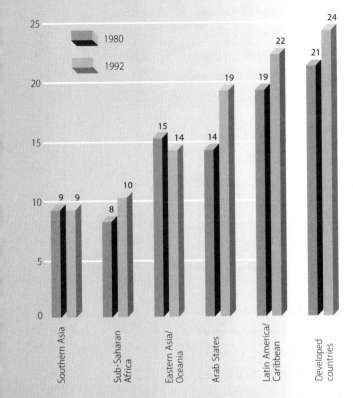

Figures compiled by UNESCO's Division of Statistics. The regions correspond to UNESCO's nomenclature. The countries of the former Soviet Union are considered as developed countries, and those that are in Asia are also included here.

Ken Gannicott and David Throsby, *Educational Quality and Effective Schooling*, Paris, UNESCO, 1994. (UNESCO doc. EDC/IV/2.)

it is unlikely that there will be significant improvements in quality where they are most needed.

Thus, improving the quality and motivation of teachers must be a priority in all countries. Some of the areas in which steps can be taken are listed here and described in more detail in the next sections of this chapter.

• *Recruitment.* Better screening of candidates, combined with a broadening of the recruitment basis through more active prospecting for candidates. Special measures can be envisaged to recruit candidates from diverse linguistic and cultural backgrounds to enter teaching.

• *Initial education.* Closer links between universities and teacher-training institutions for both future primary- and secondary-school teachers. The ultimate goal should be higher education, in co-operation with universities, for all teachers, but particularly for secondary teachers. Furthermore, in view of the role of the future teachers in the overall development of the pupils' personalities, their training should at an early stage place emphasis on the four pillars of education discussed in Chapter 4.

• *In-service training.* Development of in-service programmes to allow frequent access to them by teachers, in particular using appropriate communication technologies. Such programmes can at the same time serve to familiarize teachers with developments in information and communication technology. In-service training is on the whole as effective as pre-service training, if not more so, in its effect on quality.[3] It can use distance-education techniques, thereby saving money and allowing teachers to go on working, at least part time, and it can be an effective instrument for implementing reform or introducing new technologies or methods. In-service training need not take place solely within the education system: time spent in work or study in the economic sector could produce benefits in bringing knowledge and know-how closer together.

- *Teacher educators.* Special attention should be paid to the recruitment and upgrading of the skills of teacher educators, so that they can fully play their roles in the ultimate renewal of educational practice.

- *Supervision.* Inspections should be an opportunity not only to check on teachers' performance but to maintain a dialogue with teachers concerning developments in knowledge, methods and sources of information. Thought should be given to ways of identifying and rewarding good teaching. It is essential to carry out practical, consistent and regular measurements of what pupils have learned. Emphasis needs to be placed on learning outcomes and teachers' roles in achieving those outcomes.

- *Management.* Reforms in management, aiming to ensure that schools have competent management personnel, can take the pressure of day-to-day management tasks off teachers' shoulders and introduce a certain pooling of ideas about the aims and methods of teaching within specific settings. Certain auxiliary services such as those of social workers or educational psychologists are not a luxury and should be made available everywhere.

- *Participation by people from outside the teaching profession.* Parents can be involved in the process of education in various ways, as can people who have working experience in vocational subjects.

- *Conditions of work.* Closer attention has to be paid to maintaining teacher motivation in difficult situations. To keep good teachers in the profession, salary and other conditions must be sufficiently attractive compared to other types of employment requiring comparable levels of training. Incentives to keep teachers in remote or particularly deprived areas are clearly a necessity if disadvantaged populations are not to be further disadvantaged by the lack of qualified teachers. Desirable as geographical mobility may be, postings should not be arbitrarily decided by central authorities. Mobility between teaching and other professions, for limited periods, could profitably be encouraged.

  - *Teaching materials.* The quality of both teacher training and teaching is dependent to a large extent on teaching materials, particularly textbooks.[4] Curriculum renewal is a constant

4. *Priorities and Strategies for Education: A World Bank Review*, Washington, D.C., The World Bank, 1995. (Development in Practice Series.)

process that should involve teachers at the planning and development stages alike. The introduction of technology allows wider distribution of audiovisual materials and the use of information technology to introduce new knowledge, teach skills and evaluate learners' progress holds out great promise. Communication technologies, properly used, can make learning more effective and provide an attractive way of accessing knowledge and skills which may not be readily available locally. Technology can help to bridge the gap between industrialized and non-industrialized countries, and can assist teachers and learners to attain levels of knowledge and skills that would not otherwise be attainable. Good materials can help inadequately trained teachers both to improve their teaching skills and upgrade their own knowledge.

Learning what and how to teach

The world in general is evolving so rapidly today that teachers, like most other professional groups, now must face the fact that their initial training will not see them through the rest of their lives: they need to update and improve their own knowledge and techniques throughout their lifetime. A careful balance has to be struck between competence in the subject taught and competence in teaching. In some countries, the system is criticized for neglecting method; in others, overemphasis on method, it is felt, produces teachers who know too little about their subject. Both are needed: neither should be sacrificed to the other in initial or in-service training. Teacher training has additionally to inculcate a view of teaching that transcends the utilitarian and encourages questioning, interaction and the consideration of several alternative hypotheses. One of the main functions of teacher education, both pre-service and in-service, is to equip teachers with the ethical, intellectual and emotional wherewithal to develop the same range of qualities in their pupils, as society demands.

Good-quality training entails bringing trainee teachers into contact with experienced teachers as well as with researchers in their particular disciplines. Regular opportunities should be offered for practising teachers to learn through group-work sessions and through in-service courses. The reinforcement of in-service training, offered in as flexible a form as possible, can contribute a great deal to enhancing the skills and motivation of teachers, and improving their status. Given the importance of research into the qualitative improvement of teaching, teacher education should include a stronger component of training for research, and linkages between teacher training institutions and universities should be further strengthened.

Particular attention needs to be paid to attracting and training teachers of science and technology, and to making them conversant with new technologies. Everywhere, but particularly in poor countries, science teaching leaves a great deal to be desired, although the critical role of science and technology in overcoming underdevelopment and combating poverty is well known. The weaknesses in the teaching of science and technology at elementary and secondary levels, especially in schools in developing countries, must be overcome by better teacher education in science and technology. Qualified teachers for these subjects are often in short supply for vocational education, a situation that does nothing to improve its image.

Teacher education tends to stand apart from other forms of training, isolating teaching from other professions; this state of affairs should be put right. Opportunities should be created for teachers to carry out periods of work and co-operative activities outside the classroom so that the school becomes more closely related to the world of work for which the teacher is supposed to be preparing the pupils. This will help to overcome the problems created by teachers having to prepare their pupils for the world of work, about which they themselves may know little.

Working teachers

The school and the community

Ways can be found for improving the performance and motivation of teachers in the relationship they establish with local authorities. When teachers are themselves part of the community where they teach, their involvement is more clearly defined. They are more sensitive and responsive to the needs of their communities and better able to work towards community goals. Strengthening the links between the school and the community is therefore one of the most important ways of ensuring that the school is able to grow in symbiosis with its milieu.

chool and home collaborate to raise upil achievement in the Philippines

e achievement levels of pupils have
en raised and a closer relationship
ween schools and families has been
ablished in the Philippines through the
ent Learning Support System (PLSS).
s innovative programme recognizes
ents as teachers of children and
ilitates their collaboration with
ifessional teachers.
e programme is monitored at every
ool by a teacher–parent group. Special
phasis is put on training. Teachers and
admasters are trained in managerial
lls such as effective collaborative
chanisms and shared decision-making
hniques as well as skills in
cher–parent and teacher–pupil

dialogue. At parent-education seminars,
parents are counselled as to ways in
which they can contribute to the
education of their children. Some
seminars involve both parents and
children.
During the implementation of the
programme, parents are drawn into the
teaching–learning processes. With
guidance from teachers, they assist their
children in their assigned learning tasks
at home or in school. They also help
teachers in conducting classes. Parents
are asked to observe their children's
behaviour in the classroom, as well as the
teaching methods. Their comments and
suggestions are discussed at regular

teacher–parent conferences, and specific
measures are collectively agreed upon.
The first PLSS experiments were carried
out in a rural community in Leyte
Province and a squatter area in Quezon
City, Metro Manila. In view of the
considerable gains in pupils' achievement
levels and greatly reduced drop-out, PLSS
has been extended to other parts of the
country with positive results.

Source: taken from I. D. Cariño and
M. Dumlao Valisno, 'The Parent Learning
Support System (PLSS): School and Community
Collaboration for Raising Pupil Achievement in
the Philippines', in: S. Shaeffer (ed.),
*Collaborating for Educational Change: The Role
of Teachers, Parents and the Community in
School Improvement,* Paris, UNESCO-IIEP, 1992.

The administration of the school

Research, as well as empirical observation, shows that the school head is one of the main factors, if not indeed the principal one, in determining school effectiveness. A good school head who is capable of establishing effective teamwork, and is seen as being competent and open-minded often achieves major improvements in the quality of his or her school. Care should therefore be taken to ensure that headships go to qualified professionals who have had special training, in management in particular. This training should result in school principals being given increased responsibilities and adequate remuneration for the discharge of their sensitive obligations. In the context of education throughout life, where everyone is in turn teacher and learner, people from outside the profession who are recruited for fixed periods or specific tasks can bring into schools certain skills that are needed and not available among the teaching staff – teaching in minority languages, teaching refugees, or linking education more closely with the world of work, for example. Involving parents in teaching activities in collaboration with trained teachers has in some circumstances proved to be a useful factor in improving school attendance, the quality of teaching and social cohesion.

Drawing teachers into decision-making on educational matters

Teachers should be more closely involved in decision-making on educational matters. The preparation of syllabuses and of teaching materials should be carried out with the participation of practising teachers, since evaluation of learning outcomes cannot be dissociated from the way that teachers teach. Similarly, the system of school management, school inspection and teacher evaluation can only stand to gain from including teachers in the decision-making process.

Favourable conditions for effective teaching

Greater professional mobility, both within the teaching profession and between it and other professions, is also desirable, in order to widen teachers' experience. And, for teachers to do a good job, they must not only be trained but must receive adequate support. This implies, in addition to appropriate conditions and resources, a system of evaluation and supervision that helps diagnose difficulties and surmount them, and that uses inspection as a means of recognizing good teaching and encouraging it. It also implies that each community or local authority should look to see how talents present in the community can be used to improve education: inputs by outside experts to classroom teaching or to out-of-school learning experiences, involvement of parents in appropriate ways in school management or in raising additional resources, links with voluntary groups to organize work experience, outings, cultural activities, sports and other learning activities not directly linked to classroom work, and so on.

Clearly, there are no easy answers to the different problems inherent in improving the quality of teachers, the teaching process and teaching content. Teachers deservedly claim recognition for their endeavours, in terms of their working conditions and status. They must be given the tools to carry out their various roles as well as possible. In return, their pupils and society as a whole are entitled to expect them to discharge their duties with dedication and a strong sense of their responsibilities.

Pointers and recommendations

• While the psychological and material situation of teachers differs greatly from country to country, an upgrading of their status is essential if 'learning throughout life' is to fulfil the central function assigned to it by the Commission in the advancement of our societies and the strengthening of mutual understanding among peoples. Their position as master or mistress in the classroom should be recognized by society and they should be given the necessary authority and suitable resources.

• The concept of learning throughout life leads straight on to that of a learning society, a society that offers many and varied opportunities of learning, both at school and in economic, social and cultural life, whence the need for more collaboration and partnerships with families, industry and business, voluntary associations, people active in cultural life, etc.

• Teachers are also concerned by the imperative requirement to update knowledge and skills. Their professional lives should be so arranged as to accommodate the opportunity, or even the obligation, for them to become more proficient in their art and to benefit from periods of experience in various spheres of economic, social and cultural life. Such possibilities are usually provided for in the many forms of study leave or sabbatical leave. Those formulae, suitably adapted, should be extended to all teachers.

• Even though teaching is essentially a solitary activity, in the sense that each teacher is faced with his or her own responsibilities and professional duties, teamwork is essential, particularly at the secondary level, in order to improve the quality of education and adapt it more closely to the special characteristics of classes or groups of pupils.

• The Commission stresses the importance of exchanges of teachers and partnerships between institutions in different countries. As is confirmed by current activities, such exchanges and partnerships provide an essential added value not only for the quality of education but also for a greater receptivity to other cultures, civilizations and experiences.

• All these lines of emphasis should be the subject of a dialogue, or even of contracts, with teachers' organizations which go beyond the purely corporatist nature of such forms of collaboration: over and above their aims of defending the moral and material interests of their members, teachers' organizations have built up a fund of experience which they are willing to make available to policy-makers.

Chapter 8

Choices for education: the political factor

All over the world, education systems are being asked to do more and do it better. Under pressure from all sides, they must respond, as we have seen, to the need for economic and social development, especially vital to the poorest groups in the population. They face a variety of cultural and ethical demands. They must take up the challenge posed by technology which – with all the risks this entails – is one of the main gateways to the twenty-first century. In other words, everyone expects something from education. Parents, working or jobless adults, business and industry, communities, governments and, of course, children, pupils and students place great hope in education.

It is impossible for education to do everything, however, and some of the hopes it inspires will inevitably be dashed. Choices have to be made and these can be difficult, especially where the equity and quality of education systems are concerned. Such choices, between different types of society, will vary from country to country, even though some of the underlying principles are the same. The strategies adopted must, though, be consistent, in both time-frame and social context, with the choices made. Among the strategies looked at by the Commission is the use of the information society's technologies, along with the opportunities offered by innovation and decentralization. However, such strategies will require overall regulation of the education system. That is the role of the political authority, which consists in taking a long-term view of the future, ensuring both the system's stability and its ability to reform itself, guaranteeing the coherence of the whole while setting priorities and, lastly, ensuring a genuine public debate on the economic and financial options involved.

Choice of education means choice of society

The demand for education

Education systems cannot continue indefinitely to satisfy a demand which can only keep on growing. They are being asked to give the same educational opportunities to all and to respond to all the demands made on them. Given budgetary limits that afford little leeway, they must allocate resources as best they can, so as to balance quantity with relevance and quality with fairness. Since there is no one optimal allocation model, the distribution of resources must clearly reflect and give effect to each society's choices of economic, social and cultural development.

In developing countries, a heavy demand for education often goes hand in hand with a severe shortage of resources. Particularly hard to make, choices involve dropping some subjects. In the industrialized countries, which are, comparatively speaking, less asphyxiated by financial constraints, the policy choices are less a matter of drastic alternatives; they are more a matter of balancing the different options in education budgets, in educational reforms or in pupil selection and streaming, and of responding to criticisms that the education system is partly to blame for the mismatch between labour market supply and demand.

In both cases, the pressure of these demands, which fall largely upon the public authorities, necessitates organizational choices which are often in reality sociopolitical ones. Policy-makers are faced with conflicting interests: industry demands more and more skills and aptitudes; science wants funds for research and the kind of top-flight higher education that produces young researchers; the arts and academia want the wherewithal for improving school enrolments and general education; and parents' groups militate for more high-quality education, that is to say, a better supply of good teachers. The dilemma becomes especially acute when it becomes impossible to satisfy all these demands, since what is at issue is not normal choice between particular interests: each demand is based on legitimate expectations that all correspond to one or other of education's basic functions.

Evaluation and public debate

Choices in education thus concern the whole of society and require the establishment of a democratic debate, not only on the resources to be made available to education but also on its ultimate goals. The principles this report has endeavoured to outline must be a feature of that debate, and none of the basic building-blocks of knowledge – learning to learn, learning to do, learning to be, learning to live together – must be neglected in favour of the others.

The debate must be founded on an accurate evaluation of the education system, which is based on premises acceptable to all and which must not be narrowly economic in character. While it is proper to speak of a market for vocational education inasmuch as some of its services may be evaluated in cost–benefit terms, this is clearly not the case with all educational activities, some of which lie outside the economic order – those, for example, which relate to participation in the life of the community or self-fulfilment. Furthermore, the education system forms a whole in which the parts are so completely interdependent and the integration with society so thorough that it can be difficult to pinpoint the origin of particular malfunctions. The evaluation of education should be understood in the broad sense, covering not only educational provision and teaching methods but also financing, management, general direction and the pursuit of long-term objectives. It brings in such concepts as the right to education, equity, efficiency, quality and the overall allocation of resources, and it is largely a matter for the public authorities. Evaluation at local level is also a possibility for such matters as school management and teacher quality.

It is at any rate important, if public opinion is to understand the overall education system and its impact on the rest of society, to establish an impartial, public evaluation system. The size of public education budgets amply justifies public demand that accounts be rendered before any move is made to increase them further. Public discussion – in parliament, for example, or even in the media – can thus become a debate on the future of society, founded on unbiased and relevant assessments.

It should also be borne in mind that any evaluation exercise is itself instructive. It gives the parties involved a better understanding of what they are doing. It may spread the capacity for innovation by highlighting successful initiatives and explaining the context of their success. At a deeper level, its findings lead to reappraising priorities and compatibility between choices and resources.

Opportunities offered by innovation and decentralization

Involving the stakeholders in the educational undertaking

The debate over how centralized or decentralized the management of the education system should be is essential to the success of strategies for improving or reforming the system.

The Commission agrees with many observers that, at the present time, educational reforms are viewed with considerable scepticism. Almost everything has been tried, yet the results rarely live up to expectations. In many countries, repeated and contradictory attempts at reform have seemingly only intensified their education systems' resistance to change.

Many reasons have been advanced to explain why this should be,[1] but they all include the procedure for implementing reforms, which is frequently decided upon by central ministries without any real consultation with those concerned and without any impact study. Ways must be found of making educational institutions sensitive to the needs of society and of instilling dynamism into the internal management machinery of education.

One of the main aims of education reform – and probably the best means of going about it – is to involve the stakeholders in decision-making. This is the context – relating both to public policy and to process – within which the Commission stresses the importance of decentralization measures in education. Obviously, the issues are different according to the traditions and administrative structure of each country, and no ideal model can be held up, but there are a number of arguments in favour of transferring responsibility to regional or local level: improving the quality of decision-making; encouraging individuals and communities;

1. Juan Carlo Tedesco, *Curre Trends in Educational Reform*, Paris, UNESCO, 1993 (UNESCO doc. EDC/1/1.)

and, more generally, encouraging innovation and participation by all. In the case of minority groups, decentralized procedures can allow further consideration to be given to cultural and linguistic aspirations, and can enhance the relevance of the education provided through the careful working out of appropriate programmes.

There are conditions to be met, however, for better local co-operation to be achieved among teachers, families and the general public. The first condition is the willingness of central government to open a forum for democratic decision-making where the wishes of the community, teachers, parent–teacher associations or non-governmental organizations can be voiced and heard. The institutions which make up the education system must for their part be genuinely prepared to adjust to local realities and adopt an open attitude towards change. Lastly, school autonomy is a vital factor in furthering local initiatives, since it goes with collegial decision-making that can break down teachers' traditional isolation from one another. The 'mission statement' approach adopted in some countries is a good illustration of how a common determination to achieve particular aims improves school life and the quality of teaching.

Encouraging genuine autonomy

There are various aspects to schools' autonomy. It applies first to resource management: the school should be able to decide how to use a substantial portion of its allotted resources. Ad hoc bodies, such as committees composed of parents (or pupils) and teachers, can in some cases be set up to advise on school management and the curriculum. More generally speaking, there should be procedures in each school for defining the role of all the parties concerned and promoting co-operation among teachers, school principals and families, as well as broader dialogue with the community. The practice of negotiation and collaboration where school management and school life in general are concerned is in itself a democratic learning process. The autonomy of educational institutions also strongly encourages innovation. In over-centralized systems, innovation tends to be confined to pilot projects which, if successful, are meant to give rise to broader measures. These are, however, not necessarily relevant to every situation. There seems to be wide agreement that innovations depend largely for their success on local circumstances. It may, therefore, be more important to propagate the capacity for innovation than to disseminate the innovations themselves.

The Commission favours a broad decentralization of education systems, based upon school autonomy and the effective participation of local stakeholders. The need for an education pursued throughout life and the emergence of learning societies using the resources of informal education should, in its view, accentuate this trend. It is at the same time aware that methods of educational organization and management are not ends in themselves but are instruments whose value and effectiveness depend largely on their political, economic, social and cultural context. Decentralization measures can form part of a democratic process or, equally well, of authoritarian processes leading to social exclusion. There are many instances, especially in Latin America, in which decentralization has aggravated existing inequalities between regions and between social groups. The weakening of the state's role with decentralization may then prevent the introduction of corrective measures. On the whole, 'international experience shows that the successful instances of decentralization are ones in which the central administration is strong',[2] whence the need for overall regulation and a clear definition of the role of the public authorities in that regulation.

The need for overall regulation of the system

Education is a collective asset that cannot be left only to market forces. Thus, whatever the organization or degree of decentralization or diversification of a system, the state must assume certain responsibilities to its citizens, including creating a national consensus on education, ensuring that the system forms a coherent whole and proposing a long-term view for the future.

One of the first tasks of government is to generate broad public agreement on the importance of education and its role in society. In developing countries in particular, only an on-going dialogue among all political parties, professional and other associations, unions, business and industry can ensure the stability and sustainability of education programmes. Such dialogue must begin at the earliest stages and go on, leaving room for review and modification, throughout implementation. Experience shows that a consensus in society is essential to any reform process, but that it

2. Tedesco op. cit.

rarely occurs spontaneously. This means that it must be given institutional form and allowed to express itself through democratic procedures.

It is also necessary to handle in an organized way the interdependence between the various components of the education system, without losing sight of the organic links between the different educational levels. Individuals proceed from basic schooling either to other levels or to other types of education. The parts of the system are interdependent: secondary schools supply higher education with students, but the universities supply secondary (and often primary) schools with teachers. In terms of both numbers and quality, the different educational levels form an indivisible whole, a fact that must be remembered when it comes to regulating flows or defining course content and assessment methods. The attention paid to interdependence is crucial to obtaining the best value from choices where resources are limited. While priorities will naturally vary from one country to another, care must be taken not only to maintain the system's coherence but also to respect the new requirements of learning throughout life. The relationship between education and the needs of the economy must likewise be preserved.

Education policies must be long-term instruments, presupposing continuity in the choices made and in the implementation of reforms. In the field of education, it is important to rise above short-term responses or reforms one after another that risk being reversed at the next change of government. Long-term planning should be based on in-depth analysis of reality (accurate diagnoses, forward analysis, social and economic background information, awareness of world education trends and assessment of results).

These are the main justifications for the role of the state, as representative of the whole community, in a pluralistic and partnership-based society where education is a lifetime affair. That role relates mainly to the societal choices that set their mark on education, but also to the regulation of the system as a whole and to promotion of the value of education; it must not, however, be exercised as a strict monopoly. It is more a matter of channelling energies, promoting initiatives and providing the conditions in which new synergies can emerge. It is also a matter of insisting on equity and quality in education. The principles of equity and the right to education require, at the very least, that access to education should not be denied to certain persons or social groups; more specifically, the state should play a redistributive role, to the benefit of minorities and the underprivileged especially. Guaranteeing educational quality moreover implies the establishment of general standards and various monitoring devices.[3]

The formal institutions at the heart of the education system, whether public or private, must clearly proceed in concerted fashion and in accordance with a long-term view. It is therefore the task of public policy to ensure coherence in space and time; in other words, to set guidelines and to regulate. Co-ordination between the different levels of education – primary, secondary and post-secondary – and development of a lifelong provision of education are essential for avoiding dysfunctions. In tomorrow's world, the need to master forces well outside the formal system will give government yet another role, with two complementary aims: on the one hand, to maintain the visibility and intelligibility of the education system while ensuring its stability; and, on the other hand, fostering partnerships and encouraging innovation, thereby releasing new energies in the service of education. The paramount importance of governance is clear in such a context: all the parties involved in education must be guided towards collectively agreed objectives within a context of shared values.

Economic and financial choices

The force of financial constraints

Collectively agreed objectives entail economic and financial choices which, even though problems differ from one main category of countries to another, are difficult to make everywhere. Industrialized countries have to deal with a sharply increasing demand for education and must find the means to cope with it. Yet their financial constraints bear no comparison with those of the developing countries which, between the increasing needs stemming from population growth, the low enrolments and the limited nature of their resources, are being financially squeezed on all sides.[4]

The school population amounts to over a quarter of the world's population, whereas public spending on education amounts to about 5 per cent of the world's aggregate gross national product (GNP). That average conceals wide variations

3.   See, for a discussion of the state's role in education, Twelfth Conference of Commonwealth Education Minister Islamabad, Pakista 27 November to 1 December 1994, *The Changing Role of the State in Education: Policies and Partnerships*, London, Commonwealth Secretariat, 1994.

4.   Serge Péano, *The Financing of Education Systems* Paris, UNESCO, 1993. (UNESCO doc. EDC/1/2.)

blic expenditure on education, 1980–92

	US$ (billions)				Percentage of GNP			
	1980	1985	1990	1992	1980	1985	1990	1992
ORLD TOTAL*	526.7	566.2	1 017.0	1 196.8	4.9	4.9	4.9	5.1
veloping countries which:	102.2	101.2	163.4	209.5	3.8	4.0	4.0	4.2
b-Saharan Africa	15.8	11.3	15.2	16.0	5.1	4.8	5.3	5.7
ab States	18.0	23.6	24.7	26.0	4.1	5.8	5.2	5.6
tin America/Caribbean	34.2	28.9	47.1	56.8	3.9	4.0	4.1	4.4
stern Asia/Oceania	16.0	20.1	31.8	41.4	2.8	3.2	3.0	3.1
F which: China	7.6	7.7	9.1	9.8	2.5	2.6	2.3	2.0
uthern Asia	12.8	14.7	35.8	60.4	4.1	3.3	3.9	4.4
F which: India	4.8	7.1	11.9	10.0	2.8	3.4	4.0	3.7
ast-developed countries	3.1	2.7	4.2	4.1	2.7	2.8	2.9	2.8
veloped countries* which:	424.5	465.0	853.6	987.3	5.2	5.1	5.1	5.3
orthern America	155.1	221.6	330.2	369.7	5.2	5.1	5.4	5.7
ia/Oceania*	73.0	79.3	160.8	225.5	5.8	5.1	4.8	4.8
rope*	196.3	164.2	362.6	419.3	5.1	5.1	5.0	5.2

xcluding countries of the former USSR.
urce: *World Education Report 1995*, p. 109, Paris, UNESCO, 1995.

Eduard Bos,
y T. Vu, Ernest
assiah and Rodolfo
Bulatao, *World
pulation
ojections,
44–1995 Edition:
timates and
ojections with
lated Demographic
atistics* (published
r the World Bank),
ltimore/London,
e Johns Hopkins
niversity Press,
94.

which reflect not only the uneven distribution of wealth throughout the world but also the relatively greater financial effort made by the industrialized countries (5.3 per cent of GNP in 1992) compared with the developing countries (4.2 per cent of GNP).

Population forecasts for the early twenty-first century predict, despite an assumed drop in fertility rates, large increases in the number of births. World Bank projections show that, in low-income countries, children under 5 will in 2025 still form the largest group in the age structure.[5] The impact of these population trends on the intake capacity of education systems will be magnified by rising school attendance. With the single exception of primary education in the industrialized countries, the rise in school populations is everywhere outstripping population growth.

Low school enrolments, taken in conjunction with population growth, particularly high in those countries where the education system is the most deficient, means that the effort required of developing countries is particularly daunting. UNESCO projections[6] lead to the conclusion that enrolments will continue to rise. They are expected to increase, taking all levels and countries together, from a little over 1 billion today to about 1.15 billion in 2000 and 1.3 billion in 2025. The relative share of the industrialized countries should, owing to the predicted decline in birth rates, continue to fall. The sharpest increases are expected in the developing countries, largely as a result of higher enrolment figures in sub-Saharan Africa, the Arab States and Southern Asia. The rise in school attendance in developing countries will extend to all levels of education: primary (589 million by 2000 compared with 522 million in 1992); secondary (269 million as against 227 million); and post-secondary (40 million compared with 32 million).

While needs are rising, available resources are dwindling in many cases, especially in such regions as sub-Saharan Africa, for reasons that range from the slowing of economic activity to the burden of foreign debt. Education systems must, in addition, compete for public funds with the other sectors under state responsibility, and they tend to suffer from general austerity measures and policy choices relating to budget allocations. The Commission feels that, given the key role which it attributes to education in social development, public resources devoted to education should be increased. It is obvious that situations vary greatly, especially in an overall comparison between the developing countries and the industrialized countries: the latter face less population pressure, have more resources at their disposal and already high school-enrolment rates. The share of GNP allotted to public spending on education in the industrialized countries has remained relatively steady over recent years. This near-stability has gone together with population trends that are very different from those in the developing countries: from 1970 to 1990, the population under 15 years of age shrank by 6 per cent, in contrast to the 31 per cent increase observed in the developing countries. Even in the developed countries, however, such factors as the gradual move towards education for the bulk of the population, up to and including post-secondary level, the growing need for in-service training or the likely reduction in working hours (which will offer new opportunities for learning) are almost certain to contribute to an increased social demand for education.

The Commission realizes that, given the differences between countries in their degree of economic development

6. *Trends and Projections of Enrolment by Level of Education, by Age and by Sex 1960–2025 (As Assessed 1993)*, Paris, UNESCO, 1994 (Current Surveys and Research in Statistics Series CSR-E-63, UNESCO doc. BPE-94/WS.1.

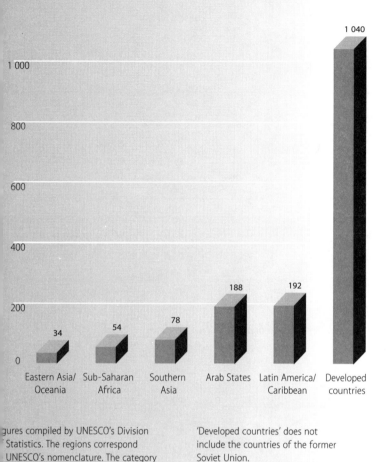

ublic expenditure on education (all levels) per head of adult population, 992 ($US)

gures compiled by UNESCO's Division
Statistics. The regions correspond
UNESCO's nomenclature. The category

'Developed countries' does not
include the countries of the former
Soviet Union.

Péano,
. cit.

and in their education systems, there is no single answer to the problem of financing education. It will therefore merely propose some general pointers, keeping in mind the distinction between developing and industrialized countries.

Pointers for the future

Increasing public spending on education, in place of expenditure under other budget heads, should be regarded as a necessity everywhere, and especially in developing countries, since it is a vital investment for the future. As a rule of thumb, not less than 6 per cent of GNP should be devoted to education, in those countries which have not yet attained that target. From the standpoint of human development, the transfer of a portion of the military budget, which is often larger than the education budget, is worth considering along with other possibilities. Promoting education can in fact do much to alleviate the causes of insecurity: unemployment, exclusion, disparities in development between nations, and ethnic and religious conflicts.

It should, however, be remembered in this connection that spending on education has more than just a social dimension: it is also an economic and political investment yielding long-term benefits: 'The purpose of education systems is to train people for citizenship, provide for the transmission of knowledge and culture from one generation to another and develop people's talents. Education systems also have to provide the skills economies will need in the future.'[7] National development hinges on the ability of working populations to handle complex technologies, and to demonstrate inventiveness and adaptability, qualities that depend to a great extent on the level of initial education. Investment in education is thus essential to long-term economic and social development and as such must be safeguarded in times of crisis.

The Commission feels that it is not only justifiable but also desirable to raise money from private sources in order to ease the pressure on national budgets. Recourse to private funds will, of course, vary in each country, but it can on no account release the state from its financial commitments. The latter remains of prime importance in the poorest countries, where private sources alone are incapable of providing education with sound and sustainable financing. Private funding can come from a variety of sources: contributions, even of modest sums, by families and students towards school fees; an undertaking by the local community to meet part of school building and upkeep costs; sharing costs with business and industry in vocational training; research contracts enabling technical and vocational schools, or universities, to shoulder part of their own costs.

Another possibility is mixed financing, which combines public and private sources in proportions that vary according to the level of education, while keeping basic education free. The Commission took particular note of the proposals made by the World Bank along those lines, concerning the developing countries. Ideas of that kind can form a sound basis for setting public resource

Education expenditure by source of funds, all levels of education combined*, selected countries, 1991 (percentages)

Group and country	Public sources	Private sources
OECD countries		
Australia	85.0	15.0
Canada	90.1	9.9
Denmark	99.4	0.6
Finland	92.3	7.7
France	89.7	10.3
Germany	72.9	27.1
Ireland	93.4	6.6
Japan	73.9	26.1
Netherlands	98.0	2.0
Spain	80.1	19.9
United States	78.6	21.4
Low- and middle-income countries		
Haiti	20.0	80.0
Hungary	93.1	6.9
India	89.0	11.0
Indonesia[a]	62.8	37.2
Kenya[b] (1992/93)	62.2	37.8
Uganda (1989/90)	43.0	57.0
Venezuela (1987)	73.0	27.0

* Primary, secondary and higher formal education. – Ed.

Source: Priorities and Strategies for Education, p. 54, Washington, D.C., The World Bank, 1995.

Notes:
[a] Public institutions only. Private sources refer to households only.
[b] Primary and secondary levels only. Private sources refer to households only.

mphasis on basic education
1 public investment

1ore efficient, equitable, and
tainable allocation of new public
estment on education would do much
neet the challenges that education
tems face today. Efficiency is achieved
making public investments where they
yield the highest returns – usually,
education investments, in basic
cation. To achieve equity, the
ernment needs to ensure that no
lified student is denied access to
cation because of inability to pay.
ause the gap between private and
ial returns is larger for higher
cation than for basic education,
dents and parents may well be willing
bear part of the costs of higher
cation. Governments can also
ourage private financing by taking on
ne of the risks that makes financial

institutions reluctant to lend for higher
education.

A policy package of fees and efficient
expenditure in the public sector might
consist of:

• Free basic education, including cost-
sharing with communities and targeted
stipends for children from poor
households

• Selective charging of fees for upper-
secondary education, combined with
targeted scholarships

• Fees for all public higher education,
combined with loans, taxes, and other
schemes to allow needy students to defer
payment until they become income-
earners, and a targeted scholarship
scheme to overcome the reluctance of
the poor to accumulate debt against
uncertain future earnings

• Assurance of quality primary
education for all children by making that
level the top priority for public spending
on education in all countries

• Improved access to quality general
secondary education (initially lower-
secondary and later all levels of
secondary) as the second priority, once all
children are receiving good primary
education

• Efficient public spending at the
school and institution level.

Fiscal sustainability also requires the
continuous projection of the implications
of public expenditure and consistent
efforts to ensure that financing plans and
mechanisms are in place.

Source: Priorities and Strategies for Education,
p. 10, Washington, D.C., The World Bank, 1995.

allocation priorities on a country-by-country basis. The Commission
also stresses the important role played by public funds in higher education: private financing must not be allowed to threaten the nature
and existence of higher education in developing countries, where it is
not only essential to the coherence of the system but is also an
important factor in scientific and technological progress. The proceeds
from the charging of tuition fees can, however, help in improving the
quality of university education, with public financing remaining at a
constant level.

The Commission considers that private funding must not be used
as a stop-gap measure; such a practice can result in wastage, incon-
sistencies and inequalities. It is the responsibility of governmental
authorities to organize the financial partnerships and take compen-
satory measures in some cases. Since education must, above all, not
be allowed to heighten social inequalities, large-scale resources
must be channelled towards the most severely disadvantaged, so
that, for example, special measures can be put in place to tackle
under-achievement, or allow quality education be provided for
ethnic minorities or the inhabitants of remote regions. Public
funding is in these cases needed to ensure equity and social
solidarity.

In short, what is wanted is to improve the management of existing resources, without detriment to equity and quality, and to put it on a long-term basis. For this purpose, various ways of improving the efficiency of the education system must be examined. For example, reducing the repeating and drop-out rates, particularly high in Africa and Latin America, should lead, by cutting the total numbers to be catered for, to greater effectiveness and better targeting of education expenditure. It has been estimated that, in a country such as Brazil, grade repeating costs $2.5 billion per year; such a sum could usefully be invested in pre-school education so as to better prepare children for their subsequent schooling. Administrative decentralization and increased school autonomy can, thanks to better adjustment to local needs, make education more cost-effective. They must, however, fit into an overall regulatory scheme, so that inconsistencies can be avoided. The cost-effectiveness of education in developing countries may be improved by a series of measures such as lengthening the school year, building lower-cost premises and developing distance education. At the same time, any attempts to boost short-run productivity that might jeopardize educational quality must be firmly rejected. Increasing the number of pupils in a class, for example, would be unjustifiable where the number is already very large, as it is in worst-placed countries. Above all, one should never lose sight of the fact that any measure that reduces teacher recruitment or training poses a threat to educational quality and seriously compromises the future.

The Commission considers that the principle of an education pursued throughout life should lead all countries, starting perhaps with the developed countries (where financial constraints are lighter), to reappraise the system of financing education within a broader framework, endeavouring to reconcile equality of opportunity with the need for a variety of individual learning paths at the end of publicly funded compulsory schooling. Alternation between time in the workplace and time spent on training or other forms of education presupposes more than one form of financing. It is fair that employers should be asked to contribute when it is a question of raising the skills of their labour force and that individuals should participate in what is for them not only an investment offering the hope of a better-paid job but also a means of self-fulfilment. Public funding is also amply warranted in view of the benefits accruing to society as a whole from the development of edu-

---

cation. The funding of higher education may be viewed in the same light: the trend towards large-scale post-secondary education justifies a wider imposition of tuition fees, offset where necessary by scholarships for the neediest students and student loan schemes.

The Commission also discussed the merits of a bolder proposal. Given the move towards learning throughout life, it might be worth considering granting a study-time entitlement, covering a certain number of years of education, to every prospective school-goer. The entitlement would be placed in a 'bank' which would manage each pupil's 'chosen time capital', backed by the appropriate funds. Each student could draw on that capital in accordance with his or her school experience and career choices. He or she could set aside part of the capital for continuing further education in the post-school years or during adult life. Each person could add to the capital by depositing money in his or her account at the 'chosen time bank', as in a sort of educational provident fund. This may seem too radical or too sweeping a reform from the viewpoint of the practices or possibilities of certain countries, but its rationale – combating inequality of opportunity – could be retained in the form of a credit granted at the end of compulsory schooling, leaving teenagers free to follow their chosen path without signing away their future.

Using the resources of the information society

The impact of the new technologies on society and on education

The Commission obviously could not discuss the major societal choices facing education without considering the new information and communication technologies. The issue goes beyond their simple use for teaching purposes; it calls for general consideration of how knowledge will be accessed in tomorrow's world. The subject can be merely touched upon here, since it is still too difficult to form an accurate idea of these technologies' effect on knowledge and learning. The Commission wishes to stress that these technologies are in the process of accomplishing nothing short of a revolution before our very eyes, one that is affecting activities connected with production and work just as much as those connected with education and training.

The inventions that have left their stamp on the twentieth century – records, radio, television, audio and video recording, computers, or air, cable and satellite broadcasting – have a more than technological dimension; their significance is essentially economic and social. Most of these technologies have become sufficiently miniaturized and cheap to have penetrated into most homes in the industrialized countries and to be used by a growing number of people in the developing countries.[8] There is every reason to believe that the impact of the new technologies, consequent upon the development of computer networks, will very rapidly make itself felt worldwide.

Today's societies are all, to some extent, information societies, in which technological development can create a cultural and educational environment capable of diversifying the sources of knowledge and learning. A feature of these technologies is their growing complexity and the ever larger range of possibilities they provide. They can, for instance, combine a very large information storage capacity with more or less personal access and wide distribution. Yet however vast their potential may seem in theory, they must be considered within specific social and economic contexts. The Commission is fully aware of the marked disparities between industrialized and developing countries as regards investment capacity, research and design potential, trading outlets and rates of return, added to which the developing countries also have different education priorities, owing to their lower school attendance rates and less-developed infrastructures. Consequently, their priorities concerning the use of technology for educational purposes are also different: 'In the developing world, it is the possibility of outreach and of economies of scale which is most immediately attractive, rather than individualized access and interactivity; in the industrialized world, the position is reversed, since distribution and access are more or less guaranteed, and individualization can count for much more.'[9]

Most of the projects undertaken in developing countries accordingly aim at reaching mass audiences or audiences which are otherwise beyond reach (use of satellite transmission in India to reach remote villages; educational radio network set up in Thailand in the 1980s; national distance education programme in China). In the industrialized countries, the aim is rather

8. See on this subject Alan Hancock, *Contemporary Information and Communication Technologies and Education*, Paris, UNESCO, 1993. (UNESCO doc. EDC/1/3.)

9. Ibid.

he National Open School in India

e National Open School (NOS) is a oneering institute of open learning at hool level. Set up in 1989 by the overnment of India, it plays a key role in e process of universalizing basic ucation for all, in enhancing equity and cial justice and in creating a learning ciety.

The National Open School offers sic, secondary, senior secondary, ocational education and life enrichment ogrammes. The students are free to oose the courses and frequently opt

for combinations of academic and vocational courses. Its courses are offered in English and a variety of local languages.

The school caters to students of all ages over 14 and has succeeded in attracting women to the extent that they make up 38 per cent of those enrolled. Marginalized groups in general, including women, comprise over 50 per cent of its enrolment. In making use of the different media, it puts great emphasis on quality aspects of the technology of text, but

does not shy away from more advanced technologies, such as instructional television, and audio and video programmes for enrichment of courses, in addition to face-to-face contact with the students. Its unit cost is less than a quarter of the cost per student in the formal school. By making use of the existing school network to serve its students, it benefits from that infrastructure while at the same time enriching it by bringing in facilities not normally available to the schools.

to use the audiovisual media as means of illustrating lessons or reaching particular minority or underprivileged groups.

It is worth remembering that the use of information and communication technologies for education purposes is not new: educational radio appeared before the First World War, for example. What has changed with the passage of time is not only the range of technologies used and their complexity; it is also the endeavour to reach wider and wider audiences, outside the formal education system, whose age range extends from pre-school children to the entire adult population. All sorts of experiments have been conducted, periods of optimism have followed periods of doubt and the variety of systems in operation makes it difficult to establish an overall picture of what has actually been achieved. The thorough evaluation made of certain experimental programmes (such as educational television in Côte d'Ivoire or the Satellite Instructional Television Experiment (SITE) in India) shows that technology alone is not a miracle answer to education systems' problems. It should, for one thing, be used in conjunction with conventional forms of education and not considered as a self-sufficient substitute for them.

A wide-ranging debate

Conscious of the wealth of experience accumulated, the Commission would like to enumerate some points upon which the international community might in future care to focus its attention and efforts as regards the educational use of the new technologies.

The use of these technologies for distance education, already firmly established in many places, appears to be an avenue full of promise for every country in the world. The education community can draw on a solid fund of international experience, beginning with the United Kingdom's Open University, founded in the early 1970s. Distance education employs a variety of delivery systems: correspondence courses, radio, television, audiovisual materials, telephone lessons and teleconferencing. The place occupied by the media and education technologies within different distance education systems varies greatly, and can be adjusted to each country's situation and infrastructure: developing countries, for example, generally prefer radio to television.

While the latest technologies may not yet have been brought into this process, they seem capable of producing significant improvements, especially in individualizing the act of learning. Another possibility is a growing convergence between distance education and the other kinds of remote activity, such as 'teleworking', that are likely to be further developed. In the case of distance learners and teleworkers alike, technological convergence is liable to blur the dividing lines between education, work and even leisure, with a single channel offering a variety of possibilities.

There is every reason to think that the new technologies will have an important role to play in adult education, different in each country and in line with the 'learning throughout life' that the Commission has attempted to outline. Modern technology has already been successfully used for in-service training in business and industry, and is a vital component in the education potential, present throughout society, that needs to be mobilized as the twenty-first century looms in sight.

The Commission wishes to make clear its position in the debate on the introduction of the new information and communication technologies into education systems: to its way of thinking, there is a decisive issue at stake here, and it is important that schools and universities should have a central place in a profound change that is affecting the whole of society. There is no doubt but that individuals' ability to access and process information is set to become the determining factor in their integration not only into the working environment but also into their social and cultural environment.

It is thus essential, in order to avoid a further aggravation of social inequalities, for education systems to teach all pupils how to master and handle these techniques. Two objectives of the utmost importance in that respect are: to ensure better

Towards a learning society

Teaching is an art, and nothing can entirely replace face-to-face tuition. Yet the media revolution is there and we should use it to our best advantage. New technology has created a host of new tools for use in the classroom, in laboratories, at home and on the move:

• computers of all sizes and sophistication;
• cable and satellite TV education broadcasting;
• multimedia equipment;
• interactive information exchange systems, including electronic mail and on-line access to libraries and public data bases;
• computerized simulators;
• virtual reality systems.

Using these tools, both students and teachers are equipped to become researchers. Teachers then coach their students to evaluate and use effectively the information they have gathered for themselves. This is far closer to real life situations than the older styles of teacher transmission of information to students. A new partnership is developing in the classroom.

Source: ERT Education Policy Group, *Education for Europeans: Towards the Learning Society,* p. 27, Brussels, The European Round Table of Industrialists (ERT), 1994.

dissemination of knowledge and to increase equality of opportunity.

On the other hand, as tools for the education of children and adolescents, the new technologies offer an unprecedented opportunity to satisfy an increasingly widespread and diversified demand, while maintaining quality. The possibilities they open up, along with their advantages for teaching, are vast. Computers and multimedia systems, for instance, make it possible to design individual learning paths along which each pupil can move at his or her own pace; they also make it easier for teachers to organize knowledge acquisition in mixed-ability classes. Compact-disc technology seems to hold out special promise, since it offers the possibility of handling large amounts of information, complete with sound, picture and text, without requiring previous familiarity with computers. Interactive media allow pupils to ask questions, look up information themselves or delve deeper into particular areas of subjects treated in class. It has often been remarked that pupils who are under-achievers in the conventional system reveal their talents better and are more motivated when the new technologies are used in the teaching process. Using the new technologies is also a way of combating under-achievement: pupils who experience difficulties under the traditional system are sometimes better motivated when they come to use them and are thus better able to show where their talents lie.

Taking these various advantages into account, the Commission is therefore of the opinion that the use of the new technologies in education is a matter of financial, societal and political choice that should be central to the concerns of governments and international organizations. Since the developing countries are at present placed at a disadvantage by their relatively lower technological capacities and limited financial resources, everything possible should be done to prevent the gap between them and the wealthy countries becoming wider: priority should be given to strengthening their infrastructures and to spreading these technologies throughout society, and international aid should be made available for these operations. A relatively inexpensive way of ensuring the broad dissemination of information and knowledge would be to set up experimental centres to which schools would be linked by network. In many cases, a kind of technological 'short cut' could be envisaged: there is no need for developing countries to go through all the successive stages that the industrialized countries have been through and they would often be well advised to go for the most advanced technologies from the outset. The formulation of policies for the dissemination of the new technologies in the developing countries therefore represents a challenge to education, calling for close collaboration between business and industry, governments and international organizations to bring into being a world of greater unity and solidarity. The Commission wishes, however, to stress that the development of these technologies, far from taking place at the expense of the written word, restores to it an essential role, and that books, although they may no longer be the only instrument of teaching and learning, nevertheless retain a central place therein since they remain the cheapest of media and the easiest to handle, illustrating the teacher's lessons while allowing the pupil to revise what has been learned and to gain independence.

A crucial point worth recalling in this regard is that the development of the new technologies does not at all diminish the role of teachers – quite the contrary – but it does change it profoundly and it offers them an opportunity they must seize (see Chapter 7). True, in an information society teachers can no longer be regarded as the sole repositories of knowledge that they have only to pass on to the younger generation: they become as it were partners in a collective fund of knowledge that it is up to them to organize, positioning themselves firmly in the vanguard of change. It is therefore essential that teachers' initial training and even more so their in-service training should give them a real command of these new tools. They need, in addition, to be sensitized to the profound changes that modern technologies effect in our cognitive processes. It will no longer be exclusively a matter for teachers of teaching pupils to learn, but also of teaching them how to seek, link up and appraise facts and information. Given the considerable quantity of information available on information networks, accurate navigation through knowledge becomes a precondition to knowing. This competency is becoming what some people consider to be a new form of literacy. This 'computeracy' is becoming more and more of a necessity for proper understanding of the real world of today. It is thus a pre-eminent means of acceding to independence, enabling individuals to play their part as free and enlightened members of society.

The Commission is indeed convinced that, in this respect as in many others, choosing a particular type of education amounts to choosing a particular type of society. It firmly believes that choices in education should be directed towards greater responsibility for every citizen, while preserving the basic principle of equity of opportunity. The measures it advocates are therefore not purely technical but in large part political: successful decentralization involves the different people and institutions active in society in the decision-making process and gives free play to innovation, without making overall regulation any less necessary. Funding from a variety of sources, based on a philosophy of partnership, requires arrangements to be instituted that allow for a diversity of learning paths. Attention to the social and educational implications of the new information and communication technologies will, provided that the necessary precautions are taken, lead to a fuller mastery of knowledge. Learning throughout life makes it possible to give direction to this social dimension of education. It presupposes the existence of universal basic schooling of good quality and accessible to all, irrespective of geographical, material, social or cultural circumstances. It offers to all the opportunity of seizing fresh chances after the completion of the initial education cycle. It also requires that talents of every sort be encouraged, that a broad variety of learning paths be opened up, and that all the resources existing in society be mobilized for that purpose.

Pointers and recommendations

• Choosing a type of education means choosing a type of society. In all countries, such choices call for extensive public debate, based on an accurate evaluation of education systems. The Commission invites the political authorities to encourage such debate, in order to reach a democratic consensus, this being the best route to success for educational reform strategies.

• The Commission advocates the implementation of measures for involving the different persons and institutions active in society in educational decision-making: administrative decentralization and the autonomy of educational establishments are conducive in most cases, it believes, to the development and generalization of innovation.

• In view of the foregoing, the Commission wishes to reaffirm the role of the political authority, which has the duty clearly to define options and ensure overall regulation, making the required adjustments: education is a community asset which cannot be regulated by market forces alone.

• The Commission none the less does not underrate the force of financial constraints and it advocates the bringing into operation of public/private partnerships. In developing countries, the public funding of basic education remains a priority, but the choices made must not imperil the coherence of the system as a whole, nor lead to other levels of education being sacrificed.

• It is essential that funding structures be reviewed in the light of the principle that learning should continue throughout individuals' lives. The Commission hence feels that the proposed study-time entitlement, as briefly outlined in the report, deserves to be discussed and explored.

• The progress of the new information and communication technologies should give rise to a general deliberation on access to knowledge in the world of tomorrow. The Commission recommends:
– the diversification and improvement of distance education through the use of the new technologies;
– greater use of those technologies in adult education and especially in the in-service training of teachers;
– the strengthening of developing countries' infrastructures and capabilities in this field and the dissemination of such technologies throughout society; these are in any case prerequisites to their use in formal education systems; and
– the launching of programmes for the dissemination of the new technologies under the auspices of UNESCO.

Chapter 9

International co-operation: educating the global village

As we have seen in the earlier chapters of this report, globalization points up the scale, urgency and interconnected nature of the problems facing the international community. The accelerated pace of population growth, the wastage of natural resources, environmental damage, the chronic poverty in much of the world, and the oppression, violence and injustice from which millions still suffer all call for large-scale remedial action that can be implemented only by reinvigorating international co-operation and putting more resources into it. Globalization, henceforth irreversible, calls for global responses: building a better – or less bad – world has become as never before everyone's business.

Education is without any doubt one, perhaps the most fundamental, of these responses. Co-operation in education should thus be viewed in the broader context of what the international community must do to stimulate awareness of all the problems requiring solution and achieve a consensus on the issues needing concerted action; this action will involve international and intergovernmental organizations, governments, non-governmental organizations, business and industry, professional and labour organizations and, of course, in the area which concerns us directly, those actively participating in the education system and the intellectual community, all working together as partners.

In this connection, the holding of a series of major world conferences under the auspices of the United Nations[1] and the recent founding of the World Trade Organization have blazed a trail for the type of collective action made necessary by the inter-dependence between nations. These conferences, the follow-up to them and the implementation of the specific projects arising out of them have fixed the framework and outlined the shape of what might be called the great worksites of international co-operation at the close of the twentieth century. Milestones along the path to a truly world-oriented approach, the conferences bear witness to the deter-mination of many actors on the world stage to make co-operation the instrument for transforming the globalization of problems into a force for good. The strength of these trends is similarly evident from the work of such international commissions as the Brandt Commission, the Brundtland Commission or the Commission on Global Governance.

This growing recourse to international action in the quest for col-lective solutions to worldwide problems is also reflected in the signifi-cant increase in recent years in United Nations interventions to ensure peace and security in various parts of the world. The United Nations has stepped in (using preventive diplomacy or conducting peacekeep-ing operations) in a growing number of conflicts: 11 in 1989, 53 in 1991, 78 in 1994. Admittedly, the results in this area and others have on occasion been disappointing, so that, at a time when the organiza-tion has just been celebrating its fiftieth anniversary, questions have to be asked about the kinds of reform that need to be carried out in the United Nations system and in its methods of action, if it is going to enhance the effectiveness of its interventions. A broad tendency can nevertheless be discerned which, it may be hoped, foreshadows the emergence in the twenty-first century of a truly global society.

Since its fields of competence touch upon matters of vital import-ance, UNESCO, working alongside other international organizations, clearly must shoulder great responsibilities. More particularly, at a point in history when the key role of education in national and human development is, in the words of its Director-General, 'uni-versally recognized and proclaimed',[2] it is right and proper that it should be associated with many of the projects by means of which the international community aims to lay the groundwork for its future. For this reason, several of the Commission's recommenda-tions follow directly on from the work of the United Nations world conferences.

1. World Conference Review and Appraise the Achievements of the United Nations Decade for Women: Equality, Development and Peace (Nairobi, Kenya, July 1985); World Conference on Education for All: Meeting Basic Learning Needs (Jomtien, Thailand, 5–9 March 1990); United Nations Conference on Environment and Development (UNCED) (Rio de Janeiro, Brazil, June 1992); International Conference on Population and Development (Cairo, Egypt, 5–13 September 1994); World Summit for Social Development (Copenhagen, Denmark, 6–12 March 1995); Fourth World Conference on Women (Beijing, China, 4–15 September 1995).

2. Speech by the Director-General of UNESCO at the opening ceremony of the Twenty-eighth Session of the General Conference, 25 October 1995.

Women and girls: education for equality

The Commission stresses the importance of the Declaration adopted by the Fourth World Conference on Women (Beijing, 1995). The Declaration outlines the different forms of discrimination practised against women and girls, particularly in regard to education and training, and sets a number of fundamental goals for the international community: to ensure equal access by women to education; to eradicate female illiteracy; and to improve access for women to vocational training, science and technology education, and continuing education.

The Commission endorses these recommendations. In general terms, it considers that the denial of equality with men to which women are still subject in most parts of the world, either on a massive scale or in more insidious forms, depending on traditions and circumstances, remains, as this twentieth century draws to a close, by its extent and its gravity a violation of the rights of the individual. The Commission, concurring with the solemn declarations made in different forums in recent years, remains convinced that it is the duty of the international community to make every effort to do away with these inequalities. Providing women and girls with an education which will, as quickly as possible, bridge the gap separating them from men and give them the chances for action and the empowerment hitherto withheld from them in the workplace, in society and in the sphere of politics, is more than an ethical imperative. A large number of studies have highlighted an important sociological reality: everywhere in the world, women have become – even though the indicators used all too often tend to belittle or bedim their real contribution to development – a major force in the economy (see Chapter 3). Seen in this light, the education of women and girls is one of the best possible investments in the future. Whether the purpose be to improve family health, the schooling of children or community life in general, the best chance societies have of succeeding lies in educating mothers and raising the status of women. Our too exclusively male-dominated world has much to learn and hope for from the emancipation of women.

Education and social development

The Commission paid special attention to the proceedings and recommendations of the World Summit for Social Development held in Copenhagen in March 1995. The conference, in dealing with poverty, unemployment and social exclusion, emphasized the contribution which education policies could make.

The pointers emerging from that summit deserve mention, since they underscore the social dimension of education policies. The participants committed themselves to promoting universal and equitable access to quality education, and ensuring for all the highest standards of physical and mental health as well as primary health care. They declared that they would make particular efforts to rectify inequalities relating to social conditions, without distinction as to race, national origin, gender, age or disability. They also pledged to respect and promote the cultures common to all of them and those specific to each of them, to strengthen the role of culture in development, to preserve the essential bases of human-centred, sustainable development, and to contribute to making the most of human resources and to social development. The aims must be to eradicate poverty, promote full and productive employment and foster social integration.[3]

The Commission naturally endorses these conclusions, which are fully in line with its own ideas on the ultimate aims of education and the areas it covers, and which lend yet more weight to its call for international co-operation based on solidarity and partnership. Although the importance of quantitative objectives should not be overstated, it seems to the Commission that, given the specific contribution education makes to social development, an appreciable proportion of development aid should be devoted to it: in liaison with the action of the international organizations, it could be set at a quarter of overall aid, which should itself be increased. The international financial institutions, beginning with the World Bank, should also accept a similar tilt towards education.

The Commission hopes there will be a regular follow-through to the Copenhagen Summit which will help in producing greater general awareness, encouraging initiatives, promoting co-operation and assessing the results achieved.

3. *Report of the World Summit for Social Development (Copenhagen, 6–12 March 1995),* New York, United Nations, 1995. (UN doc. A/CONF.166/9.)

Making debt-swaps work for education

Education, being a long-term economic, social and human invest-ment, too often gets sacrificed in adjustment plans, whereas higher school enrolment rates in fact call for increased government spend-ing. An effort must therefore be made to offset the adverse effects on education budgets of adjustment policies and policies for the reduction of domestic and foreign deficits. The Commission sees promise in recent experiments in swapping debt for education pro-grammes. A country's foreign debt is bought, discounted, in hard currency by a development agency (usually an international non-governmental organization) from the commercial banks or other creditors. It is then partly redeemed by the debtor country in local currency through its central bank, and this amount in local currency is then used exclusively for financing (sometimes over quite long periods) particular education programmes. Such debt-swap agreements are difficult to negotiate and are not always applicable, but in certain countries where the public finances are sagging under the weight of debt repayments, the outside agency that negotiates the agreement can help to boost education expenditure. In many of the most heavily indebted countries, where the percentage of GNP devoted to education is falling and school enrolments are declining, debt-relief is essential if a share of national income is to be released for education purposes. Debt-relief does not always of itself lead to an increase in social spending though, and this is where debt-swapping can give outside financial backers a certain leverage. It can also help to solve the problems faced by development aid agencies in using hard currency to finance spending in local currency or the payment of recurrent costs. The Commission, noting that the main creditors are govern-ments and official multilateral credit agencies, feels that they should investigate the possibility of taking part themselves in swap agree-ments of this kind, and in devising new schemes for linking debt-relief to long-term increases in social spending.

A UNESCO observatory for the new information technologies

While trying to identify both the financial and other barriers holding back progress in education and the new avenues becoming available to it, the Commission has given particular attention to those fields where change is occurring rapidly. One of them, reviewed at some length in Chapters 2 and 8, is that of the new information technologies. These are already transforming the societies in which they have become established by altering working relations and creating, alongside the real world, a virtual universe whose potential benefits and dangers are still very hard to estimate. They can, as many now agree, make a growing contribution to education systems. It is important to see to it that they are disseminated in all countries to avoid another gap being created between rich nations and poor nations, which could frustrate attempts to right the balance. Since the advent of the information society is one of the major facts of life for the future, the Commission recommends that UNESCO create an 'observatory' to be responsible, thinking ahead to the twenty-first century, for exploring and weighing up two aspects of the question: that is, the foreseeable impact of the new technologies on the human individual's freedom and development, and also on educational processes as such. This project would, in the Commission's view, comply well with UNESCO's role of intellectual leadership and may make it possible to cast a clearer light on a road into the future along which the modern world is advancing at great speed but with practically nothing to guide it. The intellectual, political and social harnessing of these technologies is one of the great challenges of the next century.

The Commission also feels that UNESCO should play a pivotal role as a clearing-house for information on educational software. Two main directions could underpin its work in this area: the granting of a label of quality for educational software and encouragement for the production of educational software that respects cultural diversity. To this end, UNESCO should take the initiative, in co-operation with software and computer manufacturers, of establishing and attributing a prize each year for outstanding efforts in the field.

OECS: an example of multilateral co-operation

The Organization of Eastern Caribbean States is made up of eight countries and territories (Antigua and Barbuda, the British Virgin Islands, Dominica, Grenada, Montserrat, Saint Kitts and Nevis, Saint Lucia, and Saint Vincent and the Grenadines) with a total population of around 550,000.

Although most children from those countries attend school for at least seven years and nearly half of the age group attends secondary school, there is great concern about the quality of the education provided. More than half of the 7,500 teachers are untrained, having gone into teaching directly after

completing secondary school. The higher education system, late in being developed because of the small population of these countries, so far has only 4,000 students.

Beginning in 1990, the OECS countries decided to work together to establish in common a comprehensive human resource development system through a regional education reform strategy. They are collaborating in twelve essential areas covering curriculum and teaching staff development, student assessment, reform of technical-vocational education and training, adult and continuing education, distance

education, sector resource management and management of the reform process. A continuing review of educational policies is providing the basis for a common education bill that will harmonize the legislative foundations for the education systems throughout OECS. Common data collection and evaluation will facilitate monitoring of all aspects of education.

The OECS Secretariat has negotiated with the funding sources and with technical agencies to ensure maximum co-operation with them and among them in their support for this regional educational reform strategy project.

From aid to partnership

We are currently witnessing a shift in the conception and functions of international aid. The conventional forms of aid and co-operation are being contested and acknowledgement of the need for changing 'assistance' into 'partnership' is gaining ground. Both beneficiary and donor countries are looking for new forms of co-operation genuinely based on exchange and mutual benefit. In a world where, irrespective of local factors, most problems transcend local and regional frontiers, co-operation is both a political and a practical imperative.

Views on the best methods for achieving progress can vary drastically, however, between 'donors' and 'recipients'. Receiving countries increasingly demand the right to be treated as partners. They often feel that dependence on outside expertise and foreign models exacts an unacceptably high price, both economically and culturally.

On the other hand, the economically advanced countries (and the agencies in those countries that spearhead transfers of money and technical assistance) are aware that they have no easy answers. In the past they have passed on not only expertise and material assistance, but also, in many cases, their own prejudices, fashions and errors. The economic and employment crises in many so-called developed economies have underlined the complex nature of the relationships between education and employment or between education and social cohesion. Thus, donors are accepting the need to draw more closely on the lessons of past experience in their own countries, and on previous successes and failures of international co-operation.

The Commission found, during the course of its work, some common themes that could form the basis for future reflection and for the renewal of development strategies. Among these is the importance in international co-operation, as in national policy, of seeing education systems as a whole and of conceiving reform as a democratic, consultative process related to an overall social policy concerned with respect for democracy, human rights and the rule of law. There is clearly a need to find more effective ways to target international co-operation towards the alleviation of poverty: in the field of education this means a concerted effort to reach those people who have traditionally been excluded from learning opportunities.

However urgent short-term needs and reforms may be, it is vital to devote some energy and resources to building up longer-term capacity for research and reform within poorer countries, including gathering and analysing internationally comparable information on education systems. Finally, free circulation of persons and of knowledge must be encouraged in order to attempt to bridge the knowledge gap.

A look at existing international and regional systems makes it possible to draw certain conclusions and to see what is needed to ensure sustainability of exchange schemes. The European Union, by focusing on areas of key interest to all the co-operating countries, has succeeded in catalysing intellectual co-operation, operating through a set of innovative programmes. It encourages exchanges between universities and schools, stimulates foreign-language teaching, promotes equal opportunities (notably within the European co-operation programme SOCRATES, which includes the ERASMUS, COMENIUS and LINGUA programmes) and is contributing to the establishment of a joint statistics and research fund, the Education Information Network in the European Community (EURYDICE). The aim of these programmes is to enable the participating countries to benefit jointly from the advantages they possess severally at every level of education, thereby compensating for national deficiencies. It enables young people, students in particular, to profit from the courses of study available in the different member states of the Union, thus contributing to better mutual understanding among peoples.

RASMUS*: a European programme

e ERASMUS programme launched by
e European Community in 1987 was
e first programme designed and put
to operation at European level to
omote student mobility and other
rms of co-operation between
iiversities (teacher mobility,
velopment of new joint programmes of
udy and intensive training
ogrammes). Since 1995, ERASMUS has
en incorporated into the new European
nion programme SOCRATES, which
vers all types and levels of education
d stresses the notion of 'European
ucation for all'.

The success of ERASMUS is
deniable, as may be seen from the
erall figures. From 1987 to 1995, about
0,000 students have had the

opportunity to follow a recognized period
of study in another EC academic
establishment, while 50,000 teachers
have been able to deliver courses in
another university; 1,800 establishments
have taken part in European co-operation
activities. This figure includes nearly all
universities as well as a large number of
non-university higher education
institutions.

ERASMUS is organized around two
main forms of action: the grant of
financial aid to universities for Europe-
related activities and promotion of
student mobility, with the accompanying
distribution of study grants. Thus, within
the framework of the new 'Institutional
Contract', financial aid is given to
universities to promote student and

teacher mobility, and to develop courses
common to universities in the different
member states. A number of provisions
facilitate the academic recognition of
periods of study carried out abroad.
ERASMUS study grants provide financial
aid to students going to another member
state for a period of study. The grants
(extending over 3 to 12 months) cover
mobility costs connected with study
abroad, such as language preparation,
travel expenses and cost-of-living
differentials.

* European Community Action Scheme for the
Mobility of University Students. – Ed.

Sources: European Commission and Education
Information Network in the European
Community.

Other groups of countries, including the Commonwealth and the French-speaking community, have used features of a shared past, language especially, to build up exchange and aid networks that help developing countries. Several regional and subregional organizations are gaining importance as leading spirits in co-operation among countries with common interests. Through partnerships, centres of excellence or joint programmes, it is clearly possible to create, for the benefit of smaller countries, synergies that are more effective than isolated action. The industrialized countries too can reap appreciable benefits from entering into partnerships.

Scientists, research and international exchanges

The fundamental role of scientific research in consolidating national potential is now an accepted fact. The tendency at present is for research programmes to be for the most part decided on in the wealthy countries and to serve those countries' concerns, which is not the best way to develop the spirit of partnership. Yet there are certain encouraging signs, such as the launching of endogenous research (in the exact and natural sciences as in the social sciences) and the setting up of South–South networks.

The effectiveness of such networks depends to a large extent on teacher, student and research-worker mobility, which needs to be encouraged as much as possible, and, in so far as UNESCO is concerned, on the setting of appropriate standards. It is important that facilities for research into education should be created all over the world, so that its long-term effects can be studied.

In the rich countries, co-operation between scientists working in the same field transcends national boundaries and serves as a powerful tool for internationalizing ideas, attitudes and activities. The networks set up or reinforced by the European Union work as a kind of Europe-wide research laboratory in certain fields, producing scientific and cultural spin-offs. As to the world's poorest regions, their potential continues to be sapped by the outflow of highly qualified scientists seeking research posts in the major centres. Yet there is a ray of hope: we are beginning to see graduates and researchers returning to their home countries whenever an opening, however small, occurs.

While there is no denying that the wealthy countries are doing more and more to remedy the knowledge deficit of the rest of the world, the measures for aiding the poorer countries to boost their research capacity must be unremittingly reinforced. Aid for setting up centres of excellence (see Chapter 3) is among the most useful of these measures. These centres enable countries with insufficient means of their own to combine their efforts and so advance beyond the critical threshold below which nothing viable can be done in research, higher education or investment in expensive technology, such as that needed for distance education.

New tasks for UNESCO

The remit assigned to UNESCO within the United Nations system and the place it actually occupies in international co-operation make it a key institution for the future. Its mandate, defined half a century ago in the tragic aftermath of a world war, has lost nothing of its topicality, but changing circumstances in the world oblige UNESCO to change accordingly.

Although UNESCO is neither a funding agency nor a simple research institution, it has always had the task of developing human potential, in co-operation with its Member States and its many partners and associates on the international scene. The intellectual collaboration which it fosters serves both as an instrument for rapprochement and mutual understanding between peoples and individuals, and as an essential tool for action. More than ever before, the transfer and sharing of knowledge, the interplay of ideas, high-level consultation, the organization of networks for innovation, and the dissemination of information and of the results of successful experiments, research and evaluation – all of which the Organization encourages in its fields of competence – are seen to be vital to the building of a more mutually supportive and peaceful world. It is important that these sides of its activity should be further developed.

The distinctive character of UNESCO lies in the scope of its responsibilities – not only education, but also culture, research and science, and communication – which make it an intellectual organization in the broad sense, less subordinate than others to a purely economic view of the issues. Its many-sidedness matches the complexity of today's world, in which so many phenomena are symbiotically related. As a moral authority and a setter of international standards, it pays as much heed to human development as to purely material progress. In the field of education, all these attributes predispose it to undertaking action on several fronts: helping Member States to build and reform their education systems and obtain the most benefit from the scientific and technological revolution, but also making the right to education a reality for all people throughout the world and promoting everywhere the idea of peace and the principles of justice and tolerance.

The Commission's express wish is that UNESCO's Member States should provide the Organization with the means to carry out this multi-faceted task successfully. This means, in the first place, that it should in the coming years be able to expand and reinforce a whole series of actions, based on its experience and on innovative ideas, for furthering, through alliances and partnerships between countries, the development of national education systems. The Commission also urges UNESCO to use its programme to promote the concept of learning throughout life, as set forth in this report, so that it gradually becomes a reality in the educational context of the modern world.

At another level, UNESCO can make a powerful contribution to opening people's minds, through education, to the pressing needs of international solidarity. As international organizations and individual nations are preparing to take up the challenges of the twenty-first century, the concept of world citizenship is still remote from the realities of the situation and still but dimly perceived. Yet our horizon is that of the global village, as interdependence increases and problems become worldwide. For lack of awareness of the changes at work, tension is mounting between the global and the local. This is a reason for encouraging grass-roots initiatives, developing exchange and dialogue, and lending an ear to the daily concerns of men and women. The work done by non-governmental organizations is capital in this respect, in reducing fear and incomprehension and in weaving the many bonds upon which tomorrow's global society will be based. UNESCO, with whom the non-governmental organizations have long been especially favoured partners in the field, would do well to call even more on their collaboration as a means for rooting its action in reality.

Here, the social sciences have an important place in education for international understanding, and in the development of awareness of the need for global solidarity. UNESCO could, for example, encourage the undertaking of a wide-ranging interdisciplinary inquiry into the principal questions facing human society on the eve of the twenty-first century.

Strengthened by this immediate contact with the world we live in, UNESCO will be able to fully exert its moral authority. The Commission believes that UNESCO's ethical mission, to which its Constitution assigns priority, is today enhanced by the new tasks required of education in the modern world, be it promoting sustainable development, ensuring social cohesion, encouraging democratic participation at every level, or responding to the demands made by globalization. In all these areas, the ultimate societal aims of education should never obscure the primacy of the human individual and the ideals proclaimed by the international community when the United Nations was founded. The ethical imperative, then seen as primordial, thus turns out in the final analysis to be what attunes the work of UNESCO most profoundly to present realities, with all their doubts and uncertainties. While rooting its action securely in a Utopian vision, a purposeful, balanced view of progress, it is pointing that action, as the new century draws near, towards the establishment of a genuine culture of peace.

ointers and ecommendations

The need for international -operation – which itself has to be dically rethought – is felt also in e field of education. This is an issue t only for education policy-makers d the teaching profession but r all who play an active part in mmunity life.

At the level of international -operation, a policy of strong couragement for the education of ·ls and women should be promoted, the spirit of the Beijing Conference.

So-called aid policy should be ade to evolve towards partnership fostering, among other things, -operation and exchanges within gional groupings.

A quarter of development d should be devoted to the funding education.

Debt swaps should be encouraged order to offset the adverse effect adjustment policies and policies for e reduction of domestic and foreign ·ficits on educational spending.

National education systems ould be helped to gain strength · encouraging alliances and ·-operation between ministries at gional level and between countries cing similar problems.

Countries should be helped · stress the international dimension ' the education provided (curricula, e of information technologies ıd international co-operation).

New partnerships between ternational institutions dealing with lucation should be encouraged ırough, for example, the launching ' an international project for

disseminating and implementing the concept of learning throughout life, on the lines of the inter-agency initiative that resulted in the Jomtien Conference.

•   The gathering, at international level, of data on national investment in education should be encouraged, in particular by the establishment of suitable indicators: total amount of private funds, investment by industry, spending on non-formal education, etc.

•   A set of indicators should be developed for revealing the most serious dysfunctions of education systems, by cross-relating various quantitative and qualitative data, such as: level of spending on education, drop-out rates, disparities in access, inefficiency of different parts of the system, poor-quality teaching, teachers' status, etc.

•   With an eye to the future, a UNESCO observatory should be set up to look into the new information technologies, their evolution and their foreseeable impact on not only education systems but also on modern societies.

•   Intellectual co-operation in the field of education should be encouraged through the intermediary of UNESCO: UNESCO professorships, Associated Schools, equitable sharing of knowledge between countries, dissemination of information technologies, and student, teacher and researcher exchanges.

•   UNESCO's normative action on behalf of Member States, for instance in relation to the harmonization of national legislation with international instruments, should be intensified.

Epilogue

One of the most original features of an undertaking such as that of this Commission is the diversity of background and experience, and therefore viewpoints, that each Commissioner brings to the task. Out of this diversity, though, came a very broad agreement on the overall approach to be adopted and the main thrust of the conclusions. The text of the report was debated at length, and although certainly each Commissioner would have written certain passages, or even chapters, differently as an individual, all concurred with its overall direction and content. Yet, in aiming to focus on a few themes that can shed light on major issues, the process of selection necessarily left aside some of the particular concerns of individual Commissioners, important though they are. Thus, towards the end of its work, the Commission agreed that each of its members would be asked to contribute a personal statement as a complement to the common report; it felt that these texts would give a clearer idea of the richness of the composition and debates within the Commission, and provide a wide range of angles of vision on the issues raised in the body of the report. Eleven of the Commissioners contributed texts, and these follow here.

n'am Al Mufti

Excellence in education: investing in human talent

At the present juncture in history, major innovations in science and technology, changes in economics and politics, and transformations in demographic and social structures are taking place throughout the world. These upheavals, which are likely to accelerate in the future, will place considerable strain on the educational community, in particular, to respond to growing needs and to meet the emerging challenges of a rapidly changing world. The exigencies of our time demand the dynamic interplay of creativity, courage and determination to make effective changes and the will to rise to the challenges before us.

In response to this situation, educational reform plans on both the national and international levels need to transcend adequate planning and financial resource allocation. Educational reform policies should aim at achieving educational excellence.

Education for All

In the past two decades in particular, governments and international agencies in the developing world sought to respond to developmental challenges by focusing increasingly on expanding educational opportunities. This drive by developing countries was in fulfilment of UNESCO's mission to achieve 'Education for All'. But the expansion in education was concentrated on coping with the growing demand for schooling, while the quality of education itself was not given priority. The result was over-crowded schools, outdated teaching methods based on learning by rote and teachers who have become unable to adapt to more modern approaches such as democratic participation in the classroom, co-operative learning and creative problem-solving. These are now obstacles to better education.

Significantly, the vast and rapid expansion of the education system, and its overburdening in many countries, have resulted in the inability to attend adequately to the question of *educational equity, which calls for providing learning experiences appropriate to the learning needs of students with varying abilities.* In the overwhelming ambition to provide education for all, the needs of students with high potential have been neglected and students with differing abilities have been treated equally. As Jefferson once said: 'There is nothing more unequal than equal treatment of unequal people.' Notwithstanding the good intentions of traditional policies, *to deprive outstanding students of appropriate educational opportunities is to deprive society of the best human resources that lead towards real and effective development.*

As we move into the twenty-first century, developing countries face a multiplicity of challenges in their quest for development. Taking up those challenges requires well-trained and prepared leaders to confront socio-economic needs. The specific educational requirements of outstanding students, the 'leaders of tomorrow', must be recognized and met.

To address the situation

To address the situation, additional educational opportunities that provide a more advanced content and methodology must be established to cater to individual differences. Classroom teachers should be trained to accommodate the different learning needs of talented students. One of the top priorities of every school should be to develop and set challenging curricula that offer advanced comprehensive learning opportunities, in order to meet the needs of outstanding students. This is of the utmost importance for the preparation of future leaders who will spearhead the march towards sustainable development. The regular school curriculum needs to be developed to offer talented students a challenge.

Excellence in education

To strive for excellence in education means to strive for a richer curriculum, based on the varying talents and needs of all students, the realization of each student's potential, and the development and nurturing of outstanding talent. It is also most important to ensure that teachers receive better training in how to teach high-level curricula. Otherwise, society's message to students would be to aim for academic adequacy, not academic excellence.

The role of the family, community and non-governmental organizations

To identify talent and to nurture it is not the responsibility of the school alone. The role of the family and the local community in developing potential provides the basis for and complements the efforts of the school. In turn, the non-governmental organizations can play a key role in assisting communities to assume their social responsibilities. They can be very effective in developing awareness and efficiency and in promoting participation of all members of the community.

And, most importantly, women

The backbone of community involvement remains the increased participation of women in the development process, an issue that has become central to human development and which will be increasingly recognized in the future. Women are currently under-represented in almost all advanced education programmes and in most top administrative positions. *The key to increasing the participation of women is education.* Educating women is probably one of the most rewarding investments a nation can make. *Expanding opportunities for women, and especially for women and girls of outstanding abilities, opens up avenues for the emergence of women leaders* and allows them to make a valuable contribution to decision-making for the benefit of educational progress and sustainable development.

A pertinent educational response in Jordan

In Jordan, approximately 1 million children, constituting 25 per cent of the population, are enrolled in schools. Compulsory education in the country and the boom in school enrolment at all levels resulted in an over-burdened education system which has not been able to cope with the issue of educational equity. To remedy the situation, Jordan has been engaged, over the past ten years, in a comprehensive educational reform programme to improve the quality of education. Legislation has paid special attention to students with outstanding abilities, and to developing the skills and training of teachers to meet the demands of these students.

After identifying the national need for excellence in education and in an effort to address the issue, the Noor Al Hussein Foundation (NHF) launched an innovative educational project. NHF, a non-governmental non-profit organization, was established in 1985 to identify and meet different development needs throughout Jordan, to introduce innovative and dynamic integrated community development models, and to set national standards of excellence in human and socio-economic development, education, culture and the arts. NHF's philosophy is characterized by a comprehensive approach to development, based on democratic participation and intersectoral co-operation at all levels.

Working with the government to implement the directives of the national educational reform plan and to provide educational opportunities for talented students, NHF established the Jubilee School in 1993 after devoting a decade to planning, extensive research, curriculum development and teacher training.

The Jubilee School, a co-educational secondary boarding school, offers a unique learning experience. Its academic programme is geared to students' intellectual needs, capabilities and experience. It offers an educational environment that motivates and challenges students to achieve their full potential through discovery, experimentation, creative problem-solving and possibly invention. Applicants to the school are carefully selected through a rigorous multiple-criteria system that includes school achievement, ratings of behavioural characteristics, general intellectual level, specific mathematical abilities and levels of creativity.

To ensure equality of opportunity for students from various socio-economic backgrounds, all students receive scholarships and much emphasis is placed on enrolling students from remote and under-privileged areas of the kingdom, where educational facilities are unable to meet the challenging needs of talented students. It is hoped that the Jubilee School's graduate students will return to their local communities, after further training or education, to assume leadership roles and to contribute to the development of the community.

Committed to a democratic learning environment, the school encourages freedom of thought and expression. Through their educational experience, students learn how to become effective users of knowledge. The school seeks not only to equip its students with a solid academic base, but also to build strength of character and to instil in them a deep sense of social responsibility.

In addition, the Jubilee School contributes to improving the quality of education for talented students in the community through its Centre for Excellence in Education, which works in co-operation with the Ministry of Education and with both the private and public sectors. The centre seeks to develop educational and instructional curricula, manuals and information that can be used by other schools throughout Jordan. It also helps to develop and make widely known innovative approaches to and advances in mathematics, science and the humanities, which can become resources for secondary-school teachers in Jordan. The centre functions as a resource library and an educational research facility. In addition, it sponsors training workshops, programmes and activities for teachers and talented students from all parts of Jordan, which focus on training teachers in the most effective teaching techniques, in curriculum development, and in providing for individual differences in their own classroom situations. Training programmes also address the issues of increasing access to early childhood education, increasing learning opportunities for disadvantaged and minority children with outstanding talents, and broadening the definition of the gifted through the observation of students in settings that enable them to display their abilities rather than through reliance solely on test scores.

The Jubilee School and its Centre for Excellence in Education represent a successful synthesis of research and innovation to enhance human potential, of modernization in training laboratories to promote national development, and of co-operation and commitment by public and private organizations to serve Jordanian society as a whole. In its first two years of operation, Jubilee School students have achieved outstanding results in their academic and social development. The school's success is reflected most clearly in what one Jubilee student had to say about it:

I used to regard school as a prison. But the Jubilee School is the place where I could learn and feel completely free. The Jubilee is the place for friends, science and imagination. At the Jubilee, the teacher is a friend, knowledge is a friend, and books are friends.

Isao Amagi

Upgrading the quality of school education

The modern school education systems developed by nation-states have greatly contributed to shaping not only individuals but also society as a whole. For that very reason, they are apt to be subjected both to public criticism and to undue demands as society evolves.

Every country has to engage in educational reform from time to time in terms of teaching, content and management of school education. Yet, however extensively the system may be reformed, the present basic functions of school education are likely to survive in the coming century and the key words for their survival might be the 'quality' and 'relevance' of school education.

Educational policy should address the question of the quality of school education from the following three aspects:

1. *Upgrading the quality of teachers*, through the adoption of the following policies and measures:
• *The level of pre-service education of teachers*, which is carried out at secondary-school level in some countries, should be raised to higher education level, as in the case of many industrially developed countries, which have created teachers' colleges and universities. In some of those countries, graduate courses are offered in teacher education.
• *Teachers' certificates* should indicate whether they are for primary school, secondary school, technical or vocational education, teaching the handicapped etc., according to the pre-service education.

- *Recruitment and placement* of teachers should reflect an equitable balance between the various subject-areas, experienced and less-experienced teachers, urban and rural areas, etc.
- *In-service training* is strongly recommended as lifelong education of all those engaged in the teaching profession to upgrade teaching capacities both in theory and practice. Curriculum development and related matters (see (2) below) should be taken into account in the in-service training of teachers.
- *Working conditions of teachers* – such as class size, working hours/days and supporting facilities – should be considered.
- *Teachers' salaries* should be high enough to attract promising young people to the teaching profession and a reasonable balance achieved between their salaries and those of other civil servants.

The formulation of a comprehensive teacher policy, combined with above-mentioned measures, should be a matter of prime concern to the authorities concerned.

2. *The design and development of the curriculum and related matters* should be carried out by the authorities and professional groups concerned. The school curriculum reflects the contents of teacher-training courses.

Teaching methods, textbooks, teaching materials and aids should be developed at the same time as the curriculum. In particular, computers and other information media should be utilized to enhance the process both of teaching and learning.

Academic research achievements in natural and social sciences, and humanities should be taken into account in curriculum development. The important role of experimental studies, and experience of working and living with nature, should also be considered in the development of teaching and learning methods.

3. *The improvement of school management* is the third area in which school education can be upgraded. School is a fundamental educational establishment where practical educational activities are carried out systematically. Although in most cases teachers work alone in classrooms, they are members of a group which works together to develop what could be called a 'school culture'. We can hardly expect high-quality school education without good leadership on the part of the headmaster and active co-operation of teachers in school management.

Finally, *improving the quality of school education* considered from the three aspects mentioned above should be a fundamental policy issue in all countries, whatever their circumstances, in the coming century.

Roberto Carneiro

Revitalizing the community spirit: a glimpse of the socializing role of the school in the next century

The century now drawing to a close has opened deep wounds, but the dominant theme of the coming century will be one of hope. In this new age, with its new social demands, learning the art of *living together* will be seen as the means of healing the many wounds inflicted by the hatred and intolerance that have prevailed throughout so much of the twentieth century.

Humanity can hardly recognize itself in the distorting mirror in which the ills affecting our societies take the form of marks and scars. The new direction in which history has been moving since 1989, a direction determined by the triumph of an implacable economic logic based on the law of the strongest and subjected to the dictates of a soulless neo-liberalism, make it essential that there should be *a reawakening of consciences, a moral revival* to tackle the fundamental social issue of worsening inequality in the world. This is a complex equation, defined by a set of variables chief amongst which are:

• Disturbing symptoms of *poverty fatigue*, stemming from situations of extreme poverty.

• A new, many-faceted form of destitution, reflecting the ever-worsening impoverishment of cultural, material, spiritual and emotional life, and also civic life.

• The declining importance of social capital in a society that cultivates risk and in which egoistic drives that completely undermine trust in inter-personal relations predominate.

• The conflictual and vertical nature of social relationships, defined by a logic comprising many different strands and representing the action of a variety of interest groups, as well as the gradual replacement of the class struggle by ethnic or religious and cultural conflicts, heralding the emergence of large-scale widespread tribalism.

- The abandonment of the civic domain, which underpins civilization, to an entrenched money-making philosophy that generates dualism and social exclusion.

The twenty-first century is thus faced with a major challenge, that of the *rebuilding of human communities.* Signs of impatience abound; human societies sense that a linear projection of the trends prevailing at the end of the present century holds out no promise of better times to come. The mass society and individualism that characterized the first generation of information and communication technologies, raising the triumphant economic model to its zenith, are now being superseded by a second technological generation in which the idea of networking and the value of (virtual) neighbourhood relations are beginning to reappear. The learning society, based on a code of knowledge-sharing and on learning experiences created by the unrestricted interpersonal relations that globalization makes possible, seems bound to encourage the emergence of post- materialistic values.

In this way, solidarity and the new community spirit can once again, quite naturally, be seen as constituting a life-ordering organic principle, and as an alternative to exclusion and the suicidal devitalization of the social fabric. In this context, fundamental and stable socializing institutions such as the family and the school have to reassume their role as the core around which a lasting basis for the society of the future can be established.

Education has always been and is still a highly social exercise. The full development of the individual's personality is the outcome of the consolidation of personal independence and, at one and the same time, of the cultivation of a concern for others, in other words, of the process of discovering other people on the basis of a moral outlook. Humanization, defined as the internal growth of the individual, finds its fullest expression at that fixed point where the paths of freedom and responsibility meet. Education systems are a source of *human capital* (Becker), *cultural capital* (Bourdieu), and *social capital* (Putnam). Instead of being 'a wolf to his fellow man' (*homo homini lupus*), man may thus become 'a friend to man' (*homo homini amicus*) through an education that has remained faithful to its community goals.

The task, though immense, cannot be postponed, since the construction of the social order of the next century depends on it. Above all, however, only *education for justice* will make it possible to reconstruct a core of moral education presupposing a civic culture characterized by non-conformism and the rejection of injustice, and preparing individuals for an active citizenship in which the responsibility to participate in the life of the community replaces mere delegated citizenship. Indeed, it is through the acquisition of a sense of abstract justice (equity, equality of opportunity, responsible freedom, respect for others, protection of the weak, and awareness of differences) that attitudes predisposing people towards taking practical steps to promote social justice and defend democratic values are created.

Thus, on the principle that education is, or comes close to being, a public good, the school should be defined first and foremost as a social institution or, more precisely, as an institution belonging to civil society; in other words, it must cease to be a mere component of an economic juggernaut that crushes the tenuous links of human solidarity.

According to Hannah Arendt, social life comprises three spheres, the *public,* the *market* and the *private*. While the public sphere is expected to promote the values of *equity,* Arendt believes that the market and the world of work generate discrimination, whilst the private sphere is characterized by exclusion, the corollary of individual choice.

On the basis of these fundamental concepts, the *school*, whatever its specific status – private, co-operative or state – is defined as a *sphere of public action*, as an environment and *locus* of socialization, which at the same time contributes to the economic and private spheres by virtue of the accumulation of the qualifications and human capital that it produces. In societies that are becoming increasingly complex and diversified in cultural terms, the emergence of the school as a part of the public sphere accentuates the indispensable role it plays in the promotion of social cohesion and mobility, and in training for community life.

In the end, nothing that happens in the school is without significance for the process of building stable societies.

Indeed, it is through the establishment of *plural educational communities*, governed by rules of democratic participation, in which emphasis is placed on dialogue between different points of view and in which the resolution of naturally occurring conflicts by any form of coercion or authoritarianism is rejected, that education for a fully fledged citizenship can be provided. In the context of this kind of education, passive tolerance is replaced by positive discrimination in favour of minorities, given that the primary purpose of democratic education is equal, universal access to fundamental political rights.

Schools of this kind are of crucial importance to *learning throughout life.* It is these schools that will provide the skills essential for lasting socialization, that is, for the consolidation of cultures in such a way that they can resist the processes of exclusion through pro-active attitudes that can fashion novel and stimulating social roles at each stage of life. *Education and socialization go hand in hand throughout life.*

A new century, by definition, means *fresh prospects*. These prospects, specifically human-centred and humanizing, necessarily imply that priority be given to education.

Fay Chung

Education
in Africa today

Africa, more than any other continent in the world, needs to re-think its education systems in line with, on the one hand, the globalization of the world economy, and on the other hand, the real situation. In addition, all too often, the inherited colonial systems of education have been preserved more or less intact, generally with the rationale of 'preserving standards', although these so-called standards were more illusory than real, with a very small élite enjoying exactly the same education as in the metropolitan country and the vast majority being deprived of any form of modern education at all. That this educated élite was unable to transform their countries from feudal social structures and traditional subsistence agriculture contrasts greatly with the success of the East Asian élites who have managed to move their countries to a stage where they are more economically efficient than the Western economies that they had begun by imitating. It is pertinent to ask why the African élite has failed whereas their counterparts in East Asia have succeeded so spectacularly. It is also pertinent to ask what role education played in the success of East Asia as compared to what has happened in Africa.

East Asia has been heavily influenced by the Japanese model. Beginning with the Meiji era, primary education was made compulsory for all in Japan by 1870. After establishing primary education for all, secondary education for all became the goal, and after the Second World War, it was possible to institute tertiary education for the majority. Moreover, even in the nineteenth century, the Japanese were very conscious that it was essential for their very survival as a nation to appropriate for themselves Western mathematics, science and technology, whilst eschewing Western culture and social values. With a certain cultural arrogance, they insisted on the primacy of their own language, literature, culture and religion, jealously preserving them. At the same time, with an equally determined humility, they sought to imitate, and later even to surpass, Western science and technology.

Africa has not made such a conscious choice. The introduction of Western education into Africa by Christian missionaries meant that the educated élite was more steeped in Christian theology, history, literature and culture than in science and technology, and this heavy bias towards the humanities has remained up to today. Probably the most visible symptom of this Western orientation was the rejection of a role in the education system for African languages. Up till today African languages are not taught in most French-speaking or Portuguese-speaking countries, and even some Anglophone countries have denigrated the use of African languages as 'divisive' and 'tribalistic'. In contrast to the Japanese, there was no conscious rejection of Western culture and values. Nor was there a conscious espousal of Western science and technology. To the African Christian convert, African culture was synonymous with superstition and backwardness, and was generally rejected as 'uncivilized'. In other words, the educated African took on the European conception of traditional African culture.

Not only has education in Africa retained its colonial systems and structures, but it has remained highly exclusive. Very few African countries have attained primary education for all, despite the fact that many have been independent for some thirty years. At secondary level, the record is even worse, with many African countries able to provide secondary education to only 4 or 5 per cent of the age-group. Most African countries can boast of less than 1 per cent of the relevant age-group attaining any form of tertiary education, compared to between 25 per cent and 75 per cent in industrialized countries. And those who do attain tertiary education are unlikely to specialize in science or technology.

It is within this context that we need to re-examine the connection between education and economic development on the one hand, and education and cultural values on the other hand. 'Development' must be defined more clearly and with greater specificity. At present Africa's development strategy appears to be based almost exclusively on *structural adjustment*, although this is clearly a far too narrow and too purely an economic conceptualization of development which does not take into consideration other extremely important factors, such as the level of human resource development or the level of economic diversification and industrialization in a country. Education also needs to be redefined so that the systems and structures of the past are not retained uncritically. Education must serve a purpose. Africa needs to decide what that purpose is. Education has a critical role to play in economic development. It has an equally important role in creating and defining the values that will make Africa politically and culturally united, coherent, and forward-looking. Only when the purpose of education has been clearly defined can Africa decide what type of education is suitable for its development.

In deciding on that purpose, the *global village* and the *global market* must be kept in mind. It is no longer possible for Africa to perpetuate its colonial and feudal heritages by continuing with the education systems and structures of the past whilst ignoring the transformation of the rest of the world into technologically advanced industrialized economies. On the other hand, as the latest entrant into the modernization process, it is possible for Africa to avoid the terrible environmental and human damage caused by that process. Africa, as the least polluted and least environmentally damaged continent, needs to use its advantages to good effect by entering the modern age without inheriting the adverse effects visible elsewhere. The damage to human and societal relations by so-called progress also needs to be avoided. The question is: can Africa reach a high level of industrialization that will give it the level of economic independence that it has so far failed to attain and at the same time can it develop a successful sociopolitical system that preserves the best of the past while incorporating the universal values that will characterize the twenty-first century?

Bronislaw Geremek

Cohesion, solidarity and exclusion

As the twentieth century draws to a close, we must with some bitterness acknowledge that the hopes raised in 1900 have been disappointed and that the extraordinary technological and scientific progress which has marked the century has not led to a better balance between human beings and nature, or to more harmony in human relations. On the threshold of the next century it is important to identify the challenges and the tensions of the present, in order to point the way for education and propose educational strategies. It is from this angle that social cohesion should be seen as one of the goals of education.

The very concept of social cohesion is somewhat ambiguous from the axiological standpoint. Modernization processes differ considerably from one place, or one time, to another. In the Euro-Atlantic zone, modernization went on between the sixteenth and the nineteenth centuries; in the rest of the world it has been, and still is, proceeding in the twentieth century. On all sides, however, a feature of the process is the increasing intervention of state power in social relations. Military service and compulsory schooling, law and order, or public health justify any efforts made by the modern state to establish – or impose – the social cohesion which should underpin it. And yet the twentieth century also brought the totalitarian experience with all its ideological and political constraints – a form of social training, which encompassed the education system, designed to impose social cohesion and cultural uniformity. This applies not only to Fascism/Nazism and Communism, but also to certain authoritarian regimes. The totalitarian temptation seems to be omnipresent in the twentieth century, barring the way to the universalization of democratic principles.

It was after the acknowledged failure of the totalitarian and authoritarian systems that the preponderance of the rights of the individual, over the rights of the state in particular, was re-established in the last quarter of the twentieth century. The philosophy of human rights has become a universally accepted standard; the direct interference of the state in the economy or in social affairs has come to be regarded as suspect and superfluous; individual freedom has been recognized as a value and as an overriding political directive. The year 1989, which was marked by the bicentenary of the French Revolution and by the non-violent revolution of the countries of Eastern Europe, was the culminating point of this individualistic trend. Overriding the climate of the end of this century, however, a strong plea for solidarity made itself heard: as early as 1980, a Polish trade union under the name of 'Solidarity' opposed the Communist system, while the French Government established a 'Ministry of Solidarity', thus bridging the contradiction between individualism and social integration. Ensuring the cohesion of our societies today means, in the first place, respecting the dignity of human beings and forming social bonds in the name of solidarity. No particular philosophy or cultural tradition can claim such an approach as its own: it emerges as one of the universal aspirations which are shaping the course for education at the turn of the century. State action in various fields is directed towards social cohesion. True, the state is the emanation of a collective identity in which it finds its justification, and all its action is aimed at supporting that identity – national or civil – by basing it on the memory of a common past or the defence of common interests. The state may also consider solidarity as both the basis and the objective of its various policies: social policy designed to help the weak or reduce material inequalities; educational policy ensuring free access to knowledge and creating opportunities for communication among people; and cultural policy supporting creative activity and participation in cultural life. The future of social integration depends also, however, on the action taken by the societies themselves, on the efforts of the non-governmental organizations, of the institutions of civil society, on the relations between capital and labour, and on human attitudes and sensibilities. This calls for lifelong education, involving not only the school, but also the home, the workplace, the trade unions or the army, which can also educate and train. On the threshold of the twenty-first century, 'Learning to Be' reminds us of the paramount importance of respect for the individual in social and political relations, in the relationship between human beings and nature, in the confrontation of civilizations and economies. When trying to understand reality – that of humanity and that of the world – we must recognize the interdependencies which create the need for different forms of solidarity. These forms of solidarity do not come from good intentions; they result from the constraints of our time. They are to be found at different levels and in communities differing in size. The phenomenon of globalization, which is clearly apparent today in all fields of human activity, allows us to see North–South relations, international co-operation problems and peace strategies from this angle.

In the educational philosophy of the late twentieth century, social cohesion and solidarity appear as indissolubly linked aspirations and purposes, in harmony with the dignity of the individual. Respect for human rights goes hand in hand with a sense of responsibility and inclines men and women to learn to live together. Yet among the principal problems which the present-day world must face is the increasing burden of exclusion.

Exclusion is not an invention of the end of the twentieth century. It runs through the history of humankind, which bears the mark of Cain. It is described in the mythologies and in the holy scriptures of the great religions; and exclusion, in the past and in the present, is analysed by cultural anthropology and social history. Over the last third of the twentieth century, however, since the events of the 1960s in Europe and the United States of America, it has become a current concept in the human sciences and in political language. This may be seen as a sign that it has become a social problem, or that the phenomenon has taken on unprecedented dimensions, or again that the need for social cohesion has made exclusion a more serious matter. At all events, exclusion has become one of the great challenges of the end of this century and it is for the education of the next century to address it.

Historians of poverty have shown that modernization processes have at different times in history led societies to regard the poor as outcasts. The phenomenon is apparent at the end of this century, first of all in the alarming character of the increasing poverty in the countries south of the Sahara, then in the unemployment that has become an enduring feature of the capitalist economies, and – last but not least – in the migration to the affluent countries of populations fleeing the poverty and lack of prospects in their countries of origin. The experience of the last decades of the century goes to show that there is no remedy for these evils except economic growth and the fundamental role of education in this connection is well known. However, it is mainly social attitudes to poverty which are a matter for concern: instead of compassion and solidarity, we observe only indifference, fear or hatred.

It is important to try to change these attitudes. Education dealing with universal history, societies and cultures all over the world, combined with a genuine education in civics, may be effective and lead to a better understanding of social otherness. To cope with the problem of unemployment we would have to rethink our present conception of education, take schooling out of its cramping context, go beyond the limits of compulsory education and, with lifelong education in view, provide for several periods of learning. Besides, the concept of an educational society should lead us to narrow the gap between skilled labour and unskilled labour, which is one of the basic causes of inequality in the world today. The transition from technologies requiring a large workforce to technologies which are labour-saving leads inevitably to emphasis on the quality of labour, and therefore to emphasis on education, but it also offers everyone an opportunity of devoting more time to learning. The problem of unemployment is not thereby solved, but it no longer has the same character of a stark segregation from a society based on work.

Immigration cannot be analysed solely in labour market terms, and the hostility shown towards immigrants cannot be reduced to the fear of competition. In most cases immigrants occupy jobs in the host country for which there are no local applicants because they are jobs requiring few skills or jobs that are looked down upon. Cultural difference is another aspect of otherness. Traditional societies had at their disposal channels of acculturation which made it possible to urbanize rural populations – apprenticeship in guilds, communal life in confraternities, and domestic service. Present-day societies should develop means of acculturation which would enable immigrants to be integrated into the existing social fabric. Realization that there is a problem here should influence present-day education systems and fit them to train adults, too, by giving them qualifications, teaching them how to learn and providing them with cultural facilities.

If education is to play a determining role in the struggle against exclusion of all those who for socio-economic or cultural reasons find themselves marginalized in present-day societies, its role seems still more pre-eminent in the integration of minorities in society. Legal norms concerning the status of minorities have already been established and await application, but the problem is more a matter of social psychology than of legislation. To change collective attitudes to otherness, we should have to envisage a joint educational effort involving the state and civil society, the media and the religious communities, parents and associations, but also – and above all – the schools. The teaching of history and of the social sciences in the broadest sense of the term – indeed, every form of civic education – should inculcate in the young a spirit of tolerance and dialogue, so that the legitimate aspiration to preserve traditions and retain a collective identity is never seen as incompatible with a spirit of fellowship and solidarity, and so that the maintenance of social cohesion never implies a closed, inward-looking attitude or fundamentalism.

Lifelong education is, of course, a safeguard against the most painful form of exclusion – exclusion due to ignorance. The changes occurring in the information and communication technologies – sometimes referred to as the computer revolution – increase the risk of this form of exclusion, with the result that education has a crucial role to play in the run-up to the twenty-first century. All educational reforms should therefore be undertaken in full awareness of the risks of exclusion and with an eye to the need to preserve social cohesion.

Aleksandra Kornhauser

Creating opportunities

For every member of the International Commission on Education for the Twenty-first Century, it was a pleasure to be associated with the efforts resulting in this report. However, what really counts now is not the satisfaction of the work accomplished, but the reflection about the implementation of ideas and recommendations.

The mirror of experience shows a world in a dramatic situation. The report's call for optimism is more than justified: because if those in leading positions show pessimism and cynical approaches, what hope has the majority? Enthusiasm for efforts to overcome the critical situations should lead our endeavours if we wish to reach the noble goals presented in the report.

Taking opportunities as they come is not sufficient. We have to create them. This contribution tries – using three examples from countries in transition – to convey some ideas and efforts for the implementation of the recommendations.

Understanding the concept of sustainable human development

This concept is, in educational practice, all too often vague. It is mostly explained as an urgent need to protect the environment by limiting the world's consumption, particularly of non-renewable resources. The developed world, in reality, is not very enthusiastic about these requirements. The developing countries oppose it in practice with the well-justified statement that they have lived at the limits of consumption since long ago and have the right to take a greater share in future. Similar is the situation in the countries in transition where the collapse of the economy has caused a most severe social crisis and the problems of future development are overshadowed with the struggle for daily survival. The model of limits does not create enthusiasm.

Another approach to sustainable human development is needed. 'Development' must be the optimistic promise for a better life for all people. 'Human' should mean another value system giving more weight to non-material richness and solidarity, and introducing more responsibility of mankind towards the environment. 'Sustainable' should mean primarily 'better' which will allow a higher living level to be reached with lower consumption. Sustainable human development should therefore be understood as progress through increasing quality in every human activity.

For achieving higher quality, we need better knowledge. We need achievements of science and technology, of social sciences and humanities. This knowledge needs to be integrated into national and local expertise. To recognize quality in human terms, we also need an improved value system. Knowledge interwoven with values creates wisdom.

The report pays major attention to the values needed for the twenty-first century. They are rooted in local, national and global cultures. We have to learn to talk to each other again: people in science and people in culture. The present gap is neither natural nor historical. This alienation is mainly the characteristic of the twentieth century caused to a large extent through educational neglect for human integrity.

How can we make these ideas of sustainable human development, as a movement towards quality, operational? An example comes from involvement in UNESCO and UNDP activities aimed at catalysing the design and implementation of national sustainable human development programmes.

In several countries in transition in Central and Eastern Europe, the following strategy has been proposed and already partially implemented. A National Board at the level of Presidency or Parliament has been formed (or proposed) consisting of leading personalities from politics, the economy, science and culture. The Board is responsible for the general policy, launching of initiatives and development of strategies for their implementation. It motivates for action and evaluates trends. The Board's implementation body is the Executive Co-ordination Committee. Its members are representatives of all major sectors: governmental institutions, production, commerce, science, education, culture, non-governmental organizations and mass media. The Executive Co-ordination Committee is responsible for taking initiatives and making strategies operational, mobilizing sectors for their contribution, integrating efforts, evaluating specific results and promoting best practice. Each sector creates is own working groups attached to selected projects.

Where is education in this initiative? Everywhere! The universities and the academies of science (both educational institutions integrating knowledge and values) play a major role in the National Board and in the Executive Co-ordination Committee. The governmental institutions cannot master new tasks without new knowledge; consequently a programme for courses bringing ideas and examples of good practice needs to be developed and offered to this sector. Production needs to introduce new, clean(er) processes and products. Bearing in mind the limits in capital investment, knowledge-intensive processes are of high priority. The development and transfer of knowledge occurs by research going hand-in-hand with education. Commerce needs knowledge of the world market and entrepreneurial skills; both are lacking in the countries of transition.

It is again education (understood in a wide scope) which can provide such skills and integrate sociocultural values. Last but not least, education of journalists, readers and television-viewers is needed for the motivation of the general public. Environmental awareness is more often oriented towards protesting than towards active involvement for the prevention of degradation and improvement of the environment in work and everyday life.

Education is the cement for building sustainable human development. Comprehensive environmental education strategies and programmes need to be developed to cover both formal and informal education, with a lifelong perspective, and implemented by governmental institutions, the production sector, commerce and local communities.

Some might consider this approach too complex, yet it appears to be working in several countries in transition. The tradition of centrally planned economies often favours initial top-down approaches. The need for creating numerous opportunities soon brings in bottom-up initiatives.

As soon as we start to implement the concept of sustainable human development, the new concept of education – presented in the report of the Commission – is essential. Experience shows that the integration of knowledge and values for a more humanistic society, development of high responsibility towards the local, national and global environment, and strengthening the readiness to share an enthusiasm for living together, need special consideration and support. Co-operation of leading personalities from the world of politics, production, science and culture in the relevant mass-media programmes proved to be highly catalytic.

To tolerate – or respect?

Another much discussed concept, particularly in the countries in transition, is tolerance. In the years to come this might not be sufficient and we will have to change tolerant coexistence into living together in active co-operation. The latter implies joint efforts for the protection of diversity. We will have to replace 'I am tolerant . . . ' with 'I respect . . . '.

Numerous examples of intolerance followed the collapse of political systems based on pressure. This collapse raised the hopes of many nations to reach freedom, including the freedom of choice on their future integration into larger alliances. In several countries, this crossroad situation has been misused for introducing intolerance and hate, bringing the danger of war, or its reality. What is so sad is that people who lived for half a century or more peacefully together, either in the same country or as neighbours, now deeply hate each other. Why have they accepted the 'explanation' that the other nation, the other religion, or the other culture, has through centuries limited, or even threatened, their lives?

Education has to be blamed. If it were not manipulated for political goals of questionable values, if it were more objective in the evaluation of the past, and if it integrated individual and local values with global ones, then people would not be such easy victims of propaganda.

For a better mutual understanding, the idea of writing history textbooks by joint teams of historians from neighbouring countries has been proposed, but even many historians laughed. And yet, we must go ahead with this. We need such 'crazy' ideas in the situation where the established approaches obviously do not work. What hope is there for the future if we are not given a more accurate account of the past? If the presentation of the events were more accurate and their explanation less nationalistic or hegemonistic, and more in the light of individual and global human values, it would be more difficult to mislead public opinion.

At least two additional efforts are needed in education to avoid manipulation of people's beliefs: strengthening the use of the scientific method which is based on objective observation and draws conclusions from data difficult to manipulate; and stressing global cultural values which go beyond tolerance and foster love for cultural diversity. We have rich programmes for the protection of biodiversity. Entering the twenty-first century, protection of cultural diversity must become an essential part of all educational programmes for lifelong education.

Linking education with the world of work

This is another urgent task. However, bringing work situations into education is often regarded as a slippery slope in the efforts for improving the quality of education, particularly at universities in the countries of transition. The fact that employment patterns rapidly change is used to avoid any direct connections with future employers and to declare basic knowledge as sufficient in the preparation for a changing world.

The achievements of many internationally highly recognized universities deny such an approach. Co-operation with industry and agriculture has also proven to increase the quality of tertiary education in the countries in transition and in developing countries, particularly if supported by national authorities.

Several university–industry projects show that direct involvement of university students and teachers brings a wealth of advantages, for instance learning to work in a group; facing real problems which reach from the idea to the market; recognizing that the newest information is hardly good enough for economic competition at the global level, and that international information systems have to be used; learning to acquire and organize information from different sources; looking for patterns of knowledge which could support the formation of hypotheses; designing interactions between information processing and experimental work; co-operating in pilot production; looking for market opportunities and learning about market development; recognizing opportunities for the transfer of knowledge and technologies, and listing technologies which should not be transferred; including environmental standards in technological and economic considerations; developing entrepreneurial skills; and recognizing self-employment opportunities, that is, replacing 'waiting for jobs' by 'creating jobs', etc.

Values are an integral part of any university–industry or university–agriculture project, particularly if technological and socio-economic parameters for sustainable human development are taken into account. Development of clean(er) processes and products, pollution prevention and waste management are the fields where numerous opportunities can be created.

Solving real problems by research-educational methods in tertiary education, and inquiry approaches at pre-university levels, benefits particularly the countries in transition and developing countries where urgent actions are needed for the improvement of the transfer of knowledge and technology, both nationally and internationally.

Follow-up

The report is based on experiences and hopes worldwide. What will its future be? Will it be a cornerstone in the development of education? Will it be a basis for a new beginning, bringing greater awareness of the need for learning to know, to do, to be, to live together? Or will it be just another event, sparkling maybe, but not changing much? The answer depends primarily on the actions of national authorities.

In their activities, international support will be crucial. The main danger is that new ideas will be extinguished by the pressures of existing practices, before they are strong enough to survive in often harsh conditions. An international programme for the recognition and dissemination of good practices, independent from the present educational routine, might be a nursery for the survival and further development of the main features stressed by the report.

Michael Manley

Education, empowerment and social healing

I am availing myself of the opportunity provided to each member of the Commission to add a brief personal comment. I do so not to add anything new – the Report is comprehensive – but by way of emphasis.

I raise five points:

First, the educational process in the future, to the extent that we can anticipate coming events by studying present experience, will have to shoulder a contradictory burden.

On the one hand an education system is the guardian of standards: standards of academic excellence, scientific truth and technological relevance. As such the system tends to be exclusionary, concentrating energy on those students who demonstrate abilities and aptitudes that are consistent with norms of excellence. The rest will tend to be relegated to a lesser process of training for life as part of a process of exclusion from the best that society can offer.

On the other hand we live in a world which is being increasingly torn apart by intractable divisions. There is the United States in danger of entrenching a permanent dichotomy between a largely black underclass and the rest of the society, largely white.

European social fabric is beginning to fray under the strains which are surfacing between native majorities and migrant worker minorities. Ethnic tensions have torn apart Bosnia and Sri Lanka, while their tribal equivalents create similar instabilities in Nigeria, Angola or Rwanda. In short, the world is crying out for inclusionary, healing, uniting influences. These cannot begin with political endeavour with much prospect of success. Often politics is driven by these very tensions. The same is true of parents who are, of necessity, often the seat of the problem. It is the education system and, in particular, the school that provides the best, perhaps the only hope of starting the healing, inclusionary social process.

The school of today and tomorrow must plant the seeds of caring so that underclasses do not become the victims of an ideology of exclusion; must nurture the concept of an over-arching humanity in which the brilliant, the average and even the disturbed, the Muslim and the Christian, the Hausa and the Ibo, the Irish Catholic and the Protestant, all occupy an equal place in a process of permanent social inclusion.

In this sense the school, which must be the guardian of standards, must be the catalyst for human values which are as universal as the scientific truths which must be protected. Indeed, if we do not achieve a widely effective breakthrough in multicultural education, we may find that increased success in the imparting of skills can have an ultimately negative impact. It is not fanciful to anticipate a situation in which highly educated people are trained to fight each other with increasingly deadly effect. For example, more cost-effectively achieved ethnic cleansing could be the price of failure to address both sides of the educational challenge.

Secondly, the role which education must play in the process of empowerment can be seen in both an obvious and a more profound way. Clearly, a young person will be empowered to the extent that education imparts marketable skills. At the same time, empowerment involves social skills beginning with an understanding of how societies work; what are the systems of power and the levers to which they respond; how to influence decision-making and the extent to which this is affected by social dynamics. The examples can be multiplied almost indefinitely. If all of this is not facilitated by the educational process, the underclass in prosperous societies will remain permanently frozen in powerlessness; developing countries will never develop the means to advancing because they will be unable to take profitable advantage of the opportunities in the global marketplace. Furthermore, all societies, at whatever stage of development, will be increasingly subject to wrenching social tensions as the gaps between rich and poor become ever more deeply entrenched, ever more intractable.

A tragic and potentially disastrous situation now exists in the world. The corrective programmes imposed by the International Monetary Fund and the structural adjustment programmes by the International Development Bank have massively invaded and compressed the capacity of developing countries to finance the delivery of education in terms of quantitative and qualitative improvement. Recent moves to ameliorate this process are coming far too little and too late. Thus, far from being the moving force behind individual and collective empowerment, education is in retreat in many parts of the world.

It is the ultimate irony that UNESCO calls for the development of new paradigms for the twenty-first century while the multilateral financial institutions, themselves the creatures of Bretton Woods and the United Nations system, conspire to ensure that the pervasive paradigm in recent years can be summed up as 'compression and retreat'. We must press for a dramatic reversal as the pre-condition of a credible set of recommendations.

The paradoxes which are implicit in the first two points lead us to the third question of emphasis. To be effective, an education system must operate within the context of a social compact, understood and supported by all. Governments have a huge responsibility to act as the brokers of this compact, a process which should begin within the political system itself. Unity among political leaders is the indispensable prerequisite for unity in society are large about the education system. Only by these means can we ensure that it serves the need for standards and the imperative of a broad national consensus directed towards social justice.

Fourthly, the first three points have an implication for the work which should follow the publication of the report. How will we capture the attention of governments and societies so that these years of work have an impact globally and within each society?

The report is being presented at a time when the state itself is in substantial retreat in many countries. In addition to pressures exerted by the multilateral financial institutions, governments have become the targets of minimalist ideology or the victims of shrinking resources. For these reasons alone it is possible to predict a diminishing role for the state in education systems in much of the world. Something will have to take up the slack if individual societies are to hope to improve or maintain their position in the global market-place and solve the problems posed by increasingly bitter social division. The provision of adequate resources is not the least of the issues which must be addressed by each society.

Accordingly, UNESCO needs to organize teams of persons who take the report, its analyses, its conclusions and its recommendations to every corner of the globe. The report should become the basis for governmental discussion; parliamentary debate; examination by research departments of political parties; within the ranks of educators and the wider body of academe; among religious leaders and last, but by no means least, in schools themselves, perhaps in simplified form.

My final comment is about the members of the teaching profession and the role which they must continue to play as individuals. Economic reality requires and improving technology facilitates the delivery of more and more of the substance of education by impersonal means such as video and audio tapes or even more indirectly, as in the case of distance learning. These technical advances are entirely desirable if education is to be provided in the most cost-effective way to the greatest number of people around the globe. However, there is an inherent danger against which we must guard.

Throughout history teachers have played a role more profound and subtle than that of instruction. Bringing to their vocation a passion for ideas and values together with a love of children and an understanding of the process by which you plant the seeds of motivation, the profession has inspired millions of people to become everything from community activists to loving parents; from distinguished professionals to valued leaders in every aspect of a society's life. It is imperative that we never lose sight of the teacher in this personal, interfacing sense as the critical instrument in the educational process.

aran Singh

Education for the global society

As we move through the last decade of this extraordinary century, which has witnessed unparalleled destruction and unimagined progress, the cruellest mass killings in human history and the most amazing breakthroughs in human welfare, the advent of weapons of unprecedented lethality and creative probings into outer space, we find ourselves at a crucial point in the long and tortuous history of the human race on Planet Earth. It is now quite clear that humanity is in the throes of a transition to a global society. We live in a shrinking world in which the malign heritage of conflict and competition will have to make way for a new culture of convergence and co-operation, and the alarming gap between the developed and the developing world will have to be bridged if the rich promise of the next millennium is not to evaporate in the conflict and chaos that is already overtaking many parts of the world. This is the basic challenge to education in the twenty-first century.

It is not that we lack the intellectual or economic resources to tackle the problems. Scientific breakthroughs and technological ingenuity have given us the capacity to overcome all those challenges, but what is missing is the wisdom and compassion to apply them creatively. Knowledge is expanding but wisdom languishes. The yawning chasm will need to be bridged before the end of the century if we are ever to reverse the present trend towards disaster and it is here that education in the broadest sense of the term assumes such vital importance. National education systems are almost invariably postulated on beliefs that flow from pre-nuclear and pre-global perceptions, and are therefore unable to provide the new paradigm of thought that human welfare and survival now requires. Outmoded orthodoxies and obsolescent orientations continue to deprive the younger generations of an adequate awareness of the essential unity of the world into which they have been born. Indeed, by fostering negative attitudes towards other groups or nations, they hinder the growth of globalism.

The astounding communications technology which today encircles the globe seldom uses its tremendous potential to spread global values and foster a more caring, compassionate consciousness. On the contrary, the media are full of violence and horror, cruelty and carnage, unbridled consumerism and un-abashed promiscuity, a situation which not only distorts the awareness of the young but dulls our sensitivity to the problems of human suffering and pain. What is urgently needed, therefore, is a creative revolution in our education and communications policies. We need to develop carefully structured programmes on a global scale based unequivocally on the premise that human survival involves the growth of a creative and compassionate global consciousness. The spiritual dimension will have to be given central importance in our new educational thinking.

We must have the courage to think globally, to break away from traditional paradigms and plunge boldly into the unknown. We must so mobilize our inner and outer resources that we begin consciously to build a new world based on mutually assured welfare rather than mutually assured destruction. As global citizens committed to human survival and welfare, we must use the latest array of innovative and interactive pedagogic methodologies to structure a worldwide programme of education – for children and adults alike – that would open their eyes to the reality of the dawning global age and their hearts to the cry of the oppressed and the suffering. And there is no time to be lost for, along with the emergence of the global society, the sinister forces of fundamentalism and fanaticism, of exploitation and intimidation are also active.

Let us, then, with utmost speed, pioneer and propagate a holistic educational philosophy for the twenty-first century based upon the following premises:

• that the planet we inhabit and of which we are all citizens – Planet Earth – is a single, living, pulsating entity; that the human race in the final analysis is an interlocking, extended family – *Vasudhaiva Kuktumbakam* as the Veda has it; and that differences of race and religion, nationality and ideology, sex and sexual preference, economic and social status – though significant in themselves – must be viewed in the broader context of global unity;

  • that the ecology of Planet Earth has to be preserved from mindless destruction and ruthless exploitation, and enriched for the welfare of generations yet unborn; and that there should be a more equitable consumption pattern based on limits to growth, not unbridled consumerism;

• that hatred and bigotry, fundamentalism and fanaticism, and greed and jealousy, whether among individuals, groups or nations, are corrosive emotions which must be overcome as we move into the next century; and that love and compassion, caring and charity, and friendship and co-operation are the elements that have to be encouraged as we transit into our new global awareness;

• that the world's great religions must no longer war against each other for supremacy but co-operate for the welfare of the human race, and that through a continuing and creative interfaith dialogue, the golden thread of spiritual aspiration that binds them together must be strengthened instead of the dogma and exclusivism that divides them;

• that a massive and concerted drive is needed to eradicate the scourge of illiteracy worldwide by the year 2010, with special emphasis on promoting female literacy, particularly in the developing countries;

• that holistic education must acknowledge the multiple dimensions of the human personality – physical, intellectual, aesthetic, emotional and spiritual – thus moving towards the perennial dream of an integrated individual living on a harmonious planet.

Rodolfo Stavenhagen

Education for a multicultural world

The challenges to education are great in a world which is increasingly multicultural. As the process of globalization becomes a more immediate reality for the planet's population, so also comes the realization that 'my neighbour may no longer be like me'. For many people, this may come as a shock because it challenges traditional stable visions of neighbourhood, community and nation; it questions long-established ways of relating to one's fellow human beings and it turns ethnic diversity into the stuff of everyday life.

On the one hand, economic globalization brings the producers and the consumers of different continents and regions into functional relationship with each other. Today's global corporations are organized in such a fashion that a single product may contain parts made in dozens of factories in as many different countries. The managers and employees of these giant firms often spend more time shuttling between countries than they do at home with family and friends, rather like the soldiers of fortune of olden times. It would be disingenuous to believe that the current restructuring of the world's economic relations has no effect on the personal attitudes and values of everybody involved – from the unskilled worker in an assembly line in a poor nation to the consumer of a product which says on a tag that it was 'Made in . . .' a faraway country.

On the other hand, the rapid expansion of communications networks, especially the audiovisual media, has brought what used to be considered unrelated events in faraway places into the intimate space of millions of homes from metropolitan neighbourhoods to urban slums to remote villages. The exotic is no longer distant and the distant becomes ever more familiar. To the extent that the cultural industries promote the lifestyles of the Western, urban-industrial, middle-class sectors by way of satellite dishes and video stores, the multicultural world draws closer together, and the cultural values of those lifestyles become, as it were, international standards against which local populations (particularly the young) measure their achievements and aspirations.

The counterpoint to globalization is reflected in the massive movements of populations across international borders. Whereas in earlier times colonial settlers spread out from Europe into the so-called undeveloped areas, in recent decades millions upon millions of migrant workers and their families have flocked into the industrial heartlands of Europe and North America from all over the former colonies and the economic periphery, in search of better livelihoods and, frequently, to escape oppressive political and social conditions as well. Even as the former industrial economies are in fact 'de-industrializing' and exporting many of their manufacturing operations abroad, massive migrations of culturally diverse peoples from Third World countries impose increasing strains on traditional labour markets and the social fabric of the host countries.

Most modern nation-states are organized on the assumption that they are, or should be, culturally homogeneous. That is the essence of modern 'nationhood', upon which contemporary statehood and citizenship are founded. No matter that in most cases the facts differ from the model; nowadays, mono-ethnic states are the exception rather than the rule. But the idea of the mono-ethnic, culturally homogeneous nation has been used more often than not to disguise the fact that such states are more adequately described as ethnocratic, that is, where a single majority or dominant ethnic group manages to impose its own vision of 'nationhood' upon the rest of society. In such circumstances, ethnic groups that do not conform to the dominant model are treated as 'minorities', not only numerically, but mainly in sociological and political terms. This contradiction leads not infrequently to social tensions and conflicts that have escalated in recent years in a number of countries. Indeed, many of the current ethnic conflicts in the world can be traced to the problems inherent in the way the modern nation-state manages ethnic diversity within its borders.

Those problems are directly reflected in the social, cultural and educational policies adopted by states with regard to the various peoples, nations and ethnic groups that live within their borders. One of the most important roles assigned to formal schooling in many countries has been to fashion good, law-abiding citizens who will share a single national identity and who will be loyal to the nation-state. Whilst this no doubt served a noble purpose, and may even have been necessary in certain historical circumstances, it also led in many instances to the marginalization and even the destruction of numerous ethnically distinct peoples whose cultures, religions, languages, beliefs or ways of life did not conform to the so-called national ideal.

Religious, linguistic and national minorities, as well as indigenous and tribal peoples were often subordinated, sometimes forcefully and against their will, to the interests of the state and the dominant society. While many people thus acquired a new identity and national consciousness (particularly emigrants to new shores), others had to discard their own cultures, languages, religions and traditions, and adapt to the alien norms and customs that were consolidated and reproduced through national institutions, including the education and legal systems.

In many countries there are tensions between the purposes and requirements of a 'national' system of education, and the values, interests and aspirations of culturally distinct peoples. At the same time, in an increasingly interdependent world, conflicting tendencies pull in different directions: on the one hand, the trend toward national homogenization and world uniformization; on the other, the search for roots, community and distinctiveness, which for some can only be found by strengthening local and regional identities, and keeping a healthy distance from the 'others', who are sometimes perceived as threatening.

Such a complex situation represents a challenge to the education system and to state-sponsored cultural policies, as well as to the functioning of market mechanisms in (among others) the fields of communications and entertainment, those vast networks in which global cultural industries call the shots. In recent years, traditional educational policies based on the premise of a single national culture have come under increasing critical scrutiny. More and more states not only tolerate expressions of cultural diversity but now recognize that instead of being an obstacle to be overcome, multicultural and pluri-ethnic populations are the true mainstays of democratic social integration. Education in the twenty-first century must come to grips with that challenge, and education systems (in the widest possible sense) must be flexible and imaginative enough to be able to strike a creative balance between the two structural tendencies mentioned above.

A truly multicultural education will be one that can address simultaneously the requirements of global and national integration, and the specific needs of particular culturally distinct communities, both in rural and urban settings. It will lead to an awareness of diversity and to respect for others, whether those others are my next-door neighbours, workers in the field, or my fellow human beings in a faraway country. To achieve such a truly pluralistic education it will be necessary to rethink the objectives of what it means to educate and be educated; to remodel the contents and the curricula of formal schooling institutions; to develop new teaching skills and educational methods; and to stimulate the emergence of new generations of teachers/learners. A truly pluralistic education is based on a philosophy of humanistic pluralism. This is an ethos that prizes the social realities of cultural pluralism. The values of humanistic and cultural pluralism that are necessary to inspire such educational transformation are sometimes lacking; they must be generated in the educational process itself and will in turn be strengthened by it.

Many observers, however, have serious doubts about cultural pluralism and its expression in multicultural education. While paying lip service to cultural diversity (which can hardly be denied in today's world), they nevertheless question the wisdom of furthering diversity through education. They fear that this may lead to the crystallization of separate identities, the strengthening of ethnocentrism, the proliferation of ethnic animosities and, finally, to the disintegration of existing nation-states. There are certainly many current examples of exaggerated ethnic nationalisms leading to political separatism and societal breakdown, not to mention genocidal massacres and hate-filled ethnic cleansings. Yet ethnic diversity cannot be wished away and it is unrealistic to blame multiculturalist policies for the numerous conflicts that in many instances arise precisely because ethnic diversity goes unrecognized or is suppressed.

The criticism of multiculturalism (and the term means different things in different contexts) may come from ethnic nationalists who feel that the 'essence' of their nation is being undermined by foreign elements (immigrants, culturally differentiated minorities). But it may also come from concerned liberals who want to build the 'civic' nation in which every single individual has the same worth as any other, regardless of race, language, nationality, religion or culture. They feel that by emphasizing cultural or ethnic distinctions, borders and walls are erected between otherwise equal – if not always identical – human beings. It is only through education tending toward a truly civic culture to be shared by all that differences will cease to beget inequalities and distinctiveness will no longer generate enmity. In such a world view, ethnic identities will belong to the purely private domain (like religion in the modern secular state), and should be of no concern to public policies.

While that is surely a worthy vision, we see all around us that ethnic groups do mobilize around cultural symbols and beliefs, and that education systems are in fact at stake in today's 'cultural wars'. Whether such struggles are deeply embedded in the collective psyche (as some would hold) or are simply manipulated by opportunistic 'ethnic entrepreneurs' (as others might argue), it is not by relegating them to the backroom that democratic, humanistic values can be fostered. Surely the world in the twenty-first century is mature enough to know how to foster a democratic civic culture, based on individual human rights, and to encourage at the same time mutual respect for the culture of others, based on the recognition of the collective human rights of all peoples around the world, great or small, each as deserving as every other.

This is the challenge that must be met by education in the twenty-first century.

Myong Won Suhr

Opening our minds for a better life for all

Everyone is born egocentric. But from early childhood, each human being gradually realizes that he or she has to live together with others in order to survive. The constraints arising from the egocentric nature of human beings give rise to many difficulties, conflicts, frustrations and even hatred against others, including family members, but the fact remains: everyone has to learn to live with others. Everyday observation of the animal world gives ample illustration of that truth.

The following are some thoughts on why it is so important for education systems all over the world to open our minds and so help us to live in harmony with our fellow human beings and also with nature.

Living together in harmony must be the ultimate goal of education in the twenty-first century

Unfortunately, that reality does not inform our daily life, whether at home or in school, whether at community or national level. At international level, the situation is even more difficult. Education systems tend to be nationalistic; the danger arises when they are aggressively so, to the detriment of peaceful worldwide coexistence. One of the greatest barriers to world peace is the ethnocentrism that exists everywhere in the world.

Because of the rapid advances made in science and technology, we have become a worldwide community, one 'global village'. However, most people do not realize this fact, while those who do often prefer to devote themselves to the details of their day-to-day life and notably to the attainment or preservation of personal prestige.

In the Republic of Korea, the university entrance examination constitutes the most harmful barrier to 'wholesome education'. The examination has adverse effects on all levels of education, as well as on the cause of world peace. The Ministry of Education has tried every kind of remedial measure to minimize the negative effects of the examination, so far in vain. Any new system has immediately provoked fresh counter-tactics.

Education reform for change

In terms of the number of students engaged in higher education per 100,000 inhabitants, the Republic of Korea comes third, immediately after Canada and the United States of America. Qualitatively, however, there are many weaknesses and failures in producing world citizens who will live peacefully alongside others in the twenty-first century. Specifically, the ethical or moral dimension of education today in the Republic of Korea is much poorer than in ancient Korean education. While students now have more factual knowledge, their moral conduct is unacceptable to their elders. However, while the public is sharply critical of students' behaviour, it is at the same time strongly in favour of preparing young people for the entrance examination. In other words, the public does not see the contradictions inherent in today's higher education system.

Aware of the problem, the country's universities have recently been changing their curricula drastically in order to reconstruct the contents of education. Emphasis is now less on education oriented toward economic growth (that is to say, science and technology) and more on education oriented toward human or social development, drawing on age-old human values. Nowadays, we Koreans are beginning to realize that economic-growth-oriented policies in all fields have resulted in our paying a heavy moral price for having neglected the traditional values.

The open society and attendant fears

We foresee an open society in the near future. But many people in the Republic of Korea are not yet fully ready to accept the idea of an open society and some are apprehensive about an uncertain society. For many centuries, Koreans were at the mercy of the powerful nations surrounding them and the old law of the survival of the fittest might still apply. Thus, the General Agreement on Tariffs and Trade (GATT) was not popular, especially among farmers. Enlightened people have some reservations about the globalization of the intellectual and cultural sphere, fearing that education and cultural affairs will be prey to 'neo-cultural imperialism' on the part of the world's major economic powers. Likewise, the general public is rather reluctant to accept the World Trade Organization, the successor to the GATT, because of the probable pre-eminence in it of the United States, the European Union and Japan.

On the threshold of the twenty-first century, we see that there is an urgent need everywhere in the world for the public to receive constructive information and education to dispel apprehension about the coming century, the result to a large extent of the past closed policies of each nation, including its education. The Republic of Korea is no exception. It may even be stronger because of past sufferings at the hands of foreign powers.

A common destiny in the global village

For some years, we have been stressing the importance of East–West understanding for world peace. But frankly speaking, people in the Western world know less about those in the Eastern world than the reverse. At the same time, people in the Eastern world know almost nothing about their close neighbours, preferring, in nearly all cases, to learn from the technologically advanced West in order to emerge from the underdeveloped state.

From now on, however, East–West understanding may well become an important factor for worldwide cultural, as well as economic well-being. Through East–West understanding and co-operative organizations, the Eastern nations can contribute both to world peace and to common prosperity among near neighbours.

We have entered an age in which there are, so to speak, no longer any national boundaries. The world's peoples have to live together, whether they wish to do so or not. We all have to appreciate that fact and educate our future world citizens accordingly. It is therefore incumbent upon governmental and non-governmental bodies to stress the importance of open policies and open education.

Eastern misapprehension of Western culture

Among Eastern nations, there has been until quite recently a widely held view that Western culture is materialistic whereas Eastern culture is ethical or spiritual, and is in general superior to the Western model, and that the Eastern nations should therefore confine themselves to learning Western science and technology, and shun the other aspects of occidental culture. That opinion was not peculiar to the Republic of Korea: it can easily be found also in Chinese and Japanese books.

However, that general assumption is wrong. Unless we comprehend

Western logic, critical thinking, curiosity about the unknown, experimental practices for truth-finding and objective approaches to issues, we cannot appreciate Western culture. In spite of a certain prejudice in the East against Western culture, it is not difficult to find abundant examples of Westerners' love for truth (including scientific truth), ethics and logic, without material reward for their endeavours.

Hostility towards Western attitudes

In science and technology, which have changed the world so much and been so rapidly developed in the West, Western scientists have tended to treat nature as something to be conquered by human intelligence and skills. And that approach did indeed lead to great discoveries and inventions, and hence to advanced civilizations. However, all those positive contributions to human well-being have also brought in their train major problems. The damage to nature through pollution of the air, water and soil is already serious and will become more so. The protection and preservation of our environment has also become a vast problem for us, our children and our grandchildren.

In the East our ancestors chose not – or dared not – to control nature, considering it essential to live in peace and harmony with it. Since they regarded human beings as part of nature, there was nothing to fight, control or conquer. Those attitudes prevailed for many centuries and to some extent retarded our material progress because of the very slow rate of change in nature, whereas in the West, people did not hesitate to control nature and so achieved more rapid changes. In the twenty-first century, the protection and preservation of the environment will be fundamental to all human and animal welfare. Thus, all peoples of the world will be called upon to take an active part in that vital endeavour.

Finally, despite the egocentricity I mentioned earlier that characterizes all human beings at the very beginning of their lives, I have unshakable confidence in the future of humanity. Our common treasure of wisdom and experience can and undoubtedly will enable us to find ways to increase our spiritual and material well-being and to live together in harmony.

Zhou Nanzhao

Interactions of education and culture for economic and human development: an Asian perspective

Both education and culture can be defined in various ways. In relation to culture, education might be referred to as a process of instilling in young people the traditionally inherited and contemporarily renewed values and beliefs which lie at the heart of cultures. Education is an agent of cultural transmission while culture provides a context of educational institutions and constitutes an essential part of education contents. Education has been placed 'at the core of the value order, and values as the sustaining force in education'.[1] In serving the development needs of the people, both education and culture become a means to and an end of development.

The exploration into the interrelationship of education and culture will be meaningful only when it relates to development, which is a multidimensional, world-scale, evolutionary and mobilizing process, and of which the human being is the origin, agent and ultimate purpose.[2] From an Asian perspective, this text is intended to interpret the interrelations of education with culture in developmental contexts. It illustrates both positive and negative effects of cultural traditions on education and economic development, pointing to the need for both preservation and renewal of cultural traditions. In the light of the increasing globalization in all spheres, it briefly discusses a desirable core of shared universal values to be cultivated by education and mutual learning of Eastern and Western cultures. Finally it emphasizes people-centred development as the ultimate goal of both education and culture in the twenty-first century. In view of the great diversity within Asian cultures,

1. World Commission on Culture and Development, *Our Creative Diversity: Report of the World Commission on Culture and Development,* p. 7, Paris, UNESCO, 1995.

2. *The Cultural Dimension of Development: Towards a Practical Approach,* pp. 122–3, Paris, UNESCO, 1995.

reference is confined mainly to the Confucian tradition, which reflects only part of Asian cultures despite its pervasive impacts in the region. Without running the risk of over-simplification, no attempt is made to generalize any of the arguments.

Traits of Asian cultures benefiting educational and economic development

Many studies have been done to explore relations between education, culture and development. Among the most recent are those mentioned in notes 1, 5 and 6 of this article. Citing Asian examples, the following illustrates traits of cultural values which have been conducive to educational and economic development.

• *Deep-rooted appreciation of the value of education.* The Asian stress on learning was classic. To Confucius, man is perfectible and can be led in the right path through education, especially through his own effort at self-cultivation, within himself, but also through the emulation of models outside himself.[3] He emphasized the power of education to improve society and to teach citizenship. The Confucian political ideal was 'to rule the state by moral virtues', which had to be developed by education. He even equated the roles of education to those of sufficient food provision and a powerful army for national defence. Responding to the question 'What is to be done next after population growth?', he said, 'To make the populace wealthy', and to the consequent question, 'What next?', he simply answered, 'To educate them'.[4] For centuries education has formed a foundation for the entire political, social, economic and cultural life of Asian peoples. Working Asian mothers, bending low in the rice fields, had always enshrined hope in their hearts to preserve their children, by education, from the poverty that had afflicted them. The well-known Japanese image of the 'education mother', who regarded education of the children as her prime duty; the Chinese mother who travelled a long way to take evening classes for years on behalf of her disabled son and then taught the boy with her notes taken in the class; the Korean mothers who would sell their cows to pay for their children to complete schooling; the great wisdom in the sayings of India's great poet Tagore and its great politician Gandhi about the value of education – all these illustrate the value attached to education in Asia.

• *The consequently high expectation of the young.* An ancient Chinese story tells why and how the mother of Mencius, the great Confucian scholar, moved her home three times in order that her son had good teachers, good neighbours, and good peers for a good education. Findings of many studies indicate that high expectation of parents and teachers has a positive correlation to high curriculum standards, more student hours on learning

3. John King Fairbank, *The US and China*, 3rd edition, Harvard University Press, 1971.

4. Confucius, *The Four Books*, Changsha, Hunan Press, 1992.

tasks, strict training drills in intellectual skills, more parent-children interaction at home, close teacher–pupil relations at school and consequently to higher learning achievement especially in such intellectually demanding courses as mathematics. Since there is no substantial difference in the intelligence quotient of most children and no children are ineducable, this cultural factor does to some extent account for the relatively high scholastic achievements of many Asian students.

• *Emphasis on the group rather than the individual.* By tradition, collectivism has long overwhelmed individualism in Asian cultures. Confucianism emphasized the development of the individual as a social being, as an element of the family and of the society at large. Learning the rules of social relationships was considered an essential way to become a mature and responsible member of society. Over the centuries, Chinese intellectuals upheld the moral ideals of 'bearing the worries of the world *before* anyone else and enjoying the pleasures of life *after* all others'. The group-oriented attitude, as displayed in the classic 'team spirit' of the Japanese, has been most conducive to both economic productivity and social cohesion. This explains partly why many Asians tend to dislike the concept of competition among individuals yet display a strong collective force of competitiveness.

• *Stress on the spiritual rather than the material dimension of development.* 'Spiritual' is meant here in a cultural, moral and ethical sense. Traditional Chinese culture, based on Confucianism and Taoism, was essentially ethics-based, stressing moral cultivation of the personality. Whether the Confucian ethical principles, or the Tao's self-cultivation or the Idealist School's 'keep rationality and eliminate worldly desires', all were largely philosophies of moral humanism, by which man was examined from the point of view of ethical political relations, and the realization of an individual's value depended on his interaction with the collective (the family and the state). It is widely recognized in the region that education cannot be value-free and the perception of a future is implicitly a view of the moral order of the future.[5] Up to the very present, in efforts to modernize, the building of both 'spiritual' and 'material' civilizations is made the twin goal of national development in many Asian countries, and education is expected as an active agent to contribute to both processes. The renewed stress on moral-values education is most recently displayed in the Kuala Lumpur Declaration by the fourth Asian–Pacific Conference of Ministers of Education and Those Responsible for Economic Planning in 1993.

• *Meritocracy based on performance in state examinations rather than on inherited power and wealth.* Asia had the world's longest tradition of civil examination, by which state officers and civil servants were screened and selected. In theory the ultimate goal of Confucian education was the

5. Raja Roy Singh, *Education for the Twenty-first Century: Asia–Pacific Perspectives,* p. 80, Bangkok, UNESCO/PROAP, 1991.

cultivation of the person in the ethical sense; in practice, it was concerned more with the preparation and selection of the ruling élite than with true education aimed at the full development of individual personality. This examination-performance-based meritocracy used to be a motivating force for learning and career achievement irrespective of class; however the over-emphasis on Confucian classics-focused examination had suppressed the creativity of many brilliant young minds and turned out to be a 'tail wagging the dog' of the education system in substantial ways.

•   *Legitimization of authority.* To Confucius, education was a forceful instrument of the ruling élite to govern the state. Through education the ruler should 'learn to care for the people' while the ruled 'learn to be obedient'. The care from the top and the obedience from the subordinate below were supposed to lead to a stable social order. The authority of the parent at home and that of the teacher at school accounted in one way for the high discipline of most Asian students. Extended to the political and economic sphere, the high authority of the state was beneficial to facilitating a co-operative, harmonious business–government relationship and to effecting government policy implementation. Especially when the government authority develops policy environments favourable for free enterprise and fair competition, the respect of the authority will be most conducive to healthy economic growth. An authoritative modern government has been said to be one of the factors accounting for the economic miracles of East Asian economies.

Negative elements in Asian cultural traditions impeding educational-economic development: the need for cultural renewal

Interwoven in the 'modernizing' process, elements of cultural traditions have had both positive and negative effects on economic and social life. It is only too natural to challenge the Asian cultural tradition by asking why economies with (cultural) traditions that are so conducive to development have only recently embarked on rapid growth? Some scholars even saw Confucianism as a 'conservative, anti-modernizing force'.[6] While this might be exaggerated and one-sided, it is safe to say that, apart from the more fundamental economic-political factors impeding development, elements in traditional cultures explained in part the lag or lack of development of an industrial economy in many Asian countries.

•   *'Politicization' of educational-cultural values and lack of governmental commitment to economic modernization.* Educational institutions were

6.   Peter A. Petri, *The Lessons of East Asia: Common Foundations of East Asian Success*, Washington, D.C., The World Bank, 1993.

made merely an instrument in political strife and an appendage to the government apparatus.

• *Neglect of individuality.* While the collective/societal interests were over-emphasized to the extreme, the individual was reduced to merely an instrument. At the same time, the rights of the individual were not made compatible with the duties.

• *Focus on interpersonal relationships rather than on man over nature,* which for a long time resulted in underdevelopment of positive science, engineering and applied technologies.

• *Over-emphasis on classics-oriented examination* in screening talents and potential bureaucrats.

• *Disdain for pragmatism, utilitarianism and business.* Confucian idealism gave enormous weight to classic texts and their memorization in schooling, neglecting sciences and technical applications. It separated brain from hand and scholarship from craftsmanship. The educated élite were entitled to rule simply by virtue of their 'moral superiority', without having to acquire practical knowledge of skills. Matters of utilitarian values were despised and business was listed as an occupation of low social status. Partly due to this cultural factor, vocational and technical education remain under-developed to this day in many developing Asian countries.

• *Gender bias.* Confucius once said that 'only the mean and women are difficult to raise'. For centuries women were reduced to an appendage at home and negligible in society. From this traditional bias in many Asian cultures a vicious cycle emerged, in which girls were not expected to play social roles in economic growth or in their families and therefore had much less schooling than boys. It also accounts much for the persistently high ratio of girls among the millions of school drop-outs in the Asian region (two-thirds during 1985–92). As elsewhere, the lower educational level of Asian women resulted in higher infant mortality, high population growth in the rural areas, worse conditions for child nutrition and health, and a stagnant economy.

'Crisis in human values', a worldwide phenomena, could also be observed in the Asian region. While education transmits cultural heritage to next generations, it has a mission to innovate traditional cultures. The negative elements in traditional cultures point to the need for their renewal in the light of the changing socio-economic contexts and education has an important role to play in effecting positive cultural value changes.

Universal cultural values to be cultivated by education for global ethics

While striving for preservation of cultural identity and traditions, Asian nations have been increasingly aware of interregional interdependence. In response to increasing globalization, there have been advocacy efforts made by education systems in Asian region to facilitate a desirable core of universal values, which have included the following:

• *Awareness of human rights combined with a sense of social responsibilities.* Caution is taken that rights are not separated from duties, that the concept of human rights is not imposed from a Western ethnocentric perspective but related to cultural traditions and national/regional contexts, and that the rights of individuals are linked to those of the collectives.

• *Value of social equity and democratic participation in decision-making and government,* which will be the 'central objective in all parts of life'.[7]

• *Understanding and tolerance of cultural differences and pluralism,* which is a precondition of social cohesion, peaceful co-existence and conflict-resolution by negotiation instead of force, and ultimately of world peace.

• *A spirit of caring,* a 'keynote value for future education', and an intrinsic quality of human compassion, which should be extended not only to the family members and colleagues, but to all the disadvantaged, the sick, the poor and the disabled, for the well-being of humankind and our planet.

• *Co-operative spirit.* While competition can be observed in all spheres of daily life, co-operation is all the more necessary. As Jacques Delors observes: 'The world is our village: if one house catches fire, the roofs over all our heads are immediately at risk. If any one of us tries to start rebuilding, his efforts will be purely symbolic. Solidarity has to be the order of the day: each of us must bear his own share of the general responsibility.'[8]

• *Enterprising spirit,* a quality which is needed not only for economic productivity and competitiveness but for all life situations.

• *Creativity,* which will always be needed for technological advances, social progress, economic dynamics and all other human endeavours.

• *Sensitivity to gender equality,* which has been recognized as 'the key to development and poverty alleviation',[9] and 'both a gateway to development and a measure of that development'.[10]

• *Open-mindedness to change,* which will be the only thing which will not change, and the attitude not only to accept change but to act as an agent of positive change.

• *Sense of obligation to environment protection and sustainable develop-*

7. *Human Development Report 1993,* New York, Oxford University Press, 1993.

8. Jacques Delors (speech at the United Nations Conference on Environment and Development, Rio de Janeiro, Brazil, June 1992).

9. Colin Power (speech in Beijing on International Literacy Day, 8 September 1995).

10. Federico Mayor (speech in Beijing on International Literacy Day, 8 September 1995).

ment, so as not to create economic, social and ecological debts for future generations.

It is worth noting that most of these universal values needed for the twenty-first century have long been embedded in the age-old cultural traditions of human civilizations. They encompass the moral visions and ideals of truth, kindness, beauty, justice and liberty which were elaborated long ago by our predecessors and magnificently preserved in the treasuries of thought. For example, the spirit of 'caring' was embedded in the Confucian 'benevolence', the Mohist 'concurrent loving' and the Buddhist 'mercy'. The sensitivity to environmental protection was expressed in ancient China by the concern of the Taoists about the destructive consequences of technical advances to natural resources and their advocacy of 'return to Nature'. Altruism, originating in the love of one human being for another, has been respected as the highest human value in Asia for hundreds of years. Humanity in the next century might find elements of wisdom of Confucianism as relevant as it was long ago. Therefore, one way to foster universal values for future centuries is to educate the young with great books of the past and inherit the fine traditions of humanity.

Another approach to the cultivation of these universal values for global ethics is to promote, by means of education, cross-cultural learning between Eastern and Western cultures. Culturally the East and West are compatible and complementary rather than contradictory and mutually opposing. The Confucian aristocracy ('scholar-official') of merit, rather than hereditary privilege, was closest to the ancient Greek idea of 'government by the best'. Asia's cultural learning from the West has evolved from the material dimension (modern technologies) to the institutional (political infrastructure) and the socio-psychological (values and beliefs) dimensions. It is education that has provided bridges between Eastern and Western cultures. If and when the East and West could learn and benefit from each other, integrating each other's cultural strengths – for example, the individual initiative with the collective team spirit, competitiveness with co-operativeness, the technological capacities with the moral qualities – then desirable universal values will gradually develop and a global ethic will be formed, which will be a fundamental renewal of cultures and a great contribution of education to humanity.

People-centred development: the ultimate goal of education and culture

Development, which aims at 'the full flowering of human potential all over the world', is the ultimate goal of both education and culture. In the Asian region, education is being emphasized as 'a vital force of development' and culture as both an important means and an integral component of development. As in other regions, development has increasingly been seen in Asia as a complex dynamic process, embracing economic, political, social, human and environmental as well as cultural dimensions.

As the material base upon which human beings could pursue all kinds of superstructural activities for survival and growth, economic development is of primary significance to education and culture. The importance of the effect of modernization of national economies on education and culture cannot be over-emphasized, especially for developing countries. With as many as 830 million people living in absolute poverty in the Asia–Pacific region alone, economic growth becomes an essential element of any effort in eradicating poverty and a precondition for both cultural and educational development. Without strong national industry and agriculture, educational programmes will lack the necessary resources and even political independence will be hindered. Without material civilization in terms of technological and infrastructure development, spiritual civilization will have weak support and indigenous cultural identity will be eroded by new forms of cultural colonialism transmitted by powerful information technology. That is why most Asian countries have, legitimately and rightfully, regarded economic modernization as a highest priority and made persistent efforts in striving for modernization.

However, economic and technological advances will lose their true meaning if the humanistic and cultural dimensions are not made the central component and goal of development efforts. In the twenty-first century, when industries will be more technology-intensive and human society increasingly knowledge-intensive, human capital developed through education and training will assume increasingly crucial roles.

In the East, from Confucius to contemporary Asian thinkers, the ideal of 'a harmonious one-world' and 'a coherent human society of universal peace' has been cherished and pursued for ages. In the West, from Plato, French enlightenment, English humanism and European Renaissance to the American Declaration of Independence, the ideal of equity, justice, liberty and human dignity has been sought and fought for for centuries. Humankind has never ceased its efforts to integrate economic with educational and cultural dimensions of development. UNDP's conception of 'development *of* the people *for* the people *by* the people' corresponds to our interpretation of the dialectic interrelations of education to culture in the light of Asian traditions and contemporary contexts of globalization.

Appendices

1. The work of the Commission

In November 1991 the General Conference invited the Director-General 'to convene an international commission to reflect on education and learning for the twenty-first century'. Federico Mayor requested Jacques Delors to chair the Commission, with a group of fourteen other eminent figures from all over the world and from a variety of cultural and professional backgrounds.

The International Commission on Education for the Twenty-first Century was formally established at the beginning of 1993. Financed by UNESCO and working with the assistance of a secretariat provided by the Organization, the Commission was able to draw on the Organization's valuable resources and international experience, and on an impressive mass of information, but was completely independent in carrying out its work and in preparing its recommendations.

UNESCO has on several previous occasions produced international studies reviewing issues and priorities in education worldwide. In 1968, *The World Educational Crisis: A Systems Analysis*, by Philip H. Coombs, then Director of UNESCO's International Institute for Educational Planning (IIEP), drew on the work of the Institute to examine the problems facing education, and to recommend far-reaching innovations.

In 1971, in the wake of student upheavals in much of the world during the previous three years, René Maheu (then Director-General of UNESCO), asked a former French Prime Minister and Minister of Education, Edgar Faure, to chair a seven-person panel entrusted with defining 'the new aims to be assigned to education as a result of the rapid changes in knowledge and in societies, the demands of development, the aspirations of the individual, and the overriding need for international understanding and peace' and putting forward 'suggestions regarding the intellectual, human and financial means needed to attain the objectives set'. Published in 1972 under the title *Learning to Be*, the report of the Faure Commission had the great merit of firmly establishing the concept of lifelong education at a time when traditional education systems were being challenged.

The first and perhaps the chief difficulty confronting the Commission chaired by Jacques Delors concerned the extreme diversity of educational situations, conceptions and structures. Related to this difficulty was the sheer quantity of information available and the obvious impossibility, for the Commission, of digesting more than a small proportion of it in the course of its work. It was thus obliged to be selective and to single out what was essential for the future, bearing in mind both geopolitical, economic, social and cultural trends on the one hand and, on the other, the part educational policies could play.

Six lines of inquiry were chosen, enabling the Commission to approach its task from the angle of the aims (both individual and societal) of the learning process: education and culture; education and citizenship; education and social cohesion; education, work and employment; education and development; and education, research and science. These six lines were complemented by three transverse themes relating more directly to the functioning of education systems: communications technologies; teachers and teaching; and financing and management.

The method adopted by the Commission was to engage in as wide-ranging a process of consultation as was possible in the time available. It held eight plenary sessions, and the same number of working-group sessions, to examine both the major topics chosen, and concerns and issues particular to one region or group of countries. Participants in the working-group sessions were representative of a wide range of professions and organizations directly and indirectly related to education, formal and non-formal: teachers, researchers, students, government officials, and people active in governmental and non-governmental organizations at national and international levels. A series of presentations by distinguished individuals enabled the Commission to hold in-depth exchanges on a wide range of topics related in various degrees to education. Individual consultations were carried out, face-to-face or in writing. A questionnaire was sent to all the National Commissions for UNESCO, inviting them to submit documentation or unpublished material: the response was very positive and the replies were studied carefully. Non-governmental organizations were similarly consulted and in some cases invited to participate in meetings. In the past two-and-a-half years, members of the Commission, including its Chairman, also attended a series of governmental and non-governmental meetings in which its work was discussed and ideas exchanged. Many written submissions, commissioned or unsolicited, were sent to the Commission. The Commission's secretariat analysed a considerable volume of documentation and provided the Commission's members with summaries on a variety of topics. The Commission proposes that, in addition to its report, UNESCO should also publish the working documents produced for it.

2. Members of the Commission

Jacques Delors (France)

Chairman of the Commission; former President of the European Commission (1985–95); former French Minister of Economy and Finance

In'am Al Mufti (Jordan)

Specialist on the status of women; Adviser to Queen Noor of Jordan on Planning and Development – Noor Al Hussein Foundation; former Minister of Social Development

Isao Amagi (Japan)

Educator; Special Adviser to the Minister of Education, Science and Culture, Japan; Chairman of the Japan Educational Exchange–BABA Foundation

Roberto Carneiro (Portugal)

President, TVI (Televisão Independente); former Minister of Education; Minister of State, Portugal

Fay Chung (Zimbabwe)

Former Minister of State for National Affairs, Employment Creation and Co-operatives; Member of Parliament; former Minister of Education, Zimbabwe; now at UNICEF, New York

Bronislaw Geremek (Poland)

Historian; Member of Parliament; former Professor at the Collège de France

William Gorham (United States)

Specialist in public policy; President of the Urban Institute in Washington, D.C., since 1968

Aleksandra Kornhauser (Slovenia)

Director, International Centre for Chemical Studies, Ljubljana; specialist on the interface between industrial development and environmental protection

Michael Manley (Jamaica)

Trade unionist, university lecturer and author; Prime Minister, 1972–80 and 1989–92

Marisela Padrón Quero (Venezuela)

Sociologist; former research director, Fundación Romulo Betancourt; former Minister of the Family, Venezuela; Chief, Latin America and the Caribbean Division, UNFPA, New York

Marie-Angélique Savané (Senegal)

Sociologist; member of the Commission on Global Governance; Director, Africa Division, UNFPA, New York

Karan Singh (India)

Diplomat and several times minister, *inter alia* for education and health; author of several books on the environment, philosophy and political science; Chairman of the Temple of Understanding, a major international interfaith organization

Rodolfo Stavenhagen (Mexico)

Researcher in political and social science; Professor at the Centre of Sociological Studies, El Colegio de Mexico

Myong Won Suhr (Republic of Korea)

Former Minister of Education; Chairman of the Presidential Commission for Educational Reform in Korea (1985–87)

Zhou Nanzhao (China)

Educator; Vice-President and Professor, China National Institute for Educational Research

The Commission wishes to express its thanks to Danièle Blondel, formerly Director of Higher Education in France and Professor at the University of Paris–Dauphine who, until September 1995, was Special Adviser to the Chairman. From the beginning, Danièle Blondel contributed a significant momentum to the work of the Commission. She made a substantial contribution in the form of studies and papers to its reflection and to the drafting of several chapters of the report.

3. Mandate of the Commission

At its first meeting (2–4 March 1993), the Commission examined and accepted the following mandate proposed to it by the Director-General of UNESCO:

The aim of the International Commission on Education for the Twenty-first Century is to study and reflect on the challenges facing education in the coming years and to formulate suggestions and recommendations in the form of a report which can serve as an agenda for renewal and action for policy-makers and officials at the highest levels. The report will suggest approaches to both policy and practice which are both innovative and feasible, while taking into account the wide diversity of situations, needs, means and aspirations existing in countries and in regions. The report will be addressed primarily to governments, but as one of its purposes will be to address issues related to the role of international co-operation and assistance in general and to the role of UNESCO in particular, it will also attempt to formulate recommendations which are pertinent for international bodies.

The Commission will focus its reflection on one central and all-encompassing question: what kind of education is needed for what kind of society of tomorrow? It will consider the new roles of education and the new demands made on education systems in a world of accelerating economic, environmental and social change and tension. It will study the implications for education of the major trends in the evolution of contemporary society; it will examine the state of knowledge and experience of the best educational practices in various cultural, economic and political settings in order to identify the strengths and weaknesses of contemporary policy. In doing so, it will attempt to keep at the heart of its work those most intimately involved in education: learners of all ages, first of all, and those involved in fostering learning, whether they be teachers, parents, members of the community, or other participants in education.

Initially, the Commission will need to identify a series of key questions which it will examine during its work, the answers to which will be the major recommendations it will put forward. These questions will include perennial issues facing governments, societies and educators, and which will continue to be important during the coming years. There will also be questions raised by new configurations of society and new developments in the physical and social world. The latter will imply new priorities, new study, new action. Some may be universal, based on inevitable and indispensable responses to a changing world; others will be region- or nation-specific and will focus on the widely differing economic, cultural and social situations prevailing in different countries.

Questions concerning education and education systems fall, broadly, into two main categories. The first category includes those questions relating to the purposes, goals and functions of education, including the aims of individuals and each person's need and desire for self-fulfilment. The second covers the specifically educational issues concerning providers of education, including the models, structures, contents and functioning of education systems.

The Commission will carry out a broadly based analysis both of what is known about the current situation, and of forecasts and trends in national policies and reforms in education in the different regions of the world over the last twenty years. On this basis, the Commission will reflect in depth on the major turning-points in human development on the eve of the twenty-first century, and the new demands these turning-points will make on education. It will highlight the ways in which education can play a more dynamic and constructive role in preparing individuals and societies for the twenty-first century.

Principles

In its deliberations and work, the Commission will attempt to keep in mind some underlying principles which are universal and common to the aims of educators, citizens, policy-makers, and other partners and participants in the process of education.

First, education is a basic human right and a universal human value: learning and education are ends in themselves, to be aimed at by both individuals and societies and to be promoted and made available over the entire lifetime of each individual.

Second, education, formal and non-formal, must serve society as an instrument for fostering the creation, advancement and dissemination of knowledge and science, and by making knowledge and teaching universally available.

Third, the triple goals of equity, relevance and excellence must prevail in any policy of education, and the search for a harmonious combination of these goals is a crucial task for all those involved in educational planning and practice.

Fourth, renewal and any corresponding reform of education must be the result of profound and thoughtful examination and understanding of what is known about successful practice and policy, as well as understanding of the specific conditions and requirements relevant to each particular situation; they must be decided upon by mutual agreement through appropriate pacts among the parties concerned, as a medium-term process.

Fifth, while existence of a wide variety of economic, social and cultural situations clearly calls for differing approaches to educational development, all approaches must take into account basic and agreed-upon values and concerns of the international community and of the United Nations system: human rights, tolerance and understanding, democracy, responsibility, universality, cultural identity, the search for peace, the preservation of the environment, the sharing of knowledge, alleviation of poverty, population control, health.

Sixth, education is the responsibility of the whole of society: all persons involved and all partnerships – in addition to those incumbent on institutions – must be taken fully into account.

Scope, work and report

The scope of the topic as viewed by the Commission will embrace the concept of education in its broadest meaning, from pre-school through school and higher education, including both formal and non-formal education, and covering the widest possible spectrum of agencies and providers. On the other hand, the conclusions and recommendations will be action-oriented and directed mainly to governmental and private agencies, policy-makers and decision-makers, and in general all those responsible for making and carrying out educational plans and actions. It is to be hoped that they will, in addition, stimulate a far-reaching public debate on educational reform in Member States of UNESCO.

The Commission will meet over a period of two years, on a schedule determined by it, and will submit a report in early 1995. This report will be designed to serve as an agenda for educational renewal and as guidelines for UNESCO's action in the field of education in the coming years. It will be communicated to the governing bodies of UNESCO, to its Member States and National Commissions and to the governmental and non-governmental organizations with which UNESCO co-operates.

The Commission is supported in its work by a secretariat furnished by UNESCO, and will call upon the intellectual and material resources of UNESCO as required for successful completion of its tasks.

4. Distinguished advisers

The Commission was served by a panel of eminent persons and organizations with a distinguished record of contributions to thought and achievement in a variety of fields relating to education. The members of the panel, listed below, were called upon to participate in a variety of ways, including written submissions and participation in meetings.

Individuals

Jorge Allende
Chilean biochemist and molecular biologist; Professor at the University of Chile; Fellow of the Third World Academy of Sciences; Member of the Chilean Academy of Sciences

Emeka Anyaoku
Nigerian diplomat; Secretary-General of the Commonwealth Secretariat

Margarita Marino de Botero
Executive Director, 'Colegio Verde', Villa de Leyva; former Director-General of the National Institute of Natural Resources and the Environment, Colombia

Gro Harlem Brundtland
Prime Minister of Norway; chaired the World Commission on Environment and Development

Elizabeth Dowdeswell
Executive Director, United Nations Environmental Programme (UNEP), Nairobi

Daniel Goeudevert
French business executive; Premier Vice-President, Green Cross International; former Chairman of the Volkswagen Management Body; Member of the Board of Directors, International Partnership Initiative (IPI)

Makaminan Makagiansar
Former UNESCO Assistant Director-General for Culture; Adviser to the Minister of Science and Technology of Indonesia

Yehudi Menuhin

British violinist; President and Associate Conductor, Royal Philharmonic Orchestra; Nehru Award for Peace and International Understanding (1970); member of the Académie Universelle de la Culture

Thomas Odhiambo

Kenyan scientist; Chairman of the African Academy of Sciences; member of the International Council of Scientific Unions

René Rémond

French historian; Président of the National Foundation of Political Science; Co-director of the *Revue historique*

Bertrand Schwartz

French engineer, university professor and educator; member of the Conseil Économique et Social

Anatoly Sobchak

Mayor of St Petersburg, Russian Federation; Head of the Faculty of Law at the University of St Petersburg; former Minister of Education

David Suzuki

Canadian scientist, educator, international speaker and moderator of television programmes and films on science; recipient of numerous awards in areas related to science and broadcasting

Ahmed Zaki Yamani

Lawyer; former Minister of Petroleum and Mineral Resources of Saudi Arabia; former Secretary-General and former Chairman of the Organization of Arab Petroleum Exporting Countries

Institutions

International Association of Universities (IAU)

International Council for Adult Education (ICAE)

Education International (EI)

United Nations University (UNU)

5. Secretariat

A number of UNESCO staff members, both in Paris and in field offices, contributed by commenting in writing or orally on papers submitted to the Commission or on drafts of chapters. The organization of meetings away from Paris was greatly helped in most instances by the intellectual and organizational assistance provided by staff in country offices. They are too numerous to list here, but the work of the Commission could not have been carried out successfully without them.

Colin Power, UNESCO's Assistant Director-General for Education, gave his unfailing support to the work of the Commission and its secretariat. He also chaired a steering committee that monitored UNESCO's input to the work of the Commission.

The following UNESCO staff members or consultants participated in the work of the Commission and in the preparation of its final report:

Alexandra Draxler, Secretary of the Commission

Jean-Pierre Boyer, Programme Specialist

Boubacar Camara, Assistant Programme Specialist
Eva Carlson-Wahlberg, Associate Expert
Woo Tak Chung, Associate Expert
Jean Gaudin, Consultant
Maureen Long, Editorial Consultant (final draft)
Claude Navarro, Editorial Consultant (final draft)
Brian Verity, Editorial Consultant (final draft)

Administrative staff
  Rose-Marie Baffert
  Michel Bermond
  Catherine Domain
  Karima Pires

6. Commission meetings

First session	2–4 March 1993, Paris (working methods and issues)
Second session	20–24 September 1993, Dakar (education and development, financing and organization of education)
Third session	12–15 January 1994, Paris (education and science)
Fourth session	13–15 April 1994, Vancouver (Canada) (teachers and the teaching process, lifelong education, multiculturalism)
Fifth session	26–30 September 1994, Santiago de Chile (education, citizenship and democracy)
Sixth session	6–10 February 1995, Paris (international co-operation)
Seventh session	22–25 September 1995, Tunis (education and culture)
Eighth session	15–17 January 1996, New Delhi (adoption of the final report)

Each session of the Commission except the first included as part of its programme a working group, with invited experts, to examine issues specific to the region in which the meeting was held, and the topic that was the particular focus of that session. Members of the Commission, and its secretariat, organized or participated in a range of meetings and conferences that provided valuable inputs for the formulation of its final report. The Commission organized a working group on international co-operation in education (World Bank, Washington, D.C., December 1993) and a meeting between the Chairman of the Commission and the Executive of Education International (Brussels, May 1994). It provided support to a seminar on education and social cohesion in Alicante, Spain, held with the generous help of the Spanish Government (November 1994), to a national seminar on 'Education: Challenges of the Twenty-first Century' (New Delhi, January 1995) and to a seminar on 'Education, Work and Society: The Current Crisis and Paths Towards the Future', organized at the University of Paris IX–Dauphine (March 1995) by the Special Adviser to the Chairman of the Commission. Round tables to discuss the work of the Commission were organized as part of the Fifth Meeting of Ministers of Education of Arab States (Cairo, June 1994), the Twelfth Conference of Commonwealth Education Ministers (Islamabad, November 1994), the 44th session of the International Conference on Education (IBE, Geneva, October 1994) and the Conference of the American Comparative and International Education Society (Boston, March 1995).

7. Individuals and institutions consulted

Numerous persons contributed directly or indirectly to the work of the Commission. The list below comprises those who submitted papers or other material to the Commission, and participants in meetings or hearings, with the titles they had when they were consulted. Many individuals not mentioned here were also consulted, or came spontaneously to meet with the Commission secretariat or members of the Commission. Although they are not listed here, the Commission is grateful for the knowledge and advice they provided. A large number of National Commissions for UNESCO submitted material and responded to an open-ended questionnaire. Most of the agencies of the United Nations system contributed directly or indirectly (through papers or other consultations) and a substantial number of non-governmental organizations sent material spontaneously. Again, all cannot be listed here, but these contributions formed the foundations for the final report and the Commission wishes to express its appreciation to all those who expressed an interest in its work.

Ibrahim Abu-Lughod, Professor of Political Science; Vice-President, Birzeit University (West Bank)

Inés Aguerrondo, Under-Secretary for Educational Planning and Management, Ministry of Culture and Education, Buenos Aires

Khaldoun H. Al Naqeeb, Associate Professor, University of Kuwait, Shuwaik

Virginia Albert, Co-ordinator for the Caribbean, Education International

Neville E. Alexander, Director, Project for the Study of Alternative Education in South Africa, University of Cape Town (South Africa)

Haider Ibrahim Ali, Professor, Sudanese Studies Center, Cairo

K. Y. Amoako, Director, Education and Social Policy Department, World Bank

Fame Hane Ba, UNFPA Office, Ouagadougou

Hadja Aïcha Diallo Bah, Minister of Pre-University Education and Vocational Training (Guinea)

Samuel T. Bajah, Chief Programme Officer (Science, Technology and Mathematics Education), Education Department, Commonwealth Secretariat

Tom Bediako, Secretary-General, All African Teachers Organization

Monique Bégin, Co-Chair of the Royal Commission on Education, Ontario (Canada)

Paul Bélanger, Director, UNESCO Institute for Education (UIE), Hamburg (Germany)

Olivier Bertrand, former researcher, Centre for Studies and Research on Qualifications (CEREQ) (France)

Robert Bisaillon, Chairman of the Conseil Supérieur de l'Éducation, Quebec (Canada)

Alphonse Blagué, Rector of the University of Bangui; Co-ordinator of the Comité pour l'Élaboration du Programme d'Ajustement du Secteur Éducation (CEPASE)

Wolfgang Böttcher, Gewerkschaft Erziehung und Wissenschaft (Germany)

Ali Bousnina, President of the Université des Sciences, des Techniques et de Médecine, Tunis

Mark Bray, Comparative Education Research Centre, University of Hong Kong

Nicholas Burnett, Principal Economist, Education and Social Policy Department, World Bank

Inés Bustillo, Economic Commission for Latin America and the Caribbean (ECLAC)

Carlos Cardoso, Director-General, Institut National d'Études et Recherche (Guinée-Bissau)

Raúl Cariboni, Co-ordinator for Latin America, Education International

Ana Maria Cetto, Professor, Department of Mathematics, University College, London

Abdesselam Cheddadi, Professor, Faculty of Education Sciences, Université Mohammad V, Rabat

Chua Soo Pong, Director, Chinese Opera Institute (Singapore)

Helen M. Connell, Consultant, Paris

José Luis Coraggio, International Council for Adult Education (ICAE) (Canada)

Didier Dacunha-Castelle, Professor, Department of Mathematics, Université de Paris-Sud, Orsay (France)

Krishna Datt, Council of Pacific Teachers Organizations

Goéry Delacôte, Executive Director, Exploratorium, San Francisco (United States)

Michel Demazure, Director, Palais de la Découverte, Paris

Souleymane Bachir Diagne, Technical Adviser on Education to the Presidency of the Republic; Professor, Department of Philosophy, University Cheikh Anta Diop, Dakar

Ahmed Djebbar, Minister of National Education (Algeria)

Albert Kangui Ekué, Director, Division of Education, Science and Culture, Organization of African Unity (OAU)

Linda English, Economist, Africa Region, Canadian International Development Agency (CIDA)

Jan Erdtsieck, Education International

Ingemar Fägerlind, Director, Institute of International Education, Stockholm University

Aminata Sow Fall, Official of the Centre Africain d'Animation et d'Échanges Culturels, Dakar

Yoro Fall, Professor, Université de Dakar; member of UNESCO's World Commission on Culture and Development

Glen Farrell, President, Open Learning Agency, British Columbia (Canada)

Emanuel Fatoma, Co-ordinator for English-speaking Africa, Education International

Mary Hatwood Futrell, President, Education International

Ken Gannicott, Professor of Education, University of Wollongong, New South Wales (Australia)

Wolfgang Gmelin, German Foundation for International Development (DSE), Bonn

Danièle Gosnave, Specialist in family education curricula, Family Education Project, Ministry of National Education, Dakar

François Gros, Permanent Secretary, Académie des Sciences (France)

Ingmar Gustafsson, Senior Human Resources Adviser to the President, Swedish International Development Co-operation Agency (Sweden)

Aklilu Habte, United Nations Children's Fund (UNICEF)

Jacques Hallak, Director, UNESCO-IIEP

Janet Halliwell, Chair of the Higher Education Council, Nova Scotia (Canada)

Alan Hancock, Director of Programme for Central and East European Development (PROCEED), UNESCO

Mohammed Hassan, Executive Director, Third World Academy of Sciences, Trieste (Italy)

Mary A. Hepburn, Professor and Head, Citizen Education Division, Carl Vinson Institute of Government, University of Georgia (United States)

Abdelbaki Hermassi, former Ambassador; Permanent Delegate of Tunisia to UNESCO

Steven Heyneman, Chief, Human Resources and Social Development, Technical Department (Europe, Central Asia, Middle East and North Africa Regions), World Bank

Herbert Hinzen, International Council for Adult Education, ICAE (Canada)

Phillip Hughes, Professor, University of Tasmania (Australia)

Alan King, Professor (Philosophy of Education), Queen's University, Ontario (Canada)

Verna J. Kirkness, Former Director, First Nations House of Learning, Longhouse University of British Columbia (Canada)

Fadia Kiwan, Professor, Jesuit University, Beirut

Alberto Rodolfo Kornblihtt, Senior Researcher, Instituto de Investigaciones en Ingeniería, Genética y Biología Molecular, Buenos Aires

Wolfgang Kueper, Head of Division, Education and Sciences, Deutsche Gesellschaft für Technische Zusammenarbeit, Eschborn (Germany)

Gabeyehu Kumsa, Deputy Permanent Delegate of Ethiopia to UNESCO; former Director of Educational Planning and External Services, Ministry of Education (Ethiopia)

Diane Laberge, Director-General, Institut Canadien d'Éducation des Adultes, Montreal, Quebec (Canada)

Augustin A. Larrauri, UNESCO Representative in Canada, Quebec City

Pablo Latapí, Consultant, Centro de Estudios Educativos (Mexico)

Viviane F. Launay, Secretary-General, Canadian Commission for UNESCO

Pierre Léna, Member of the Academy of Sciences; Professor, Université Paris VII, Observatoire de Meudon (France)

Elena Lenskaya, Counsellor to the Minister of Education (Russian Federation)

Henry Levin, David Jacobs Professor of Education and Economics, Stanford University, California (United States)

Marlaine Lockheed, World Bank

Noel McGinn, Institute Fellow, Harvard Institute for International Development (United States); Professor, Harvard School of Education (United States)

William Francis Mackey, Professor/Researcher, Centre International de Recherche en Aménagement Linguistique, Université Laval, Quebec (Canada)

James A. Maraj, President, Commonwealth of Learning

Frank Method, Senior Education Adviser, United States Agency for International Development (USAID), Washington, D.C.

Erroll Miller, Professor, University of the West Indies

Peter Moock, Education and Social Policy Department, World Bank

Chitra Naik, Member (Education), Planning Commission, New Delhi

J. V. Narlikar, Professor, Inter-University Centre for Astronomy and Astrophysics, Pune (India)

Bougouma Ngom, Secretrary-General, Conférence des Ministres de l'Éducation des Pays Ayant en Commun l'Usage du Français (CONFMEM)

Pai Obanya, Director, UNESCO Dakar

Victor M. Ordoñez, Director, Basic Education Division, UNESCO

François Orivel, Director of Research, CNRS, IREDU, Université de Bourgogne, Dijon (France)

Claude Pair, Professor, Institut Polytechnique de Lorraine, Nancy (France)

Paul Pallan, Assistant Deputy Minister, Student Services Department, Ministry of Education, British Columbia (Canada)

George Papadopoulos, Former Deputy Director in Charge of Education, OECD

Serge Péano, Chief of Programme, 'Cost and Financing of Education', International Institute for Educational Planning (IIEP), UNESCO

Jacques Proulx, Vice-Chairman, Sub-Commission on Education, Canadian Commission for UNESCO; Délégué à la Coopération Internationale, University of Sherbrooke, Quebec (Canada)

George Psacharapoulos, World Bank

Ana Maria Quiroz, former Secretary-General, International Council for Adult Education (ICAE) (Canada)

Germán Rama, Consultant, Montevideo

Luis Ratinoff, Inter-American Development Bank (IDB), Office of External Relations

Fernando Reimers, Institute Associate, Education Specialist, Harvard Institute for International Development (United States)

René Rémond, President of the Fondation Nationale des Sciences Politiques (France)

Norman Rifkin, Director, Center for Human Capacity Development, USAID (United States)

José Rivero, Directeur a.i., UNESCO Santiago

Gert Rosenthal, Executive Secretary, Economic Commission for Latin America and the Caribbean (ECLAC)

Antonio Ruberti, Professor, Dipartimento di Informatica e Sistemistica, Facoltá di Roma 'La Sapienza' (Italy)

Nadji Safir, former Head of Social, Educational and Cultural Affairs, Institut National des Études de Stratégie Globale (Algeria)

Mouna L. Samman, Programme Specialist, Environment and Population Education and Information for Human Development (ED/EPD), UNESCO

Alexander Sannikov, Programme Specialist, Education Sector, UNESCO

Ernesto Schiefelbein, Director, UNESCO Santiago; former Minister of National Education (Chile)

Leticia Shahani, Senate President *Pro Tempore*, Chair of the Education Committee, Manila

Adnan Shihab-Eldin, Director, UNESCO Cairo

John Smyth, Chief Editor, *World Education Report* (UNESCO)

Esi Sutherland-Addy, Research Fellow, Institute of African Studies, University of Ghana Legon, Accra

Robert Tabachnick, Associate Dean, Professor of Curriculum and Instruction, School of Education, University of Wisconsin-Madison (USA)

Shigekazu Takemura, Vice-Dean, Faculty of Education, Hiroshima University (Japan)

Sibry Tapsoba, Regional Administrator of Programmes (Social Policies), Centre pour la Recherche en Développement International, Dakar

Juan Carlos Tedesco, Director, UNESCO International Bureau of Education (IBE), Geneva

Malang Thiam, Chief of the Education and Health Division, African Development Bank

Sakhir Thiam, Professor, Université Cheikh Anta Diop, Dakar

Mark Thompson, Professor, University of British Columbia, Vancouver (Canada)

David Throsby, Professor of Economics, Macquarie University, Sydney (Australia)

Alice Tiendrébéoga, Minister with responsibility for Basic Education and Mass Literacy, Ouagadougou

Judith Tobin, Director, Strategic Issues, TV Ontario (Canada)

Rosa María Torres, International Council for Adult Education (ICAE) (Canada)

Carlos Tunnerman, Special Adviser to the Director-General of UNESCO

Kapila Vatsyayan, Academic Director, Indira Gandhi National Centre for the Arts, New Delhi

Marit Vedeld, Norwegian Agency for Development Co-operation, Oslo

Vichai Tunsiri, Adviser to the Minister of Education, Bangkok

A. E. (Ted) Wall, President, Canadian Association of Deans of Education; Dean, Faculty of Education, McGill University, Montreal (Canada)

Shem O. Wandiga, Pro Vice-Chancellor, University of Nairobi

Bertrand Weil, Professor, Faculté de Médecine, Paris

Tom Whiston, Professor, Science Policy Research Unit, University of Sussex (United Kingdom)

Graeme Withers, Australian Council for Educational Research, Melbourne, Australia

Davina B. Woods, Federal Aboriginal Education Officer, Australian Education Union, South Melbourne (Australia)

Joanna Zumstein, Senior Adviser for Education, Canadian International Development Agency (Canada)

8. Follow-up

A secretariat will ensure the follow-up to the Commission's work, by publishing the background material and studies looking more closely into aspects of the Commission's deliberations or recommendations, by helping to organize, at the request of governmental or non-governmental authorities, meetings to discuss the findings of the Commission and by taking part in activities that will attempt to put into practice some of the Commission's recommendations. The address will continue to be:

UNESCO
Education Sector
Unit for Education for the Twenty-first Century
7, place de Fontenoy
75352 Paris 07 SP, France
Tel. (33 - 1) 45 68 11 23
Fax (33 - 1) 43 06 52 55
Internet: EDOBSERV@UNESCO.ORG